Ignatow had already "scream-tested" the house—
Mary Ann screaming inside while Ignatow stood
near the busy road in front to determine if she
could be heard.

When Brenda and Ignatow came through the
front door, Mary Ann locked it behind them. As
Ignatow had ordered, Brenda Schaefer was
trapped; she had no way to run.

"Why did you bring me here?" she asked.

"You're here for sex-therapy class," he told her.

"No, I want to go home."

Ignatow grabbed Brenda's arm.

"You are not leaving."

DOUBLE JEOPARDY

DOUBLE JEOPARDY

An Electrifying True Story
of Senseless Cruelty,
Murderous Rage,
and Justice Miscarried

BOB HILL

AVON BOOKS NEW YORK

AVON BOOKS
A division of
The Hearst Corporation
1350 Avenue of the Americas
New York, New York 10019

Copyright © 1995 by Bob Hill
Published by arrangement with the author
Library of Congress Catalog Card Number: 94-38293
ISBN: 0-380-72192-9

Published in hardcover by William Morrow and Company, Inc.; for information address Permissions Department, William Morrow and Company, Inc., 1350 Avenue of the Americas, New York, New York 10019.

The William Morrow edition contains the following Library of Congress Cataloging in Publication Data:
Hill, Bob.
  Double jeopardy : obsession, murder, and justice denied / Bob Hill.
    p. cm.   Includes index.
.. Murder—Kentucky—Case studies. 2. Schaefer, Brenda, 1952–1988. I. Title.
HV6533.K4H55 1995   94–38293
364.1'523'0976944—dc20   CIP

First Avon Books Printing: October 1996

AVON TRADEMARK REG. U.S. PAT. OFF. AND IN OTHER COUNTRIES, MARCA REGISTRADA, HECHO EN U.S.A.

Printed in the U.S.A.

RA 10 9 8 7 6 5 4 3 2 1

FOR BRENDA,
THE SCHAEFERS,
AND ALL FAMILIES HURT BY ABUSE AND EVIL

ACKNOWLEDGMENTS

Because this book consumed almost two years of an already crowded life, it couldn't have been completed without the help and support of many people.

First I want to thank Louisville *Courier-Journal* writer C. Ray Hall, a good man who gave willingly of his time, his marvelous abilities, and his computer paper. I need to thank Ernie Slone, who somehow understands computers, and Charlene Williams, who patiently transcribed hundreds of hours of tapes.

The *Courier-Journal* library research staff—Sharon Bidwell, Pat Chapman, Judy Wadlington, Ed Wooter, Amy Inskeep, and Patricia Hauck—were always there at odd hours. Photo editor Cindy Stucky and photographers Pam Spalding and Bud Kraft helped with the photographs and charts, and reporters Cary Willis, Deborah Tetter, and Leslie Scanlon helped with story background. Editor Jena Monahan helped me find the path, along with Vince Staten, a critic with style.

I want to thank the Center for Women & Families in Louisville for giving me a deeper understanding of the continuum of domestic violence, sexual abuse, and the terrible chains of co-dependency. I needed the legal advice tendered by Kim Greene and Steve Snyder of Wyatt, Tarrant & Combs, and the patience and help of many people in the Jefferson County Hall of Justice, especially in the Circuit Clerk's office.

Thanks to WHAS-TV's Steve Duncan for allowing me to view news tapes, Cincinnati *Post* writer Bill Weathers, who gave me a needed tour and introductions in Covington, Kentucky, and John, Donna, and Andie Bryan, who gave me bed and breakfast, along with David and Tru Marlowe.

Finally, I want to thank the editors at the *Courier-Journal*—Judy Rosenfield, Greg Johnson, Steve Ford, and David Hawpe—who allowed me time and space to work on this book, and my wife, Janet, who knows more than anyone just how badly I needed both commodities.

To me belongeth vengeance, and recompense; their foot shall slide in due time; for the day of their calamity is at hand, and the things that shall come upon them make haste.

—DEUTERONOMY 32:35

DOUBLE JEOPARDY

CHAPTER
1

Early on a February afternoon in 1992, two brothers, one carrying a worn garden spade, the other a small black box, walked up a grassy slope near the back edge of Louisville's Cave Hill Cemetery.

Mike Schaefer, wearing a green down-filled jacket and jeans, carried the spade in one hand like a hunting rifle. Tom Schaefer, a bearded man in a red cotton jacket and jeans, carried the black box in front of him with care, palms up, like a man bearing a gift. The box contained the cremated hands of their murdered sister, Brenda Schaefer.

The brothers walked slowly, the measured steps of a funeral procession, a walk that had become much too familiar. Brenda Schaefer's body had been buried in Cave Hill in January 1990, more than two years earlier. Few outside the family knew that Brenda had been buried without her hands; they'd been severed during her autopsy to allow the FBI to better check fingerprints. Few outside the family knew about the brothers' wish to make Brenda whole again.

The afternoon was cool but sunny, a rare pleasure in Kentucky, where winters slide by gray and gloomy. Cave Hill, where Louisvillians have long been buried beneath sculpted marble and massive granite obelisks, also serves as the city's

finest arboretum. In the spring and summer, its low green
hills are decorated with bursts of pink dogwood and white
magnolia that fall away toward spring-fed lakes. In early
February the trees are bare, the cemetery's mood more somber.

The brothers walked slowly up the slope toward a gray
granite monument with

SCHAEFER

carved across its face. Beneath the wide stone, flanked by
green holly and curly arborvitae, were buried four members
of their family: their brother, John W. Schaefer, Jr.; their
mother, Mary Essie; their father, John W. Schaefer; and
Brenda.

John junior, nicknamed Jack, had been a Louisville police
detective, a likable, restless man who finally settled on police
work as a way to serve others. He and a partner were am-
bushed the night of May 2, 1971. Jack, twenty-eight, was
found facedown on a slab of concrete in an alley. He had
been shot five times—twice in the head and three times in
the back. His wallet and police badge were missing.

Carved in the gray granite beneath his name was:

GREATER LOVE HATH NO MAN THAN THIS,
THAT A MAN LAY DOWN HIS LIFE FOR HIS FRIENDS.

JOHN 15:13

Mary Essie Schaefer had died on July 13, 1990. She had
been a cafeteria worker at Our Lady of Lourdes Catholic
School for eighteen years. She had been ill with lupus, but
her death was hurried by Brenda's disappearance, then the
traumatic discovery of her body in a shallow grave sixteen
months after she had disappeared.

Essie's husband, John, who worked for a Louisville distillery most of his life, died on February 6, 1991, of a heart
attack. He had lived twenty years after the murder of John

junior, his oldest son and namesake, but never recovered from the shock. The murder of his daughter and loss of his wife ended any will to live.

The deaths—three funerals in little more than a year—were terrible tests of Tom and Mike Schaefer's strengths and weaknesses. It was only by accident the brothers learned Brenda's hands had been cut off during her autopsy; a Jefferson County police detective let the information slip out. Then the brothers learned the hands were still at the Jefferson County coroner's office, that it would take a court order to get them back.

The brothers tried to accept this final indignity as a blessing, a chance to bring some peace into their lives. Brenda's long disappearance, the arrest of her accused murderer, the almost two-year wait for the trial, had taken their toll.

Brenda was their younger sister, the shy and quiet one who played with kittens on the back porch. She'd grown into a beautiful young woman, who had moved back home to care for their ailing mother. Even at thirty-six, Brenda had never lost her little-girl vulnerability.

The brothers had no way to reconcile that Brenda with the violent, sadistic, ritualized details of her five-hour torture, rape, and murder, each brutal act planned in advance, then photographed in color before her nude body was buried deep in thick woods.

On the morning of February 2, 1992, having gained release of Brenda's hands through a contentious court battle, the brothers went to the office of state medical examiner Dr. L. C. McCloud. His office was on the seventh floor of the old Baptist Hospital, a bulky, yellow-brick building built where urban Louisville blended into two-story, tree-shaded, upper-middle-class homes.

Mike Schaefer drove their father's 1982 AMC Concord, white with a blue vinyl top. The brothers, quiet and preoccupied, became a little irritated because they couldn't find a parking place. McCloud was waiting for them in his office. The men exchanged pleasantries, then got down to business. The examiner handed the brothers a brown, heavily sealed cardboard box, the same one the FBI had used to send Brenda's hands back to Louisville. McCloud assured the brothers the hands, floating in a clear preservative in a small plastic bag, were inside in the box.

"I've looked," he said.

The Schaefers thanked him, anxious to get on with the day.

"I'm sorry," said McCloud, walking them toward the door.

Tom Schaefer carried the box to the car; he would keep it on his lap. The brothers had learned to fight off depression with gallows humor. Mike was a little better practitioner of the art than Tom, a melancholy man whose pain often seemed closer to the surface.

"What do you suppose would happen," Mike asked, "if we had to leave the box in the car and someone stole it?"

Their plan had been to drive to Vogt Cremation Service, where the hands would be cremated before burial. Tom had a thought: The hands should first be blessed by Father Robert E. Osborne at Our Lady of Lourdes Church. When the brothers reached the church, a secretary said the priest was probably in the grade school.

"Can I hold that box for you while you look?" the secretary asked.

The brothers glanced at each other.

"NO," they answered in unison.

Father Osborne was in the grade school. Sensing the importance of the mission, he led the brothers to a small counseling room in the rectory. The brothers sat on a sofa, Father Osborne in a chair, the cardboard box resting on the coffee table between them.

Tom Schaefer explained what was in the box; it was important to them the hands be blessed before burial. The priest looked shocked; he had officiated at Brenda's funeral without realizing her body was not whole. Mike Schaefer said he feared that burying the ashes next to Brenda's body might be illegal.

The priest smiled a little.

"There are things that are legal," he said, "and there are things that are right."

The priest placed his hands on the box, asking God to make Brenda Sue Schaefer's body whole again. Mike was pleased; the brief prayer seemed perfect, as if Father Osborne had somehow prepared for it.

The three men spoke briefly of the murder trial: the change of venue from Louisville, the flamboyant black prosecutor in a 97-percent-white county, the dismal performance of a prime witness, a jury with members who obviously had an agenda all their own.

Father Osborne shook his head in disgust.

"Shiiit," he said in a low voice.

It was 11:00 A.M. when the brothers reached Vogt Cremation Service. They were disappointed in its looks. It was a concrete-block building with an overhead door and metal roof located in an industrial area southeast of Louisville. Mike wanted to open the cardboard box to verify Brenda's hands were inside, but the cardboard lid was taped too tightly, and he didn't have a knife.

Company president John Vogt greeted them with suspicion; where had they gotten the hands? The brothers showed him Brenda's death certificate and the qualifications certificate naming them co-administrators of their sister's estate. Vogt recognized the Schaefer name; the murder trial had been highly publicized. He agreed to the cremation, telling the brothers to come back at 2:00 P.M.

"There won't be much left," a Vogt employee warned them.

The brothers drove to their parents' two-story, yellow-brick house; they wanted to use their father's old gardening spade to bury Brenda's hands. They returned to Vogt and paid thirty-five dollars for the cremation. The ashes were in a black plastic box roughly six inches wide, nine inches long, and three inches deep.

Mike Schaefer drove to Cave Hill Cemetery, parking the car on the blacktop road that curved below the family plot. He remained determined to peer into the black box to verify its contents, but he felt a little morbid curiosity about them, too. He removed the lid and took out a clear, Ziploc plastic bag containing the ashes. They were sand-colored, with the consistency of fine wood ashes. The individual bones, bleached white by the fire, floated in the ashes.

Working carefully, the brothers removed a piece of sod from the grassy slope and dug a deep hole. They placed the box on end in the hole, filled in the dirt, and replaced the sod, removing all evidence of any burial.

The brothers bowed their heads and stood silently on the hill, a warm sun in their faces. They said no more prayers; at that point they had heard enough cemetery prayers.

CHAPTER 2

The Schaefer family had always drawn closer together in times of crisis. Essie liked to greet family members in her big living room, a comfortable, old-fashioned mix of dark furniture, pale green drapes, and creamy wallpaper covered with ferns. John might meet them there, but more often than not he'd be found in his small, cramped room off the kitchen, staring at the television.

They were not a family comfortable with outward affection. They tried, not always successfully, to keep individual problems at some distance. But beneath those paper-thin walls they were deeply attached to home, to each other. They'd always gathered in great numbers on Christmas, Labor Day, and Memorial Day, kidding with and playing tricks on each other as their terms of endearment.

John and Essie were keepers and collectors. The top of their living-room stereo was cluttered with family pictures, their white-brick fireplace mantel decorated with homemade crafts. Carolyn Kopp, Brenda's older sister, often made dried-flower arrangements. Brenda wasn't quite as talented, but enjoyed making pinecone wreaths and lamps from hobby kits.

Seventeen years after his murder, Jack's street clothes and

7

police uniforms still hung in an upstairs bedroom. His father had saved all the newspaper stories in scrapbooks. Tom Schaefer, who shared a bedroom with his older brother when he was murdered, kept them neat. Tom kept Jack's old car for a long time after his murder, as he would his sister's.

Brenda's baby shoes, her high school ring, and the gown in which she was christened—*all* the Schaefer children were christened in the gown their father had worn at his 1913 christening—were carefully saved in boxes.

The Schaefer family had lived in the St. Matthews area nearly one hundred and fifty years. Not one member of the older generations—and they all grew up in huge German-Catholic families—ever left Jefferson County. John and Essie's St. Matthews house was less than six blocks from the place where the first Schaefer had settled in the 1840s.

The Schaefers were farmers, bakers, butchers, painters, mechanics, and distillery workers; handy, hardworking, and frugal. The first to arrive in St. Matthews—the Potato Capital of the World—was Valentine Schaefer, Brenda's great-grandfather, who emigrated to the United States from farm country near Frankfurt, Germany. Valentine Schaefer met Anna Kolb, another German immigrant-farmer, and they married soon after. He was killed in 1897 when a train struck his horse-drawn wagon.

Anna and Valentine had eight children, including John Joseph Schaefer, who was born on the family farm in 1888. In 1910 he married Catherine Lammlein, one of seven children. She had grown up near Butchertown, a hog-slaughtering center where pigs were routinely herded down streets, their bloody, stinking offal tossed into nearby Beargrass Creek.

John Joseph and Catherine would have ten children, six boys and four girls. They tried to make a living on the family truck farm, but the drought years of 1912-1914 turned their fields brown and barren, forcing them into bankruptcy.

John then went to work for Hall's Seed Company in Louisville, selling field seed. Catherine stayed home to raise the children. They eventually settled in Germantown, a neighborhood of whitewashed trees and fences, neat yards, neighborhood bars, and elongated "shotgun" houses.

Brenda's father, John William Schaefer, was their first son. He was born in the old family farmhouse in 1913, part of the first generation of Schaefers that didn't speak mostly German. He attended Catholic schools, going no farther than eighth grade, normal for the times and the family. The Schaefer boys were expected to work as soon as possible, turning their pay over to their parents, who would give some back as allowance.

"You need to stay out of school and get a job," his father had advised him.

John William was driving a Model-T delivery truck when he was nine years old. He apprenticed as a butcher, working in a downtown Louisville meat market. He worked for a wholesale grocery company, had a route selling coffee, and helped paint the interior of Louisville's elegant Seelbach Hotel.

He lived under special family grace, paying less for room and board than his brothers. John William had become very ill in the 1918 flu epidemic; a two-year-old sister had already died of spinal meningitis.

"If John gets well," his mother promised herself, and her church, "he can get anything he wants."

John lived his German heritage: shrewd, tough-minded, hardworking, stoic, unable to open up to his children. Despite his lack of formal education, he taught himself to do all the family bookkeeping and taxes. He knew the value of money, of putting something away; if there was some overtime or holiday time to be worked, John Schaefer would work it. He always found odd jobs during the months he was laid off. He would take care of his family—if you could justify an expense you could get the money—but he would be very tightfisted all of his life.

In the mid-1930s Mary Essie Downs moved to Louisville from Holy Cross, Kentucky, a picturesque, knobby, strongly Catholic area of the state about fifty miles southeast of the city. She had been born in 1915, the second youngest of a dozen children, several of whom died at birth. All the girls in the Downs family were named Mary after the Blessed Mother, so Mary Essie always went by her middle name.

Essie had come to Louisville to work as a live-in housekeeper. She and John Schaefer dated a short time, some dancing at local German bars, mostly visiting family and playing pinochle. Neither one ever drank heavily, although John could occasionally be persuaded to get a little deeper into his mug. (One year after a Christmas party he ended up in the backyard talking at length to the family dog.) John and Essie were married in Holy Cross in 1937.

Essie was plainspoken, with a quick sense of humor; she might wrap a bow around her head at Christmas, then dance the "shimmy" across the living room. Her role in life was to take care of her family, to cook, clean, bake, and sew fourteen to sixteen hours a day. John Schaefer was very content with that arrangement; he expected it.

Essie could be strict; she had her ways of gaining control. She was surprisingly strong; when her boys were young she could easily wrestle them to the ground, pinning their arms, getting their attention with piercing finger "pinches." When one of her teenage sons came home sick from too much drink, she held his head down in the toilet bowl while he did his best to fill it with vomit. Another time she found a condom in a teenage son's pocket—a grievous sin for a Catholic. She stomped loudly downstairs to tell her husband, who was working in the basement tool room.

"Look what I found," she shouted.

Her husband, who could bend the rules a little, fell silent for a second, the Schaefer boys cringing in fear in an upstairs bedroom.

"I hope to hell they know how to use them," John Schaefer said.

John and Essie Schaefer would raise six children. The oldest was a foster child named Mary Ann Parrott, who was nine when she came from the Louisville Children Center in 1942. Carolyn was born in 1939 and Jack in 1943; both of them were born at home. Hospital births followed: Tom in

1945, Mike in 1948, and Brenda in 1952, when her father was thirty-nine and her mother thirty-seven.

Brenda was born in Louisville's St. Anthony Hospital on April 25. It was a day her sister Carolyn, then thirteen, would savor. She was tired of having only brothers; she lay awake half the night praying hard for a younger sister.

Her father came home early that morning with the news:

"Well, you're not the baby girl anymore."

It was a mixed blessing. Carolyn was expected to help care for Brenda, take her along to a girlfriend's house. Yet Brenda, always so tiny and shy, was easy to care for.

By 1952 Mary Ann had married and left home. The rest of the family—two adults and five children—lived in a small, boxy, two-bedroom home on Staebler Avenue at the edge of St. Matthews. The $6,000 house was very crowded, but John Schaefer didn't want to move; the children would soon be grown and gone; the house would be fine.

John Schaefer had gone to work for the Bernheim Distillery in Louisville in November 1944. He first worked as a handyman, did some whiskey tasting, then graduated to watching pressure gauges and valves in the big vats, a "beer runner" in the language of the business. He often worked the midnight shift, walking diagonally across the tracks behind the house to catch a bus on Frankfort Avenue. The Schaefer children, Brenda in tow, would sometimes meet him at the bus stop as he came home.

In 1957, with five children ages eighteen to five at home, even John Schaefer knew it was time for a larger house. He moved about six blocks to Warner Avenue, paying $16,000 for the nine-room house where Brenda grew up. The house was typical of St. Matthews: large brick homes on quiet streets, many owned by people with blue-collar roots who were moving up but wouldn't feel comfortable in a new subdivision.

Brenda loved the big house. She would slip away to the back porch to hide, and play with her cat. She was the baby, never too far from her mother; Carolyn would call her "Mom's shadow." Brenda was special to Essie. She had become pregnant after Mike was born, but the baby died in her uterus. Essie became very sick, near death. Induced labor was out of the question; the Catholic Church could consider it abortion.

Essie felt trapped between the dictates of her religion and the needs of her family. She felt a mix of guilt, anger, and anxiety; if she died, who would take care of her children? The decomposed fetus was stillborn at home. Essie had a nervous breakdown; she was very upset for months afterward, preoccupied, crying very easily. Brenda's birth helped Essie recover.

As a baby, Brenda wasn't so much pretty as she was appealing. She was thin, frail, with dark blond hair and the liquid-brown eyes of a fawn, the only brown eyes among the children. Her eyes were so large her eyelids wouldn't cover them; she slept with her eyes open.

Brenda went to school at Our Lady of Lourdes, where the Schaefers had always gone to church. Essie, wanting some spending money of her own, went to school with Brenda, taking the job in the school cafeteria.

Brenda was an average student with an interest in art. Even in grade school her personality was constant; she could be spunky, but was often shy, indecisive, didn't like confrontation. If possible she would walk away from an argument; she worried about other people's feelings at the expense of her own.

In her teenage years she found ways to wiggle out from under her mother's thumb. Brenda and Cathy Zirnheld, a good friend at Our Lady of Lourdes, would sneak up into Brenda's bedroom, pop open a window, and smoke cigarettes. Too young to date, Cathy and Brenda would also meet boys at the Vogue Theatre, sit in the back row and make out.

Gary Zirnheld, Cathy's brother, gave Brenda rides to Waggener High School, where Brenda had a small circle of friends. Sometimes they would hang out at the local bowling alley, smoking cigarettes, acting adolescent cool. Occasionally a bunch of kids would slip into Brenda's house through the basement door, then hang out, never doing anything remotely sinful.

"Of our whole group Brenda was always the best person," Zirnheld would say. "She was afraid to do anything really daring."

Carlene Kaiser was another of Brenda's best friends at Our Lady of Lourdes and later at Waggener High School. Brenda was the only Schaefer child to attend a public high school, something she had worked out with her mother, although no one knew why. Carlene and Brenda spent nights at each other's houses. Kaiser admired Brenda; she was quietly popular, always so neat and well-dressed. The girls dated very little their first two years at Waggener. Brenda remained naive, very close to her mother, overprotected. Brenda was determined to be a virgin when she married; premarital sex was a sin. At night, talking to Carlene in the confessional atmosphere of a dark bedroom, Brenda would fret about her looks.

"Brenda," Carlene would say, "you have nothing to worry about. You're beautiful."

Brenda would disagree; her adolescent insecurities ran bone deep: Her hair didn't look good, her makeup was bad; silliest of all, she thought she was fat.

On July 4, 1967, shortly after Brenda's fifteenth birthday, her father and Tom bought a small summer "camp" along the Ohio River a few miles north of Harrods Creek. The camp was a powder-blue cinder-block building that served as a summer cabin. It was built on two fifty-foot-wide lots that ran well back from the river into a scattering of big sycamore, soft maple, and cottonwood trees. It was a peaceful place, barely a half hour from St. Matthews, with just enough amenities to be comfortable, always a breeze coming in off the river, although the mosquitoes were terrible at night.

The following summer Brenda was lying out on the dock sunning and swimming with Carlene Kaiser and another friend when two young men came by in an old fiberglass runabout. One of them was Charles "Pete" Van Pelt, nineteen, who lived across the Ohio in Utica, Indiana, a historic, out-of-the-way river town, clannish, insular, and pretty much proud of it.

Van Pelt was instantly infatuated with Brenda; she reminded him of Marlo Thomas on *That Girl*. At sixteen Brenda had grown into an attractive young woman with shoulder-length hair, her brown eyes evenly set in a perfectly tanned face. Van Pelt would be Brenda's first—and only—real high school boyfriend.

Van Pelt worked as a Louisville police dispatcher, hoping to become an officer someday, but he was too short at the time, barely taller than Brenda. Brenda was lithe, pretty, appealing, an incredible catch. Van Pelt adored her, was very possessive of her. His life experience was small-town, male-dominated; he had the right to control their relationship, spend the money, make the decisions, much as Brenda's father had done.

Brenda was just as immature. She'd had few friends, male or female, away from her family. When in doubt, she would turn home, toward her mother. Her relationship with Van Pelt dominated her last two years of high school. When Van Pelt gave her an engagement ring during her senior year, Brenda delighted in showing it off; she'd make a big show of lifting her left hand with her right hand, as if the ring weighed twenty-five pounds.

She was an average high school student with few outside interests; the only activity listed in her 1971 yearbook, *The Lair*, was "Art-4." The yearbook was signed by eight classmates, all of them girls, most of them wishing her good luck in her marriage to Pete. Friends who double-dated with them during those years said they fought often: teenage bickering, nothing serious.

Their wedding was set for midsummer of 1971, a few months after graduation. Van Pelt had pushed the marriage, and Brenda didn't object. Her friends were getting married; it was the thing to do. Her wish was for a big German wedding with a band.

Jack Schaefer, the big brother who had always delighted in teasing his baby sister, turned serious: He tried to talk her out of marrying anyone at her age. The rest of the family thought them too young, but if that's what Brenda wanted, then Pete Van Pelt—whom they accepted—would be part of the family.

Jack's brutal murder on May 2 tore the family to pieces.

Van Pelt was working on dispatch that night. He helped form a group to go tell Essie. She saw them coming down the sidewalk.

"It's Jack," she said. Then she fainted.

Brenda's senior year of high school ended with grieving for her dead brother. They had been close; at the funeral service Brenda and Carolyn both leaned over the casket and kissed their brother good-bye. The wedding was postponed until December 1971. The bride wore a white high-necked gown with a net veil and white ribbon trim. The groom wore a black tuxedo. They looked very young.

Years later Van Pelt would fondly recall the early years of their marriage, although its problems were obvious. He found Brenda to be warm and loving, although his friends might misinterpret her shyness for aloofness. Their main problem was sex; Van Pelt said Brenda liked to kiss and snuggle but was very sexually inhibited, terrified of the physical act of making love. Van Pelt would say he and Brenda weren't often intimate in the four years they were married. He said she never told him why she was so inhibited and was reluctant to talk to marriage counselors.

Although she would later admit to close female friends that she was very uncomfortable with sex, Brenda never gave them a reason; that area of her life was closed. She would say she did not like Van Pelt's sexual approach; his needs did not match hers. She never mentioned any abusive childhood incidents, physical or emotional, that could have produced sexual fears. Her naïveté, innocence, and Catholic guilt may have produced her fears, a less-than-sensitive husband may have aggravated them, but that part of Brenda was always a mystery to the people who knew her best.

Like many young couples, Brenda and Pete constantly argued about money. Van Pelt had an $8,600 income as a police dispatcher. Brenda worked part-time as a sales clerk and was taking training as a nurse's aide. Van Pelt accused Brenda of becoming too interested in money and material things, calling her "as stubborn and tight as her father."

He complained that if they went to parties and his friends started drinking too much, using bad language, perhaps even smoking a joint of marijuana, Brenda would want to go home. Brenda wanted an apartment in Kentucky near her mother. Van Pelt loved Essie, but was content with their Clarksville, Indiana, apartment about midway between families.

Brenda—and the whole Schaefer family—had a laundry list of incidents in which Van Pelt was financially irresponsible, buying things he and Brenda couldn't afford. Brenda complained he was so jealous he would follow her to her girlfriend's house, even follow her when she rode a bicycle around the parking lot.

The final year of their four-year marriage seemed very long, filled with arguments, finally bitter. Van Pelt would say he pounded on a few walls in frustration, that Brenda once picked up a butcher knife but never really threatened to use it. A divorce was inevitable. Brenda's family struggled with the decision; the Catholic Church said married couples should remain together regardless.

"My dad was against Brenda coming home," her sister Carolyn would say. "He said she made her bed, she ought to stay there and get it straightened out. Mom said, 'No, we can't do that.' "

Brenda felt embarrassed and guilty, trapped among her father, the Church, and a bad marriage. The divorce decree, saying the marriage was irretrievably broken, became final on March 23, 1976.

Van Pelt got their 1972 Pontiac Firebird and about $4,200 in unpaid bills, including $125 for marriage counseling.

Brenda, then almost twenty-four, went back to Warner Avenue with a few household furnishings, including three iron skillets and a color television set. She also received their twelve-year-old Chevrolet. She seemed relieved the marriage was over, but was very quiet about it. She later moved to an apartment, stayed there a while, then went home again.

On June 1, 1976, she had her name legally changed back to Brenda Sue Schaefer. She'd been hurt by the divorce, didn't date for a while, but was quietly determined to make a new life.

CHAPTER
3

Jefferson County Police Detective Jim Wesley worked weekends only every six weeks, always the 4:00 P.M. to midnight shift. Like everyone else in the county's seventeen-member violent-crimes unit, he had little control over assignments; the violent crimes found him.

Wesley, thirty-six, went to work on September 25, 1988, looking for a quiet day to fill out the weekend. It was Sunday, crisp and clean, a high of 76 degrees and a low of 55, a welcome change from the steady rain that had pummeled parts of the county the night before. Wesley was a popular officer, the police incarnation of a Norman Rockwell cover—handsome, resolute, ready to serve. He wore the usual plain-clothes-detective uniform: sport coat, tie, slacks, and dress shoes; county detectives normally wore suits only in court.

His violent-crimes unit was located in the basement of the Hall of Justice in downtown Louisville. The four-story building, worn-looking and overcrowded from the day it opened, held the various courtrooms, judges' chambers, support staff, and prisoners. The violent-crimes squad room was at the far end of two narrow basement corridors; nearly a dozen older desks and a sergeant's office squeezed into one area.

Wesley had no active murder investigations. He wanted to

catch up on his paperwork and get home to his wife, Anne, and daughter, Meredith. He checked the activity logs from the previous shift to see if any immediate follow-up was needed. Nothing; so far so good. He walked over to his desk and picked up a note left in his metal basket by Jefferson County detective Dave Wood.

It said police in St. Matthews, a small community within Jefferson County at the eastern edge of Louisville, were working a missing-persons case and had requested county help. A blue-over-white 1984 Buick Regal bearing Kentucky license plate XYD484 and registered to a Brenda Sue Schaefer, thirty-six, of 3716 Warner Avenue, St. Matthews, had been found abandoned along the westbound lane of Interstate 64 in St. Matthews at 6:08 that Sunday morning.

Wesley had just put down the note when his telephone rang. It was St. Matthews police detective Jim Ennis asking if the Jefferson County police might be willing to take over the case.

Ennis filled in some detail: Schaefer's car had been parked along the edge of the roadway near a limestone outcropping about one hundred feet west of the place where Breckenridge Lane passed over Interstate 64. The car's right rear tire was flat. The car had been broken into and ransacked. Papers were scattered around the floor and on the ground nearby. The car had three quarters of a tank of gas. It had 44,087.8 miles on the odometer.

The car's stereo, a Clarion model 8600, was missing. Someone had tried to pry open the trunk, and what could be blood was sprinkled across the backseat and outside the car. The police were not sure if the blood was Schaefer's or had come from someone who might have broken into an already abandoned car to steal the stereo. One of the investigating St. Matthews officers had placed his hand on the passenger seat during the examination, possibly leaving prints.

Ennis said the car was coated in dew, its engine and tailpipe cold. There was a hand mark in the dew on the right rear fender, as if someone had braced himself to stand up.

Ennis described Schaefer as being about five feet three

inches tall, 118 pounds, with dark-brown, shoulder-length hair, brown eyes, and no identifiable marks or scars. She'd been wearing jeans, a light-colored sweater, and expensive jewelry, including diamond rings and a gold necklace.

"It's my gut feeling," Ennis told Wesley, "that this could be much more than a missing-persons case."

"I'll be right out," Wesley answered.

Wesley, a county officer for thirteen years, had no immediate sense of something seriously wrong. He became the county's lead detective in the Brenda Schaefer case by chance—and by agreeing to help a fellow officer.

Growing up, Wesley had never thought of police work. He wanted to follow his father, a dentist, into the medical profession. He didn't want dentistry; he didn't foresee any joy in putting his hands in other people's mouths. Almost romantically, Wesley envisioned himself a general practitioner, a roomful of sick people outside his door waiting to be helped.

His father, Earl Bennett Wesley, and his mother, Edna Blanche Ross, grew up near Augusta, Kentucky, a historic Ohio River town where fine houses were built into the rising hills like a terraced cake. Both preferred to be called by their middle names. They met at Augusta High School, Bennett a senior, Blanche a freshman. Bennett went on to Transylvania College in Lexington. He enlisted in the navy in World War II, serving on a tanker. Blanche worked for the Army Signal Corps in Dayton, Ohio. They married during the war in New York City.

After the war, Bennett attended the University of Louisville dental school, graduating in 1949. His first office was in a hardware-store building in nearby Jeffersontown. He gave up his small private practice in the early 1950s, working at the Veterans Administration Hospital in Louisville for thirty-five years. His wife became a full-time housewife and mother.

Jim was born in 1952, the second of four children, two girls and two boys. When he was seven, his family moved to Fern Creek, a quiet, rural community a few miles south of Louisville. It was an idyllic childhood: a big wood behind his house, a loving family, his mother always near, a father he admired who often took him hunting, a solid infusion of Middle-America family values that Wesley would carry with honor. He went to Fern Creek High School, played tennis and basketball, a joy in basketball-mad Kentucky. He earned As and Bs with little effort—and learned that he had a real knack for the sciences, which fueled his dream of becoming a doctor.

He graduated from high school in 1970, following a close friend—who became a dermatologist—to Western Kentucky University in Bowling Green. Free for the first time, he partied too much, watched his grades slide, his easygoing personality a liability in the educational fast track required for med school. The next year he transferred to the smaller, more academically focused Transylvania—his father's school— where his road into med school seemed more solidly paved.

George Merriweather changed that. He had invited Wesley to the rush party at Delta Sigma Phi, led some of the hazing as pledge classes were hauled out into the countryside for forced calisthenics, then became Wesley's fraternal big brother. The two became instant friends. Merriweather, from Palo Alto, California, had money—lots of old family money—a strong physical presence, and a diplomatic charm. He had a thrill-seeking edge to him; he graduated from Transylvania in 1972 and immediately joined the Lexington Police Department just to see what the hell police work was all about. Wesley, barely twenty, began riding with him at night, fascinated by the calm way Merriweather handled tense situations, even in the tinderbox atmosphere of the Lexington low-income projects in the early 1970s.

Merriweather was a police dilettante; he quit the Lexington force in three years. Wesley felt a more permanent pull into law enforcement. It appealed to his basic instinct to want to help people, to make them safe. And his grade-point average hovered at 3.0, well below medical-school requirements. Wesley changed his goals, surprising everyone who knew him, including his parents. After graduating from Transylvania in 1975 with a double major in biology and education, he signed on with the Jefferson County Police Department. His past was so squeaky clean, he couldn't even remember getting a speeding ticket. His immediate goal was to be a uniformed officer, then a detective. He often looked ahead, sometimes at his own expense; his long-range goal was that after three years he would apply for the FBI.

It was early Sunday evening when Wesley arrived at the St. Matthews Police Department, a one-story redbrick building on Thierman Lane across the street from a condominium complex. Detective Ennis gave Wesley some more background. Schaefer's car had been towed to Coffey's Wrecker Service on Poplar Level Road, locked away in a blue, metallic storage building. The Jefferson County Evidence Technician Unit would check the car for fingerprints, palm prints, head and pubic hair samples, bloodstains, and other possible evidence. The flat tire would be removed, X-rayed for cause of damage, and sent to an Ohio company for detailed analysis.

A second vehicle, a black two-door 1982 Dodge registered to a Michael Boyd of Louisville, was found abandoned about five hundred yards west of Schaefer's Buick. Its passenger side window had been broken, but the radio was not stolen. Schaefer's car had been found by St. Matthews police officer Tom Gilsdorf. He went to the Schaefer home at 6:39 A.M. to fill out a missing-persons report and get a picture of Brenda, who had been living at home to help care for her mother, Essie, who was ill with lupus. The Schaefers told Gilsdorf Brenda had been wearing two diamond rings, a diamond bracelet, a gold bracelet, and a gold necklace, all of it appraised at more than $30,000.

Gilsdorf also contacted Mel Ignatow, Brenda's fiancé, apparently the last person to see her on Saturday night. Ignatow, fifty, who always carefully pronounced his name Ig-*nah*-toe, had been a salesman and buyer for Rosalco, a Louisville import-export company for twenty-three years.

He'd lost his job about a year earlier, failed at a real-estate venture in Florida, and had returned to Louisville, where he'd tried to get established selling water-softener equipment.

Ignatow told Gilsdorf he and Schaefer had been together most of Saturday afternoon and evening; Ignatow said Brenda drove her Buick because he had a tire problem on his 1984 Corvette. Brenda had left his house late Saturday night, probably heading home along Interstate 64. Ignatow lived in an expensive eastern Jefferson County home with his mother, Virginia. Normally the trip to St. Matthews from his house would take about fifteen minutes.

When Brenda didn't get home, a worried Essie Schaefer called Ignatow's house about 3:30 A.M. Sunday.

"Where's Brenda?" she asked. "Have you seen Brenda? Her car's not here."

Ignatow seemed surprised.

"Well, my God," he answered. "She left here about eleven-thirty P.M."

Essie Schaefer paused. She disliked Ignatow; she knew Brenda wanted to get away from him. She knew Brenda was trying to get back with Louisville dentist Jim Rush, an old boyfriend. Brenda might even be with Rush. She had to think of a story to cover for her daughter.

"Oh, wait a minute," Essie Schaefer said. "I think Brenda went over to see my daughter-in-law."

Ignatow asked her to check. Essie Schaefer never called him back. Near 4:00 A.M. Ignatow called her. Essie, still covering for her daughter, said Brenda was at her daughter-in-law's.

"Are you *sure*?" Ignatow asked.

"Yes, she's there."

Ignatow seemed stunned. He quickly called the daughter-in-law, Sandy Schaefer. She had not seen Brenda. She blamed the bizarre answer on internal family problems. Ignatow began crying on the phone, saying he was worried about Brenda.

"What am I going to do?" he asked Schaefer, sobbing loudly.

At 4:17 A.M. Ignatow dialed 911, reaching a Jefferson County police dispatcher. His voice faltering a little, he said, "I don't know if I've got a problem here or not. . . . I've got a person who's missing, or seems to be missing."

The dispatcher suggested Ignatow call the St. Matthews Police Department, which had jurisdiction.

Essie Schaefer couldn't sleep. About 4:30 A.M. she called Jim Rush and told him Brenda was missing. Rush got dressed and drove around for an hour to some of the night spots he and Brenda had visited. He cruised past Mel Ignatow's house looking for his Corvette. Tom Schaefer called Mike, who went to Brenda's condominium to look for her. Mike called Tom to report she wasn't there.

"You better come over to the house right away," Tom told him.

Mike drove quickly to Warner Avenue, arriving about the same time as Gilsdorf. The officer told them he had found Brenda's car, its right rear tire flat.

"What caused the hole?" asked Mike. "Was it a nail, a bullet . . . ?"

"I don't know," the officer said.

Tom Schaefer called his girlfriend, Linda Love, to tell her his sister was missing. Love, an attractive, dark-haired woman, had been dating Schaefer for four years. She was a hairdresser, had dealt with many beautiful women, but she was startled by Brenda's beauty from the moment they met; she was so pretty, with a good figure, very simply dressed. Brenda was one of those women who never seemed to realize how beautiful she was, the impact she made on others.

The women became friendly; Love and Tom Schaefer double-dated with Brenda and Jim Rush and always had a good time. Love found Brenda a lot like Tom: private, stoic, not prone to talking about their feelings. Tom was so sensitive and sentimental, he felt things so deeply, Love often worried about him.

A few weeks before Brenda disappeared, she and Love had gone to dinner. Brenda was in a talkative mood, the most intimate she had ever been. The women talked of their relationships. Brenda complained, sometimes bitterly, about Ignatow's possessive ways, telling a story Love found almost impossible to believe: She and Ignatow had gone on a vacation trip. Brenda woke up in their motel with Ignatow standing over her holding a cloth to her face, a cloth apparently doused in chloroform.

Brenda became hysterical.

"What the hell you doing?" she shouted, struggling to get awake.

"I just wanted you to relax," Ignatow answered. "It's something to help you go to sleep."

"I *was* asleep."

Brenda told Love she packed her bags that morning and wanted to leave. Something stopped her; she couldn't get a flight home or Ignatow had apologized. Brenda stayed with him.

Brenda made Love promise not to tell Tom about the incident; she reluctantly agreed. She didn't like Ignatow either; she had never understood what Brenda could see in him. Now she was frightened for her. The two sat in a parked car for an hour after dinner.

"Get rid of him," Love told her. "He's the worst of the worst. You are so pretty. You're smart. You have a lot to offer."

Brenda always had the same answer: "You just don't understand."

Love had spoken to Brenda on the phone the Friday night before she disappeared. Brenda was upset, very nervous.

"I think Mel followed me home," she told Love.

Love knew Brenda had plans to break up with Ignatow.

"Are you going to give him his ring back tomorrow night?"

"Oh, yeah."

"Just think, Brenda. After tomorrow night you'll never have to see his ugly face again."

When Love arrived at the Schaefer home Sunday, the family was in shock, moving back and forth between the big living room and the more secluded kitchen in back, the traditional gathering place. Love hugged Essie Schaefer; the two women had become close, often calling each other on the phone. Essie couldn't sit still, always getting up, peering anxiously out the front curtains, her long vigil begun. John Schaefer was more withdrawn; in times of stress he would often place his hands on his knees and stare off into space, or retreat to his room.

Ignatow came to the house early Sunday afternoon, parking his Corvette across the street from the family home. The Schaefers took quick note of the car, the one Ignatow said he wouldn't drive the day before because of a tire problem. Ignatow was solicitous, apologetic. He would later bring his mother with him to the Schaefer house on a sympathy call.

"I really feel bad about coming over here. Am I interfering in any way? I don't want to interfere."

Ignatow was a tall, rangy man, six feet five and 190 pounds. He had a fetish about neatness, physical appearance, but was not well coordinated, often awkward in his movements. His mood in the Schaefer home alternated wildly, one minute composed, the next on edge, weepy. His attempts to ingratiate himself with the family irritated everyone. Tom and Mike Schaefer had to tell him to calm down, he was bothering their mother.

Essie Schaefer had always thought Ignatow treated her thirty-six-year-old daughter like a child. Brenda had told her mother of Ignatow's attempt to press the chloroform-laced handkerchief to her face. Brenda told Essie she wanted to break up with Ignatow, return the jewelry he had given her, but feared his reaction.

"Bring him to the house and give him the darn rings," Essie had said. "He ain't gonna do anything around here."

Ignatow made his way to the big kitchen table, taking a seat at one end. Linda Love was leaning against the sink next to Carolyn Kopp, Brenda's sister, who was thinking of Jack's murder seventeen years earlier:

"Oh, my God, I can't believe this is happening. I can't believe this is happening."

Ignatow put his hands to his face and appeared to start

crying, his sobs the cries of a child gasping for air. Kopp instinctively grabbed his hand.

"She's going to come back, Mel," Kopp said. "I know she's going to show up. She's been kidnapped, but they're going to let her go."

"No, she's not," Ignatow sobbed. "I think she's gone. I think she's dead."

Linda Love had heard enough. She got Tom aside and told him, "We're going to the police."

While leaving, Schaefer wanted to check the tires on Ignatow's Corvette. He and Love walked down the front steps, past the massive oak in their front yard. They were halfway to the Corvette, a spotless bronze model with gray interior, when Ignatow came out the door behind them. They didn't get a close look—Ignatow's presence scared them off—but the Corvette's tires seemed fine.

Schaefer and Love went to the St. Matthews police station where they met Wesley. Schaefer was still unsure of Ignatow's involvement. The one certainty was something was wrong; Brenda always called home.

"If she couldn't get home she would always call because she knew Mom would be worried."

Love had no doubts. She told Wesley the things Brenda had told her at their dinner meeting.

Wesley decided the next person he had to see was Mel Ignatow.

CHAPTER
4

Even before Jim Wesley arrived at the St. Matthews Police Department to meet Linda Love and Tom Schaefer, its officers had done some additional investigative work.

Detective Jim Ennis called the nearby Oldham County police to have an officer check on a thirty-two-foot Bayliner Conquest pleasure boat owned by Mel Ignatow to determine if Brenda Schaefer might be there. Ignatow kept the boat, the *Motion Lotion*, at Tartan's Landing, a 177-slip, upscale marina on the Ohio River about fifteen miles north of Louisville. Ignatow had paid $68,000 for the boat in 1986, plus $15,000 for his slip and an annual $275 marina maintenance fee. The boat, sleek white with blue trim, was powered by twin 260-horsepower engines.

The boat slept six, could easily carry a dozen passengers. Its interior was beige, with teak molding and smoked glass on the galley appliances. Ignatow kept the boat spotless, sometimes spending forty-five minutes cleaning it before taking it out, always following passengers around with a rag in case they spilled a drink. It had Florida registration FL8036GA, which saved Ignatow, a Kentucky resident, tax money.

Oldham County detective Bill Bosemer made the run to

Tartan's Landing, driving carefully along North Buckeye Lane, which snaked past rolling farmland, horse farms defined by miles of black fence, and architect-designed homes tucked back in the woods, their windows angled to catch some sun. Bosemer met with harbormaster Charles Doll about 11:30 P.M. Sunday. Doll told him Ignatow, sounding worried, had already called about Brenda late that afternoon.

"Have you seen Brenda?" Ignatow asked Doll. "Have you seen her car anywhere out there? . . . Brenda's missing."

Ignatow told Doll that Brenda had been depressed about her job, was having problems with her family; no one knew what had happened to her. Ignatow said he was ready to sell the boat and move to Florida.

"Let me know if you see anything," he told Doll.

Bosemer searched the *Motion Lotion*, found only cobwebs and spiders. He relayed the information to Ennis, who would tell Wesley, a procedure typical of the early hours of the investigation. Such relays were a necessary part of Jefferson County police work; the county was Balkanized; it had almost one hundred smaller towns and communities within its boundaries, including Louisville, which meant a patchwork quilt of governmental agencies. Cooperation between the various police departments was usually good, but communication could be labored; professional jealousies could get involved.

Four police agencies were involved the first day of the investigation. Brenda Schaefer's car was found in St. Matthews. The larger and better-equipped Jefferson County police were soon called. Mel Ignatow's home was in Jeffersontown. The Oldham County police had briefly been involved. And the FBI—Brenda Schaefer could have been taken across state lines—was waiting in the wings. So out of professional courtesy, and following correct procedure, Wesley and Ennis called Jeffersontown police detective Robert O. Perkins before visiting Ignatow.

Perkins, thirty-four, had also done some work on the case; he'd been called about 10:30 A.M. Sunday by Jefferson County detective Dave Wood, who told him Brenda Schaefer apparently was missing; Mel Ignatow was the last to see her. At 4:35 P.M., Perkins drove out to Ignatow's house at 10500 Florian Road. Ignatow wasn't home; apparently he was still at the Schaefers'. The officer talked briefly with Virginia Ignatow, who remembered her son's coming home about 11:30 Saturday night.

"He shouted up the stairs at me that Brenda had dropped him off," she said.

Ignatow and his mother co-owned the two-story brick home in the booming Plainview area of Jeffersontown. They'd bought it in February 1984 for $149,000, a high price in the Louisville housing market, then one of the least expensive in the country. The spotted-brown brick was accented with dark-brown wooden trim and a dark, almost black roof. The front of the house was shaped like an A-frame which was built—a little incongruously—against the main house. There was an attached two-car garage at the rear of the home, which had a full basement.

Florian Road was lined with upper-middle-class executive homes, a repetitive flow of shuttered brick houses with landscaped lawns. Mailboxes, some built into rounded brick columns like small ovens, were precisely placed along the road. Ignatow's front yard was neat but poorly landscaped, with only a few obligatory evergreens and taller shade trees; the backyard was practically bare. Ignatow didn't have time for or interest in landscaping; nor did his mother, who had been ill and did a lot of volunteer work.

A pebbled sidewalk hooked around the front of the house to a small, open porch that protected a recessed front door. The door opened to a hallway that lead to the kitchen. The great room with a chocolate-brown rug was on the left, the living room and dining room on the right. Ahead were steps to the second floor.

Ignatow lived upstairs, his room opening to a balcony over the great room. He also had an upstairs den with a fireplace. His mother had a small bedroom in another area of the second floor, a place where she spent much of her time by herself; her son didn't like messes in other areas of their house. His guests were invariably stunned by his remodeled bathroom, which he told people had cost him almost $25,000. The pink and beige walls matched his toilet paper; his tub was pink granite with gold faucets. The bath had huge mirrors, an etched-glass shower door and controlled lighting. Ignatow kept his bathroom so spotless that guests were intimidated by it, afraid to use it.

Soon after Perkins, Ennis, and Wesley reached Ignatow's home, the three officers developed a game plan: Ennis would talk to the neighbors while Wesley and Perkins questioned Ignatow. As the officers stood in his driveway about 7:30 P.M., talking over final strategy, Ignatow popped out his front door and walked toward them.

"Excuse me," Wesley told him. "If you'll go back in the house I'll be right with you."

Ignatow waved and went back inside.

Ignatow's eagerness annoyed Wesley; he'd never met the man and he already had bad feelings about him. As Wesley and Perkins went inside, Wesley glanced around. He had never seen a home so immaculate; everything clean, dusted, and in its place. Two silver candelabra in the dining room were centered perfectly below the six glass globes of the chandelier. Black vases and white artificial flowers—much of the decor was Oriental—were spotless. The dark-brown rug looked unused. The kitchen table and counter gleamed. Wesley felt a little uneasy . . . the house was uncomfortably neat.

The three men sat down at the large kitchen table, Wesley facing Ignatow. Within minutes Ignatow was using their first names, beginning his sentences with, "Well, Jim . . ."

Ignatow spoke from carefully prepared notes, telling the officers in detail the events of the previous day. Brenda Schaefer had come by about 3:00 or 3:30 P.M. Saturday. Normally Ignatow would pick up Brenda in his Corvette, but he had problems with one of his tires; it had a whining sound and he feared it might have picked up a nail or had some type of cord separation. Saturday had been a dreary day, gray and rainy; Ignatow didn't want to risk having Brenda injured in his Corvette.

"I asked Brenda if she would drive," Ignatow said.

Brenda took equal pride in her car. It was gleaming white with a blue vinyl roof that came partway down around the rear window. She bought it used, replaced its eight-track tape system with the Clarion model 8600 and a power boost for better sound; her tastes in music ran to movie themes, some country, some top 40. She regularly washed and waxed the car herself.

"Brenda liked to drive," Ignatow assured Wesley.

Ignatow told the officers he and Brenda had no specific plans for Saturday; they both felt like driving around, a typical day for them. They left his house about 4:00 P.M., driving about six miles west in heavy drizzle and traffic to a Gold Star Chili restaurant in the Hikes Point area of Louisville. From there they drove almost ten miles—backtracking a little toward Ignatow's house—to visit a boat show at Harrods Creek Landing near the Ohio River, a show the couple had visited the year before. Ignatow said the weather was so bad they parked at the landing and talked a few minutes, but never went on a boat.

Ignatow told the officers Brenda wasn't very good company; she was depressed and worried because she had been working too hard, her mother's illness was getting worse. He repeatedly interrupted the officers' questioning to ask about Brenda's car; had it been found, what was its condition?

Wesley, believing Ignatow was trying too hard to lead the questioning, decided to lie to him, gauge his reaction:

"Mel, we don't know where the car is."

Ignatow remained smooth, smug, traits that would come to infuriate Wesley. Ignatow continued his story:

He and Brenda left Harrods Landing and drove north on U.S. 42 to the town of Prospect to visit an art fair, but rain again kept them in Brenda's car. They drove north another ten to fifteen miles along U.S. 42 into Oldham County, wanting to look at a housing development. They turned around, drove back into Louisville, arriving at the massive Oxmoor shopping center in St. Matthews near Brenda's home about 6:30 P.M. They walked around Oxmoor until 9:00 P.M., buying nothing. They drove back to the Harrods Creek area, visiting a popular Ohio River restaurant called Captain's Quarters.

"It was dark at the time," Ignatow explained, "and there weren't many people around, so we looked out at the water five or ten minutes and left."

Ignatow said Brenda wanted to see the Falls of the Ohio fountain, a floating Louisville landmark anchored several hundred yards off the downtown Louisville Belvedere, its fleur-de-lis pattern bathed in reds, pinks, and blues. Halfway downtown they changed their minds; the weather was too bad. They turned around and returned to the Hurstbourne Lane area, doing more window shopping at the new Stony Brook Shopping Center.

It was close to 11:30 P.M. when Brenda drove Ignatow home. He slid across the seat, kissed her good night.

"Drive safely," he said.

Then he went into his house.

He said he shouted upstairs to his mother, then settled down to read the newspaper and mail. About a half hour later, feeling hungry, he went to the refrigerator; nothing looked good. About midnight, driving his Corvette with the bad tire, he went to the Skyline Chili in the nearby Plainview Shopping Center.

He arrived about midnight, sat on one of the red counter stools at the short gray counter. He ordered spaghetti and chili, and a soft drink. There was a football game on the television. Ignatow made a point of talking to the waiter on duty, fussing with him over the size of a soft drink. He said he went home about 1:30 A.M. and went to bed. He slept until almost 4:00 A.M. when Essie Schaefer called to ask about Brenda.

Wesley and Perkins took careful notes. Wesley was proud of his ability to interview, to get people to open up, but this one had been less than satisfactory.

"Mel," he said, "do you realize almost everything you told me can't be corroborated by anyone?"

"Well, yeah, I understand that could be bad," he said. "I guess I could be a suspect. . . . But that's the way it is. . . ."

Wesley and Perkins later stood in the dark shadows of Ignatow's driveway, comparing notes. The officers shared bad feelings about Ignatow. Perkins found Ignatow cold and methodical; he told the story as if reading from a script. Wesley believed Brenda Schaefer might already be dead.

On his way back to the Jeffersontown police station, Perkins stopped by Skyline Chili to ask if Ignatow had been there the night before. The manager on duty didn't remember seeing him.

Early Monday morning Robert Longshore, a Skyline assistant manager, went to the Jeffersontown police station and identified Ignatow as the man who had been at the restaurant early Sunday morning.

St. Matthews detective Jim Ennis went to several houses in the area but couldn't find any neighbors who remembered seeing Brenda late Saturday night.

CHAPTER
5

Although Jim Wesley, Jim Ennis, and Bob Perkins could not know it at the time, Jefferson County authorities looking for answers to the murder of Brenda Schaefer would also get help from a distant source: Roy Hazelwood of the Behavioral Science Unit of the FBI Academy at Quantico, Virginia.

Hazelwood's unit—recently given national exposure in the movie *The Silence of the Lambs*—was part of the National Center for the Analysis of Violent Crime, which was devoted to examining the minds and methods of terrorists, sex offenders, and murderers. Located sixty feet belowground, its byzantine entry down an elevator shaft and through a warren of bomb-proof cinder-block offices, it was called "The National Cellar for the Analysis of Violent Crime" by its inhabitants.

Hazelwood's office could have been the debriefing area for the Marquis de Sade. Cardboard boxes stacked haphazardly on metal filing cabinets contained lengthy interviews with homicidal sadists, their wives, and their girlfriends. More disturbing were flat stacks of faded manila envelopes containing photographs of naked adolescent girls and young women being held in sexual bondage. The women were tied up with chains and ropes, their eyes glazed with terror. Most of them would be brutally tortured and raped, then murdered.

The pale yellow office walls were sprinkled with the plaques, certificates, and official letters typical of any public agency, commendations from one hundred police agencies around the world, each grateful for Hazelwood's expertise. High on the wall behind his desk was an unnecessary reminder from a fellow special agent:

WHOEVER FIGHTS MONSTERS SHOULD SEE TO IT THAT IN THE PROCESS HE DOES NOT BECOME A MONSTER. AND WHEN YOU LOOK INTO AN ABYSS, THE ABYSS ALSO LOOKS INTO YOU.

NIETZSCHE

Below that, another sign, the counterpoint to Hazelwood's bizarre working environment:

REMEMBER, WE ALL WORK FOR GOD.

Hazelwood, fifty-two, had a deep voice edged with the gravelly rasp of a longtime smoker. He was a compact five feet eight and 156 pounds, some settling toward his middle. His hair, neatly, combed, was the color of steel wool. Tinted glasses hid his eyes. His facial expression rarely changed: the mask of a man who often peered into the abyss. The gold chain and cross around Hazelwood's neck was his personal counterpoint. He kept his emotional balance by being a Christian, an elder in the Presbyterian Church, a Sunday-school teacher to fourth-grade children. He was a master teacher, in the pulpit or sixty feet underground. He was soothing, confident, quick with answers and explanations of matters beyond normal human understanding. His laughter, sharp and staccato, was reassuring.

When the calls for help came from Louisville, Hazelwood was ready. He had made himself one of the world's experts on criminal sexual sadism. He had studied it, sought out its practitioners and victims, helped put together profiles of both. Of the eight thousand murder cases stored in the Be-

havioral Science Unit computers, only thirty were true criminal sexual sadism, among the rarest of human depravities.

His case studies included a truck driver who abducted a
fourteen-year-old girl, shaved her head and pubic area, then
held her captive six days, often nude and in chains. The
driver took dozens of color photographs, in the cab of his
truck and with the girl chained to an old barn with a metal
ring clipped to her clitoris.

Another sadist, a multiple murderer, enlisted three of his
five wives to help him abuse and murder other women, taking pictures and making audiotapes during much of the torture.

"Those photographs and tapes were his awards," Hazelwood would say. "These people have to keep them the way
a soldier keeps his medals, or you or I keep family pictures.

"They keep collections. They keep horror flicks. I interviewed one woman married to one of these guys and he used
to make her watch pornographic videos. That's common."

Hazelwood was born in Pocatello, Idaho, the son of a bar-
ber who moved his family eight times before Hazelwood was
six. His father finally settled in Houston, eventually owning
a pair of seven-seat shops. Hazelwood went to Spring Branch
High School in Houston, then Sam Houston State University
in Huntsville, Texas, earning a bachelor of science degree in
1960. With four years of ROTC, he was commissioned a
second lieutenant in the U.S. Army military police. He was
a company commander in Vietnam, then accepted a fellowship in forensic medicine at the Armed Forces Institute of
Pathology. His graduation paper, accompanied by slides, was
a detailed examination of sixty types of the more exotic cutting and stabbing wounds.

In 1971 he left the military police with a rank of major to
join the FBI, investigating sexual assaults and homicides on
government reservations. In 1976 he moved to the Behavioral Science Unit at the FBI Academy in Quantico. The
academy, opened in 1972, was a longtime dream of J. Edgar
Hoover. It occupied five hundred acres of rolling, forested
land thirty miles south of Washington, D.C. With its excel-

lent staff and training facilities and dormitories, the academy soon developed two nicknames: The West Point of Law Enforcement and Club Fed.

Hazelwood became part of a team that collected and analyzed more than 150 cases of death during autoeroticism: victims who hanged, electrocuted, or suffocated themselves while seeking sexual gratification, usually through masturbation. He helped write papers on sexual abuse, rape, and serial rape, the latter a study of 41 men who had raped 837 women. Four of those 41 men interested him the most. They were intelligent, organized, proficient, often sexually insatiable. These men did not act from impulse; they carefully seduced their victims, fantasized about their torture, found pleasure in total domination.

They built cells to keep women captive. They preferred anal sex; it was more degrading. They kept their souvenirs: clothing, jewelry, tapes, photographs to help in further fantasy. Their underlying motivation was hatred of women. Hazelwood was fascinated by the ability of these men to seek out, manipulate, and eventually destroy women while still functioning in normal society, often with all the financial and social trappings of success.

"I wondered what made these people tick," he would say. "I wondered why. Why should they be stimulated by another person's humiliation, degradation?"

He found his answer, in part, in the writings of one of the sadists, a serial murderer:

"... there is no greater power over another person than that of inflicting pain on her, to force her to undergo suffering without her being able to defend herself. The pleasure in the complete domination over another person is the very essence of the Sadistic drive."

Hazelwood teamed up with an old friend, Dr. Park Dietz of Newport Beach, California. Dietz was a national media figure. He was the prosecution's star witness in the trial of John Hinckley, Jr., who tried to murder President Ronald Reagan. Dietz had been hired by the state of Wisconsin to examine Jeffrey Dahmer, who lured fifteen men to his Milwaukee apartment, had sex with their bodies, then ate parts of them. Often testifying for the prosecution—at fees reaching $3,000 a day—Dietz was a formidable witness, powerful, knowledgeable, and compelling. He also forged a career protecting celebrities from stalkers and working with large companies on preventing mass slayings by troubled employees.

"He's the best," Hazelwood would say to Dietz. "His strengths are his intelligence and his common sense."

Using the FBI's case studies of the thirty criminal sexual sadists, Hazelwood, Dietz, and Dr. Janet Warren of the University of Virginia developed a sixteen-page paper called "The Sexually Sadistic Criminal and His Offenses," the first comprehensive paper done on the subject since the early 1900s.

Hazelwood found three common personality disorders in the criminal sexual sadist. The first was paranoia, a basic distrust of others, a tendency to be easily slighted, a continual questioning of the loyalty of family and friends, without justification. A second was narcissism, a grandiose sense of self-importance, a need for constant attention, a preoccupation with money and power. The third was psychopathic behavior: physical and mental cruelty, lying, stealing, and cheating, a complete lack of genuine remorse.

"Criminal sexual sadists do everything for a reason," Hazelwood would say. "They may show remorse, appear to be in tremendous distress, but it's all calculated.

"People don't appreciate the ability of these people to fake everything. You can sit there and swear they are telling the truth because nobody can act like that . . . but they can.

"They have a real genius for picking on women who are not equipped emotionally to deal with that type of manipulation. They are so helpless against these guys."

Hazelwood, Dietz, and Warren also studied the long-term victims of criminal sadists. As with abused wives and girlfriends, the question was: Why did the partners stay? The study indicated the criminal sexual sadists used a very sophisticated transformation process. They selected vulnerable women with low self-esteem. They carefully seduced these women with attention and gifts. They gradually reshaped their sexual behavior beyond what had been normal limits. Then they reinforced that behavior with more gifts or, more commonly, by withholding affection, using calculated bursts of anger, pouting, or guilt trips.

Their seductions could take months, even years. What surprised Hazelwood was that the victims were almost all middle-class women, intelligent and generally well educated—an engineer, bank employee, business owner, and insurance broker among them. The victims often enjoyed a higher social and economic status than their abusers, who found their greatest pleasure in subjugating "nice women." Once they shaped their victims, the sadists would isolate them socially, become overly possessive and demanding, alienating them from family and friends, often without the victim's realizing it.

This transformation of moral, middle-class women into sexually compliant and totally dependent subjects served to confirm the sadist's image of women as common whores, deserving of punishment. At that point the women had been conditioned to expect it, to believe they deserved it. Women who refused to comply, who tried to break away, put themselves at great risk.

"In many cases if the women comply, if they give in, the men will become bored and drop them," Hazelwood would say. "But the women are not allowed to leave *them*; that's too much of a blow to their egos."

For all their study, Hazelwood and his academic colleagues had few answers to the root causes of criminal sexual sadism. Hazelwood suspected most sadists were shaped more by early events in their lives than by some genetic short circuit. The thirty criminal sexual sadists in their study showed a general background of homosexual experiences, promiscuous parents, drug abuse, risk-taking while driving, childhood sexual abuse, incest, cross-dressing, pornography collections, and mate-swapping, but not all traits fit any one man. The sadists were of above average intelligence, often were married, and had reputations as solid citizens.

Very few of them murdered their initial victims; murder became an acquired characteristic.

"They become bolder, more aggressive. It takes more and more to satisfy their needs. Once these guys murder somebody and get away with it, they're almost certain to do it again."

As part of their study Hazelwood, Dietz, and Warren listed twenty-two common characteristics of crimes committed by the thirty criminal sexual sadists. They then charted what percentage of these men used each method. The crimes— although committed across the country—were so similar in nature it was as if someone had printed a manual on criminal sexual sadism and sold it nationwide. Their one template fit many.

CHARACTERISTIC	PERCENT
A partner assisted in offense	36.7
Careful planning of the offense	93.3
Impersonation of police	23.3
Victim taken to preselected location	76.6
Victim in captivity twenty-four hours or more	60.0
Victim bound, blindfolded, or gagged	86.7
Sexual bondage of victim	76.7
Anal rape of victim	73.3
Forced victim to perform fellatio	70.0
Vaginal rape of victim	56.7
Foreign object penetration of victim	40.0
Variety of sex acts with victim	66.7
Sexual dysfunction during offense	43.3
Unemotional, detached during offense	86.6
Told victim what to say during assault	23.3
Intentional torture	100.0
Murdered victim	73.3
Committed serial murders	56.6
Concealed victim's corpse	66.6
Victim beaten	60.0
Recorded the offense	53.3
Kept personal item belonging to victim	40.0

Of the twenty-two points, Hazelwood always found one most interesting: the psychopathic need of many criminal sexual sadists to photograph or tape-record their crimes.

"I will guarantee you that once they take pictures these guys do not throw them away," he would say. "Find the pictures and you'll have your man."

Once he got more deeply involved in the Brenda Schaefer murder, eventually coming to Louisville to help direct a phase of its operation, Hazelwood would label the case "There is a God."

CHAPTER
6

Driving home late Sunday night after interviewing Mel Ignatow, Jim Wesley became certain he was going to stay with the case. Wesley had liked Tom Schaefer. He would grow close to the whole Schaefer family, something he usually avoided as a professional risk. Wesley knew John Schaefer, Jr., had been murdered in the line of duty, which made the bond even more special. Wesley owed something to a fallen officer. He believed in the fraternity of police. He took that obligation to heart.

He returned to work Monday to learn Brenda Schaefer had not shown up for work at Dr. William Spalding's office. Wesley was disappointed, but not surprised. The day's good news was that the FBI had been called in.

Wesley welcomed its help. The Jefferson County police had just worked with the federal agency on a shooting that had generated intense media coverage and racial controversy. David Price, an eighteen-year-old black man, had been shot once in the back outside an apartment complex. A friend, Keith Pointer, eighteen, said Price had been gunned down by a carload of white men who had passed by taunting him, yelling racial slurs. The story instantly became incendiary; public officials and civil rights leaders wanted an answer.

County police and the FBI dug in and learned Price and Pointer had been dealing in drugs. Pointer had shot Price, apparently accidentally.

By then Wesley's dream of becoming an FBI agent had faded away. He'd taken the FBI mental and psychological tests in 1979, then been interviewed in 1980. The officer felt very good about his chances. He'd interviewed well and didn't have so much as a speeding ticket going against him. Ronald Reagan, a man he admired, took away the dream with a hiring freeze. As time passed, new FBI applicants with better test scores crept ahead of Wesley. The officer came to see that as a blessing. He'd been working homicide cases for nine years. He was proud of his department, his fellow officers. The Jefferson County police didn't handle nearly as many murder cases as their Louisville counterparts, but were allowed total freedom on the ones they did work.

Wesley was analytical. He could have been a little more hard-nosed, a little more relentless, but he was a good detective. He'd become too much of a homebody to want the constant travels of an FBI agent, but at least he could enjoy their company.

Late Monday afternoon Wesley, Detective Dave Wood, and FBI agents Steve Shiner and Hal Davis went to Spalding's clinic, a squat, one-story brick building in a funky area of small stores, boutiques, and neighborhood bars not far from Cave Hill Cemetery. Spalding, small, bent-over, his nerves frayed, walked quickly down the hall toward Wesley, who was startled by his appearance. The doctor seemed on the edge of losing control. Several television news crews had interviewed him, police were talking to him, his patients were anxious.

"The telephone's been ringing all day," Spalding told Wesley. "Everybody's upset. I still don't know what the hell is going on."

Spalding, sixty-one, had one of the largest family practices in Louisville, with more than three thousand people on his rolls. He would routinely treat forty-five to fifty people a day in his clinic, then make hospital rounds. The doctor had grown up in Louisville. His father ran a grocery store and once dealt poker in a Louisville bar; his mother worked in an Indiana coat factory. Spalding had attended seminary school for three years, enlisted in the Naval Air Force toward the end of the World War II, returned to attend the University of Louisville Medical School. He'd opened his practice in 1954 charging three dollars a visit; it was up to only eighteen dollars now. His patients, many of them elderly, blue-collar people, would wait two or three hours for Doc Spalding, who was his own worst enemy.

"I'm in no hurry," Spalding would tell everybody. "We've got time to talk."

His staff was just as loyal. Brenda Schaefer had worked for him for twelve years, rarely taking days off, once working six weeks with a broken ankle. She'd drifted into the medical profession by taking a six-week nurse's-aide program while still married to Pete Van Pelt. Then she took a job at Baptist Highlands Hospital, working as an aide and X-ray technician. Spalding hired her after their first interview; she was beautiful, perfectly groomed, very pleasant, could do lab work, and was certified in X-ray. He came to adore her, as did his patients. She and the staff routinely worked the same ten-to twelve-hour days as Spalding. Some nights, and occasional weekends, Brenda would visit his older patients at nursing homes, usually King's Daughters & Sons, trimming their toenails and patiently cleaning wax out of their ears.

"Mel Ignatow is responsible for this," Spalding told Wesley, his voice quivering. "I know he is. I know the bastard did it."

Spalding erupted in a nervous torrent of information and unsubstantiated opinion: Brenda had seen large amounts of cash in Ignatow's house; Ignatow had once drugged Brenda into unconsciousness, then photographed her in the nude; Ignatow may have been involved in pornography as a college student.

Wesley and Davis interviewed two of Spalding's staff, Laverne Burnside and Marlene Ash, the office manager.

Wood and Shiner interviewed Schaefer's best friend, Joyce Smallwood.

Smallwood, thirty-nine, a dark-haired, very attractive woman, and Brenda Schaefer were alike, physically, emotionally, socially. Both worked hard, valued honesty and loyalty. Both had been married very young to jealous, sometimes controlling partners; their own immaturity and sexual naïveté didn't help. Both had been emotionally or physically hurt by spouses, browbeaten by insults. Their self-esteem, already low, was reaching critical levels.

"I was so insecure, so uncertain of my looks, I'd put on makeup to go to the mailbox," Smallwood would say.

Both made mistakes common to rebounding from bad marriages. Brenda dated very little right after her divorce, then, looking for security, briefly dated older men who seemed financially secure. One of them was a Louisville developer named Frank Prell, who later told police of wild escapades with Brenda so totally out of character with what anyone else ever said about her that Wesley and Wood discounted them but still had to include them in their reports.

Brenda, always uncertain of her beauty, underwent breast reconstruction in the late 1970s. The operation cost $500; the family said she borrowed the money from her mother. Brenda also had her nose reshaped. Smallwood found Brenda unusually modest and self-conscious. She had a very nice figure but was squeamish about nudity, even among women; she would often wear shorts over her bathing suit. The women went together to singles bars, but would nurse one or two drinks all evening. Smallwood never had the sense Brenda went to meet men; Brenda was pretty enough to attract men anywhere. Brenda just wanted to be out, to get away from home and her fifty-to sixty-hour work weeks. She and Smallwood always made it a point to go home with each other.

Smallwood said Brenda wasn't someone comfortable with physical contact; she didn't like to show affection. In the twelve years they were friends, Brenda hugged her maybe twice.

"I wish I could be more like you," Brenda once told Smallwood after the two had settled one brief argument with a hug. "I wish I could show my feelings better."

The women had taken a vacation together to Miami right after Smallwood's divorce. Smallwood remembered they giggled and laughed like high school kids. They flirted innocently with men, bought skimpy bikinis they never would wear at home, had campy pictures taken poolside under big umbrellas, ate any food they wanted, including meat on Good Friday, a sin in the Catholic Church. Brenda also called her mother every day.

During the twelve years Schaefer worked for Spalding, the women had no secrets from each other, although their relationship eventually frayed as both struggled with personal problems. Brenda's idea of office fun would be to suddenly jump up at the end of a twelve-hour day and shout "I *love* my job," or write "Freddy Spud" on the receptionist's sign-in sheet, then watch her struggle to find Freddy Spud's chart. They called each other "Laverne" and "Shirley." The movie *Thelma and Louise* wasn't out then, but they might better have identified with those characters, who yearned to break free of the lives others had prescribed for them.

Smallwood had introduced Schaefer to Mel Ignatow in September 1986. Smallwood had just begun dating a Louisville man named Bob Davis, a friend of Ignatow's. Schaefer had just broken up with Louisville dentist Jim Rush, ending an eight-year relationship. Brenda repeatedly confided to Smallwood that she loved Rush, whom she'd first met at TGI Friday's, a Louisville night spot. Brenda said she would have married Rush, but he drank too much and was taking her for granted. Brenda also was having a difficult time with Rush's teenage daughter, who seemed to resent her.

Rush, forty-four, had cared for Brenda, loved Brenda. He showered her with sweetly written cards on holidays and anniversaries, once even rented a billboard near downtown Louisville to express his feelings:

BRENDA,

THERE IS NOT ENOUGH ROOM
HERE FOR ME TO EXPRESS
ALL MY LOVE FOR YOU.

JIM

They traveled together to Florida and Hawaii. The Schaefer family liked Rush. He would join them on their trips to scenic Brown County, Indiana, where they all stayed in a cabin. Rush was blond, very personable, often the life of the party, although one night he'd gotten so drunk he fell through a coffee table at his house. He liked to sing, once jokingly cutting a country and western record he gave to Brenda. He also had demons of his own; he could blow up when drinking, smoked too much, gambled too much, sometimes started fights. He was never violent with Brenda, but his occasional public drunkenness would embarrass her.

Rush was frustrated by her. She could be too cool, too analytical, too stoic, unable to commit. He believed she was too much in charge of their relationship. As they slowly fell apart, Rush, hurt and confused, wrote her a long, heartfelt letter.

BRENDA,

THIS IS VERY DIFFICULT FOR ME TO WRITE BUT OUR CONVERSATIONS ARE LEAVING ME SO SAD. AS USUAL, YOU ARE HOLDING ALL THE CARDS. YOU HAVE CONTROL OF OUR FUTURE. IT'S YOUR DECISION WHETHER I AM IN OR OUT OF YOUR LIFE.

YOU TELL ME YOU FEEL SORRY FOR ME BUT YOU DON'T KNOW WHY. YOU TELL ME YOU ARE FEELING GUILTY BUT DON'T KNOW WHY. YOU DO KNOW HOW I FEEL NOW, WHAT I NEED IN MY LIFE AND HOW MUCH I LOVE YOU.

Rush wrote that Schaefer was continually bringing up things he had done in the past, things he had lived down.

I'M NOT VERY PERFECT, BUT NEITHER ARE YOU. I
HAVE TO PUMP INFORMATION FROM YOU ABOUT HOW
YOU FEEL ABOUT ME, OUR RELATIONSHIP, WHAT YOU
TRULY WANT FOR US. I LOVE YOU SO MUCH THAT I
HAVE SURVIVED THESE PAST FEW MONTHS JUST SEEING
A LITTLE CHANCE HERE AND THERE, A LITTLE RAY OF
HOPE AT A CLOUDY TIME, WHATEVER I COULD SEE.

I HAVE SPENT 7½ YEARS BEING COMFORTABLE WITH
YOU WITHOUT PICKING YOU APART FOR YOUR NEGA-
TIVE ASPECTS. I SEE THE POSITIVE AND LOVE YOU BE-
CAUSE I WAS LUCKY ENOUGH TO HAVE THE
OPPORTUNITY TO KNOW YOU AND SEE THE BAD ALONG
WITH THE GOOD.

. . . BUT IT'S NOT FAIR FOR YOU TO HAVE TOTAL
CONTROL ABOUT US. I DON'T KNOW IF I FEEL I CAN
TRUST YOU WITH MY HEART. YOU ACT SO COLD, SO
ANALYTICAL TO ME AT TIMES. . . . YOU ARE PLAYING
WITH MY HEART.

Rush told Brenda she was the only woman he had ever
loved, but he was tired of the "pattern" that had been established; he was hurt by her criticism, he always looked
forward to seeing her. Brenda, ever indecisive, couldn't make
up her mind if there should be a final break. Rush was uncertain how hard to push for reconciliation. He was trapped;
he was miserable without her, but didn't want Brenda's
inevitable feelings of guilt to be a deciding factor.

He knew her very well.

"How do you tell someone no," he asked her, "when you
know how much they love you?"

Rush added a postscript to the letter. It was more angry,
more revealing of the sexual problems that had plagued their
relationship.

I THINK YOU HAVE SPELLED IT OUT VERY CLEARLY.
YOU HAVE ALWAYS WON WHEN YOU HAVE PARTED
RELATIONSHIPS. THE MEN ALL BEGGING YOU TO COME
BACK. HOORAH FOR YOU. YOU HAVE LEFT ME WITH

THREE PROBLEMS. TWO ARE SEXUAL AND YOU KNOW
ABOUT THOSE. PERHAPS YOU DON'T KNOW ABOUT THE
THIRD ONE. THE ONE THAT MAKES ME CRY, BEGGING
AND FEELING LIKE THE WORLD HAS ENDED FOR ME.

... YOU CAN TAKE EVERYTHING FROM ME EXCEPT
FOR MY PRIDE. YOU ALMOST HAD THAT GONE FROM
ME. IF YOU CAN MEET ME HALFWAY, FOR GOD'S SAKE
DO IT. IF NOT, I WISH YOU THE BEST IN HAPPINESS, I
TRULY DO.

I HAVE LOVE FOR YOU ALWAYS. YOUR FRIEND, JIM.

P.S. II—I AM SEEING A THERAPIST ABOUT MY IM-
POTENCE.

Attached to Rush's letter was a *Newsweek* magazine article
on Inhibited Sexual Desire (ISD), low sexual desire brought
on by depression, stress, or a fear of intimacy.

Smallwood knew Schaefer was struggling without Rush,
and was still a little haunted by her marriage to Van Pelt.
Smallwood understood better than anyone how Brenda felt
about her failed marriage and her breakup with Rush.

"You just can't know how psychologically damaging a
bad relationship can be until you've been there," she would
tell her friends. "You'll just never understand."

So Smallwood suggested Brenda meet Mel Ignatow,
maybe even go out with them on a double date, as a way to
help cheer her up.

"What kind of double date?" Schaefer had asked.

CHAPTER
7

Mel Ignatow and Brenda Schaefer first met on a weekend night late in September 1986, almost two years to the day before Brenda would disappear. Bob Davis and Joyce Smallwood picked up Brenda, then drove to Tartan's Landing to meet Ignatow at his boat. The trio welcomed a boat trip. The weather had been unusually hot and muggy, with highs in the upper 80s and the constant threat of thunderstorms. The Louisville boat season traditionally ended closer to Labor Day, so this would be a treat.

The introductions were cordial. The six-foot-five-inch Ignatow towered over the tiny Schaefer. He had thinning brown hair that looked to be dyed, a wide mustache that stretched almost between the laugh lines of his cheeks, and glasses that rode high across the bridge of his nose. His face was pleasant, turning genial when he smiled. There was an air of condescension about him, the look of a tall, awkward, slightly effeminate, small-college English professor.

Their first date went well, so Ignatow invited Brenda for another boat ride, the next day. Afterward Brenda told Smallwood he seemed nice. He wasn't physically attractive, but he had a way of focusing attention on her, and she needed that. The fact that he seemed financially secure—in his big house, his Corvette, his boat—was also a big factor. Small-wood quickly learned some of Ignatow's idiosyncrasies. The second time they double-dated, Ignatow and Brenda were very late meeting them for a scheduled appointment at the boat dock. Mel had decided they should eat first.

"He didn't want anybody to eat on his boat," Smallwood would say. "Four adults would make a big mess."

Smallwood knew financial security was important to Brenda, but thought she was much too classy to date anyone just for their money. Smallwood would come to resent the implication.

"When you're thirty-something years old no one with any sense is going to date somebody that has no future," she would say. "Why would you date someone that has no drive in life? Would that make any sense?"

Smallwood quickly came to dislike Ignatow. She found him a con artist, telling stories of working for the CIA, of having $300,000 in cash hidden in China, of his liaisons with prostitutes in China. She'd even heard rumors he had once been arrested in the Far East for some sexual escapade.

"I told her one day, 'Brenda, if you don't get away from him, someday I'm going to read about you in the paper.' "

Ignatow was instantly captivated by Brenda. He could show her off, brag about her, glory in her companionship. He pushed hard for more dates, capturing what free time she had. Brenda would usually go out only on weekends; she was too tired during the week. Ignatow began carrying a picture of Brenda wearing a modest bathing suit, showing it to co-workers. He showered her with gifts, an opal ring, a Silver Shadow fox coat. Within two months of meeting, he was hinting of marriage. Three months after they met—Christmas of 1986—he tried to give her an engagement ring he'd bought on a buying trip overseas. He told her the ring cost $20,000.

Brenda refused to take it; she said it was too soon.

Brenda seemed partially blind to the arrogant, overbearing side of Ignatow that would almost instantly irritate her friends and family. If she and Ignatow did argue in public, which was rare, he would suddenly appear at Dr. Spalding's office with flowers and candy, making a grand show of his apology. Brenda accepted his engagement ring on February 14, 1987, Valentine's Day, not even five months after they met. She refused to set a date for the wedding, canceling a big engagement party Ignatow wanted to throw, and she didn't always wear the ring in public. By December of 1987 their relationship had changed. Rosalco had changed hands, and Ignatow was pushed out of the company. His high-speed lifestyle was in jeopardy. He'd become increasingly possessive of Brenda, more sexually demanding, more exotic in his sexual preferences.

"All Mel thinks about is sex and himself," Brenda had confided in a friend.

He'd badly frightened Brenda during a trip to Gatlinburg, Tennessee, near the Great Smoky Mountains National Park. They'd stayed at the Ledwell Motel. Brenda had gone to sleep, then awakened with a biting, stinging sensation in her nose and throat. Ignatow was standing over her with a cloth in his hand. She pretended to be asleep; he again put the cloth over her face.

Schaefer was angry, confused. "What the hell are you doing?"

"It's something I brought back from China," Ignatow explained. "You've been too keyed up lately. You need something to help you relax, to put you to sleep."

"I *was* asleep."

Smallwood told the police Ignatow "had a lot of weird ideas about sex." He talked to Brenda a lot about anal sex. He had really been on her about having group sex. He said there was a couple he knew to do it with, but he never would give names. She would never consent to it. It really upset her, but he kept badgering her about it.

"Brenda told me that Mel had talked her into being strapped down to his bed at home as a joke. He talked her into letting him strap down her arms and legs to the point where she was in a lot of pain. She begged him to loosen it, but he wouldn't do it, and he did whatever he wanted to do with her.''

Within a year Ignatow wouldn't allow Brenda an outside social life. He would call her two or three times a day at Spalding's office. He called her every weeknight at home, usually between 10:00 and 11:00 P.M. so she could never go out. When he made sales trips overseas to Taiwan or China, he would prearrange a time to call her at home; Brenda had to be there. Almost always calm and even-tempered in public, Ignatow would blow up in private. He was so obsessively neat he fussed when his mother dirtied their kitchen or spent too much money on an electric can opener. He once exploded at Schaefer because she hadn't torn the bathroom toilet tissue evenly across the roll, and hadn't returned the water-faucet handles to an even position.

Ignatow the salesman was relentlessly persuasive. People who knew him found it hard to escape him, not because of any special gift of language but because he wouldn't give up. Ignatow wanted a full accounting of her finances, her jewelry. He worried her jewelry wasn't covered by insurance; she put it on her father's homeowner's plan. He badgered real-estate agents when Brenda wanted to buy the condominium as an investment. Eventually she became convinced that Ignatow was following her as she drove home from work.

"It's like he wants to own me body and soul," she told Smallwood.

Ignatow was unrelenting. He blamed Brenda for losing his job at Rosalco; worrying about her took too much of his time. He blamed all their sexual problems on Brenda, telling her she was too cold, too afraid of sex; she had to learn to relax and enjoy it. He tried to use pornographic movies and marijuana to ''loosen her up.'' He wanted to give her Percodan tablets to relax. He insisted Brenda take large, almost clear capsules he called ''sex tablets.'' Ignatow would insist, shouting at her. She had once awakened nude after taking a pill; she didn't remember taking off her clothes and had no idea what Ignatow had done to her.

"I can get this pill in you somehow if I want to," he would tell her.

Ignatow tried to get her to experiment with some hallucinatory drugs made from mushrooms. One night, while Ignatow was out of the house and Brenda was looking for some medicine for a headache, she opened a drawer next to Ignatow's bed and found short pieces of rope. She never spent the night in Ignatow's house; she always left to go home to check on her mother. Smallwood believed that initially Brenda was too nice, too indecisive, to know how to deal with a manipulator of his power.

"Someone can badger Brenda very easily," Smallwood said. "I think that at some point she tends to give in rather than confront the problems. With Mel, there was no letting up."

Smallwood knew as well as anyone that people caught in bad relationships—the victims of spouse abuse or abusive partners—can find it very difficult to just walk away.

"You just don't understand unless you've been there. Brenda couldn't hurt anyone. She said she was scared of him, but Mel told her he loved her. What was she going to do?"

Smallwood told police that Brenda had tried to get away from Ignatow. She had once given back his ring for one day, ordering him out of her house. Every time she mentioned a breakup, or even a separation, Ignatow would cry, pleading with her, guilt-tripping her: How could she leave him at a time when he needed her so much?

"Brenda had become terrified of Mel," Smallwood told the officers. "When someone is hurting you and you're terrified, you don't have the strength to fight back. It's real easy to say I don't want to see you, but it doesn't work that way."

Brenda had confided in others about her problems, including Nina Stamps, owner of Elegant Lady Electrolysis, where Brenda routinely went to have hair removed from her breasts and fingers; she was self-conscious about it showing around her rings. Stamps liked Brenda, thought she was down to earth, very open up to a point. A few weeks before Brenda disappeared, she had been complaining to Stamps about Ignatow; she said she wanted to get away from him. A few weeks later, with Brenda again in a sour mood, Stamps recommended a book: *Women Who Love Too Much*.

"You need to read it," Stamps said. "It says that women, when they are little girls, are taught to go along with things even when they don't agree with what's happening. It doesn't make them happy, but they are taught not to make waves. They have learned to be submissive."

"Nina," Brenda told her, "you have just described my life."

At the time she disappeared, Brenda Schaefer was succeeding in standing up for herself. She had seen Jim Rush a couple of times briefly during the summer. It had gone well; she wanted to see him again. She had told Ignatow she was tired of his constant attention and prying, his sexual needs. In spite of all he had done to her, she still found the decision difficult.

"What am I going to do?" she had asked Joyce Smallwood. "I don't want to lie to Mel and I want to see Jim."

Ignatow had agreed to give Brenda limited freedom; he would not call her on Friday nights, although he did call her at the office during the day. Meanwhile, Schaefer had nervously arranged a date with Rush for Friday, September 9.

"I feel better knowing I don't have to lie to Mel about where I was Friday night," she told Smallwood.

Schaefer and Rush went to a movie, had a drink, then went back to the Schaefer house, where they talked with Essie. She was glad to see Rush; it seemed like old times. Rush and Brenda stood outside in her driveway for two hours afterward.

"I want to get away from Mel," Schaefer told Rush. "He frightens me. He doesn't want to let me go."

Rush knew the positive side of Brenda's curious personality: conservative, stoic, strong-willed, with a firm sense of right and wrong. He couldn't understand her torment, but he could appreciate it. Rush was feeling close to her again. They tentatively agreed that he would cook her a dinner that weekend.

They weren't able to get together. Nor could Brenda break away from Ignatow. On September 18, the weekend before she disappeared, she went for a ride on a houseboat with Ignatow, his sister, and other Ignatow family members. On September 21, the Wednesday before she disappeared, Brenda called Rush, asking to go out for a drink. She told him she had broken up with Ignatow that week, but would see him the coming weekend to return some things. Rush, apologetic, said he couldn't see Brenda that night; maybe the next week.

The Friday before Schaefer disappeared, both Rush and Ignatow called her at Spalding's office. By then the staff had noticed changes in Brenda; her private life had become very public within the small boundaries of their workplace. She had been suffering with intense headaches and was taking medicine for severe stomach problems. She was irritable. Her hair and dress weren't the normal Brenda-perfect.

The conversation with Rush was handled quietly, a quick personal call. Ignatow had demanded to talk to Brenda. She took the call on a wall phone, her voice rising in anger after a few minutes' conversation.

"I *told* you never to call me here again," she said, slamming down the phone.

Jim Wesley was able to confirm much of what Smallwood said in his interview with office manager Marlene Ash, who had worked for Spalding twenty-two years. Smallwood had also suggested the police and FBI talk to a woman named Mary Ann Shore, who had dated Ignatow for many years before he met Schaefer.

While driving back to his office, Wesley mentally reviewed what he had just learned: There was obvious conflict here. Sunday Mel had told him the only stress in his relationship with Brenda was her long work hours. . . . Today he'd been told Brenda wanted to break up with him. . . . Ignatow was in serious financial difficulty and Brenda had been wearing a lot of expensive jewelry. . . . The Friday before Brenda disappeared, Ignatow had called her at the office, very angry. . . . Ignatow had a bad temper and seemed capable of losing self-control. . . .

"We're dealing with one sick puppy here," Wesley told himself, "and Brenda didn't want anything to do with him anymore."

Wesley wanted to talk to Ignatow again. That night, joined by Jeffersontown detective Bob Perkins and FBI agent Maury Berthon, who would become very involved in the case, Wesley went back to Ignatow's house on Florian Road. His knock was answered by Ignatow's sister, Natalie Lisanby, a Louisville schoolteacher.

"Mel's not here," she said. "He went out for a few minutes."

"Can we come inside and wait?"

Lisanby led the men back to the kitchen, where Ignatow's mother was sitting. As soon as the men sat down, she grabbed the telephone and called Louisville attorney Charlie Ricketts.

"Isn't this something?" Wesley thought. "We're in the house thirty seconds looking for information to find Brenda Schaefer and her fiancé's mother is calling an attorney."

Ricketts had represented Ignatow in 1984 when Ignatow had pled guilty to two counts of willful evasion of income tax. In 1979 Ignatow reported $20,963.60 as income and the Internal Revenue Service found a gross income of $28,861.29. In 1980 he recorded $23,939.91 as income and the IRS found a gross of $32,339.27. He received a three-year sentence in November 1984, serving only the first thirty days. He also was fined $2,500 and made restitution of $11,245.78. Few if any people at Rosalco knew Ignatow was going to federal prison; he told people he was visiting family. In March 1984, knowing he faced tax problems, Ignatow had begun seeing a Louisville clinical psychologist. A battery of psychological tests determined he was suffering from anxiety and depression, with a passive-aggressive personality structure. Ignatow was prescribed no medicine and given a positive prognosis.

Virginia Ignatow had just completed her call to Ricketts

when her son came home, driving his Corvette. He came through the front door holding a fifth of liquor in one hand. He walked toward Wesley, his eyes flaring, and pointed a finger at him; Ignatow had learned Brenda's car had been found.

"You lied to me!"

"Mel, what are you talking about?"

"I asked you if you had found Brenda's car and you said you didn't know where it was. You lied!"

Virginia Ignatow stayed on the phone, describing the kitchen scene to Ricketts, who advised her to ask Wesley to leave. Lisanby, sure her brother was innocent, began arguing with Wesley. The mood was ugly, confrontational. Wesley knew they had to get out; he was beginning to fear a fight with Ignatow, and he had no real evidence against him. But the officer was sure he had seen another side of him.

CHAPTER
8

Mary Ann Shore's $125-a-month rented house at 4921 Poplar Level Road came with more history than architectural style. It had been built by an Italian immigrant around 1950 from lumber and hardwood flooring scavenged from Camp Zachary Taylor, an old U.S. Army training center.

The small frame home, about two miles south of Louisville, had a solid but decidedly homemade look. It was built on a gray cinder-block foundation, its exterior wrapped in square white shingles and covered with a low-sloped gray roof. An untrimmed bush, tall as the eaves, clawed at one front corner. Four plain windows trimmed in black faced the road, offering a clear view of the squat auto-parts store across the road. A low metal fence provided a dog run in the back-yard.

The house had two tiny bedrooms, a living room, a kitchen, and an eating area. One bedroom was used; the other was a storage area. A detached two-car garage, also white with black trim, sat about thirty feet to the rear of the house. The garage had begun to sag, and was too low and small to hold two modern automobiles comfortably. The best thing about the house was the land behind it—about five acres of dense woods that served as a buffer from Thomas Jefferson

Middle School, a remote place in an urban area. On evenings and weekends, Shore would walk back into the woods with her dog.

Poplar Level Road was actually a busy, four-lane highway, one of the feeder routes for the nearly fifteen thousand employees at the massive General Electric Appliance Park. The neighborhood around Shore's house was a random scattering of small, worn houses, weedy fields, shopping centers, middle-income apartments, convenience stores, gas stations, fast-food outlets, and a cinder-block muffler shop. Mel Ignatow was slumming when he left his manicured Florian Road neighborhood to visit Mary Ann Shore.

Acting on Joyce Smallwood's tip, Jim Wesley and two FBI agents, Maury Berthon and Amy Newton, went to Shore's house about 1:00 P.M. Tuesday, a little more than two days after Brenda Schaefer had been reported missing. They hadn't called ahead; they wanted to catch Shore off guard, a police tactic that often brought results. More than anything, Wesley was surprised by Shore's appearance. Brenda Schaefer had been well groomed, petite, and pretty. Shore was a much larger woman, five feet eight and about 140 pounds, with mousy brown hair, blue eyes, and a plain face. Her glasses were rounded with a wide frame, a little bit owlish.

"There's nothing attractive about this woman," thought Wesley. "I just can't see Mel Ignatow even associating with her."

Shore led them through her living room, a rectangular space with a hardwood floor, a television, two facing couches, and a glass-topped coffee table. She offered them chairs in a small dining area off the kitchen, which was white with blue cabinets. Its walls were papered with cheap, off-white wallpaper lined in silver and white stripes. A blue, imitation-Tiffany lamp hung over the table, an almost incongruous attempt at something better. Shore was nervous; the sudden appearance of Wesley and two FBI agents had caught her by surprise. Outside of two bad checks written back in August of 1981—both were under $100 and the charges were eventually dismissed—she had no police record, no real experience with law-enforcement interrogation.

Shore, thirty-eight, had been born in Louisville on March 23, 1950, to Charles and Mary R. Shore. Charles was a sheet-metal worker who died in 1983. Mary R. Shore stayed at home until her children were in school, then worked as a grocery-store cashier. Mary Ann Shore had one younger brother, William E. Shore, thirty-four, a Louisville computer analyst, and a younger sister, Theresa Shore, thirty-one, who worked at a day-care center. Mary Ann went to St. Raphael Catholic school, then to public Seneca High School, where she graduated in 1968.

Seneca was a high school representative of the blue-collar-to-middle-class neighborhood it served. It was well integrated, cliquish, a mix of college-prep and greasers, with excellent athletic teams. The school was mostly untouched by the general student turmoils of the late 1960s; cruising the hamburger stands still took precedence over anti-Vietnam War protests. Shore was an average student, remaining very much to herself and a few friends. She did not list a single school activity in her senior yearbook, the *Arrow*. Her picture showed an attractive girl with glasses, shoulder-length hair done in a flip, and a toothy smile. Her nickname was "Foxy." The words beneath her picture said, "There is wisdom in generosity."

Shore seldom held a job very long. She worked for a few years as a secretary in the Louisville office of the National Conference of Christians and Jews, and at Spalding College. Many of her subsequent jobs came through Manpower Temporaries or Kelly Girl. She also did yard work, and was a live-in baby-sitter. Co-workers said she was often unreliable; she lost one job for deliberately destroying a typewriter. Almost every place she worked or lived, items would begin to disappear: cameras, watches, rings, money, even food and bathroom cleansers. She was always broke, living on the edge, patching together junk automobiles, dreaming Cinderella dreams of a better life. She learned to manipulate, to cut corners, to lie when it suited her needs; she was better at survival skills than mapping out any plan for success.

Friends said she could be breezy and fun; her sense of humor was earthy and dry. She lived in dim shadows, hustling after things that were cheap and petty. She could be engaging, but there was no focus, purpose, or direction to her, nothing that suggested she would ever escape to anything better. She was, in many ways, the female equivalent of a good ol' boy.

"Street-wise, Mary Ann was pretty sharp," said a coworker, "but she didn't have enough sense to find her way out of a shopping mall."

Mel Ignatow was to be the security Mary Ann Shore never had, that Cinderella ride in the golden carriage. They met in 1973 at Rosalco, a company then dealing in very inexpensive baskets, dishes, jewelry boxes, clocks, lamps, ceramics, and juvenile chairs, most of it imported from Mexico or the Far East, where Ignatow often traveled as a buyer. As Rosalco grew, it moved into higher-priced merchandise, much of it furniture.

Shore was in her early twenties, still living at home. Ignatow was in his mid-thirties, newly divorced, a world traveler with a big salary, big stories, a nice car, and a macho need to prove himself. Shore began as a receptionist at Rosalco, then worked with Ignatow as a company secretary. They began dating in 1974, a relationship that would last, on and off, almost ten years.

In their early years Ignatow gave Shore a watch he had purchased in Hong Kong, and some other less expensive jewelry. She traveled with him to Hawaii, on two Caribbean cruises, and on three trips to Florida, trips Ignatow always controlled by listing the attractions he wanted to see in the exact order he wanted to see them. In 1982 Shore traveled with Ignatow to the Orient, but she often had difficulty with those trips; she didn't travel well.

Ignatow would send love notes to Shore at work. He kept meticulous diaries and notes, yet his handwriting was difficult to read: sloppy, childish, punctuated with random exclamation points and dashes. The notes were crude and incredibly sophomoric, filled with leering sexual suggestion, more the tone of a hormonal adolescent than a thirty-five-year-old man. In private he told co-workers he had no love or respect for Shore—she wasn't good enough for him; he used her for sex.

He nicknamed Shore "Sammie Sunshine" and would send her interoffice memos saying a six-foot-five-inch hairy ape was looking for someone who was precious, a sweetheart, please rush top priority. He suggested she had fatty tissue that needed to be "sexercised away," and gave her multiple-choice quizzes that featured people such as a truck driver from Detroit who preferred his own joy stick and a dentist from Dallas who pulled his peter better than he pulled teeth. Ignatow mentioned marriage to Shore in several notes, once saying his recipe for love cake started with sugar and tender caresses stirred over heat until well done into marriage.

In another he mentioned his first wife, Sharon Kippen Ignatow, a constant source of irritation to Shore. Ignatow apologized to Shore for something that had happened, saying he did compare her to Sharon. For her part, Shore would tell friends Ignatow was a very good sexual partner; she enjoyed being with him. Soon after Ignatow's divorce had become final in August 1973, Shore became Ignatow's live-in baby-sitter, watching the children for up to six weeks while Ignatow was on business trips to Japan, China, or Taiwan.

Ignatow's home at 2811 Thames Avenue was very ordinary, a small, nondescript brick home with attached carport tucked into a wooded area of nicer homes and better-kept yards. His mother lived nearby at 3741 Avon Court, another small brick home, this one backing up to the very busy Watterson Expressway. Shore would sleep in Ignatow's bedroom, drive his car, invite her friends into his house. She would be a part-time, live-in presence in the Ignatow children's lives for much of their adolescence. She didn't fix meals or clean house; the children—Donna, Patty, and Michael—did the domestic work. Nor did Shore take them to the movies, or the park. She made it very clear she was there only to watch them. Ignatow had given his children orders to "be pleasant to Mary Ann."

At first they got along. Patty Ignatow once left home while still in high school and moved in with Shore. The children would later talk about a constant "tension" in their house; personal items began to disappear from bedrooms. Years later Donna Ignatow would say in a court case that Shore occasionally appeared in their neighborhood even at times when Shore and her father were not getting along:

"They would break up periodically. . . . On several occasions, four or five times . . . I would find her at the end of the street watching the home. Mary Ann always wanted to marry my father. She was almost obsessive about it."

All three children left the house in their late teens, with Shore's blessing and encouragement.

"We can't get married until you get out of the household," Shore once told Donna Ignatow.

Shore told Wesley and the FBI agents that Ignatow was never possessive or violent, and she broke off the relationship around 1984 because it had become obvious there would be no marriage. She said their sex life had been "very good," nothing kinky, never any bondage, no attempts to give her strange pills, drugs, or mushroom concoctions. She'd had little contact with Ignatow while he was dating Brenda Schaefer, although he had come by once in 1987 to borrow their travel pictures to show to Brenda.

"I haven't heard from Mel since April," Shore said.

Wesley stared across the kitchen table at Shore. He didn't believe her. The employees at Dr. Spalding's office—and his own reading of Mel—had convinced him Ignatow could be possessive, even violent. There was no evidence to link Shore with Brenda Schaefer's disappearance. Wesley didn't believe she knew anything about that. But the officer was convinced she was trying to protect Ignatow.

"What did Mel Ignatow see in this woman?" he kept asking himself.

Heading back to his office, Wesley drove past the impound lot of Coffey's Wrecker Service, 4534 Poplar Level Road, where Brenda Schaefer's car had been towed for safekeeping until the Jefferson County police Evidence Technician Unit could check it for fingerprints, hair, and blood type.

Roger Coffey, the owner, had been towing vehicles from crime scenes for twenty years. He'd begun to feel part of the investigative process, the tow-truck arm of the law. At county request he had checked out the front seat of Brenda Schaefer's car. It was pushed way back, as if a tall person had been driving it. None of his workers, nor the investigating police, had moved the seat.

Coffey had his secretary, Rhonda Masters, who at five feet three and 128 pounds was about the size of Brenda Schaefer, get into the car. Masters's toes could barely touch the brake pedal, and couldn't touch the gas pedal. Another employee, about six feet two inches tall, found the seat to be perfectly adjusted for him.

Coffey passed the information to the county police. A man prone to saying what was on his mind, Coffey already was muttering about the scope of the investigation.

"Too complicated . . . when my son got there with the tow truck the St. Matthews Police had the door open and were looking inside the car. . . . Then it was inspected by the county . . . then it spiraled into federal jurisdiction . . . too many chiefs."

Yet the FBI had resources the local agencies needed. Only days after Schaefer disappeared, at the instigation of its Louisville office, FBI agents had called on Sharon Kippen Ignatow, who had remarried and left Louisville. She gave agents a twelve-page statement about her ex-husband, a report to be used by the FBI's Behavioral Science Unit to compile a profile on Ignatow.

Ignatow and Kippen, both raised Jewish, had been married before a justice of the peace on May 27, 1960, in Jeffersonville, Indiana, an Ohio River town then specializing in fast weddings. Kippen was a short, attractive, dark-haired woman with a pug nose. Friends would later say she bore some resemblance to Brenda Schaefer, both in looks and compliant personality. The Ignatows separated on March 18, 1973. In her initial petition, Sharon Ignatow had asked for custody of the children. She settled for much less. Ignatow was given custody of their three children, which was very rare in 1973. He also was given their house, all household items, his 1970 Grand Prix, his personal savings and personal belongings.

Sharon Ignatow, then thirty-one, received a 1968 Pontiac LeMans, her checking account, a color television, a rocking chair, and some personal belongings. Her alimony was $250 a month for twenty-four months. At the time she worked at the Jewish Community Center, earning $50 a week. The settlement produced intense speculation among their friends about all the reasons for the separation. Why were the children going to their father? Was Mel holding something very personal over her to force the settlement? Just how badly had Sharon wanted out?

Even allowing room for the angry comments of an ex-wife, the FBI Behavioral Science report continually portrayed Ignatow as being totally self-centered, dominating, and primarily interested in making money at the expense of everyone around him. It also said that if something went wrong around the house, Ignatow would "punish" his wife by demanding anal sex.

The FBI report was written in dry, cautious "police-speak," with Melvin Ignatow referred to as "the subject" and his ex-wife as "source" or "the spouse." The stilted language gave the report a curious kind of dramatic effect.

> The content of any conversations engaged in by the subject was usually controlled by the subject. The conversation content was moderate to deep when involving himself with peers or superiors, particularly in the business area, but when it came to substance content with the family, particularly the wife, it was very shallow. The majority of his conversations dealt with: himself, money or business deals.

Ignatow collected wine and other items as "props" to be shown off. He considered himself to be superior to others, could be very rigid in his thinking, and seemed to enjoy belittling his ex-wife in front of others. Close family friends would say he played sick mind games with her, mostly sexual in nature; he would engage in foreplay and then leave her, telling her she wasn't good enough for him. Ignatow would become enraged if she challenged him.

> Subject is described as being an individual who exhibited very little, if any, affection toward immediate family members to include wife and children . . . he seldom, if ever, hugged or kissed the wife and children.
>
> The subject was in absolute control of the household and made all money and business decisions. . . . The subject made no effort to inform or discuss with the spouse any business arrangements or endeavors, nor did any discussions take place as to the general overall operation of the home.
>
> Source advises that it was not uncommon for the subject to wear such jewelry accessories as a large diamond ring, gold chains, bracelets and a very expensive gold watch.
>
> Source advises the subject would spare no expense in maintaining his wardrobe and accessories, but would require his wife and children to purchase their limited clothing and school clothes at such locations as K-mart.

Ignatow was very cheap; he would order the least expensive meal at a lunch gathering and ask to eat what was left on others' plates. Ignatow would insult his wife at parties, picking at her tendency toward stockiness, feeding his ego at her expense. He was very careful about his body, ingesting enormous amounts of vitamins, jogging, getting stylish haircuts. The public Ignatow, the Rosalco buyer, was often different. He could be likable, easygoing, slow to anger, with a broad smile and firm handshake. He wasn't easily embarrassed, seemed to take things in stride.

Ignatow was a man who never forgot a first name and was always willing to use it. He worked very hard. He was on time for meetings. He could be moody or arrogant and act superior, especially with the men and women who packaged, assembled, and shipped products. But he wouldn't insult anyone at Rosalco who could hurt him professionally, especially a man. He was extremely organized.

"Mel Ignatow wouldn't go to the bathroom without making a list," a co-worker said.

His buying skills and competitive instincts pushed him into a very good income bracket at Rosalco, earning from $50,000 to $80,000 a year in the mid-1980s. He functioned well in a Rosalco sales society that accepted and rewarded him for twenty-three years. Beneath that he was a frustrated man, not nearly as wealthy as he wanted to be, feeling, to some extent, misunderstood and unappreciated by his superiors.

It can be said that it is not noticeably apparent if the subject likes or dislikes someone. He is a manipulative individual and does so in a manner that is not at first readily observable. . . . The subject does allow emotion to conquer his reasoning process.

Sharon Kippen Ignatow lived with evidence of that. She said that twice during their marriage Ignatow hit her, once cutting her lip, the second time bruising her arm. When she approached him for a divorce, Ignatow became very emotional, writing her a suicide note as a bargaining tool, then withdrawing from most family contact.

According to the source, the subject maintained what would be considered a normal sexual relationship within the marriage. No acts of bondage were ever performed. . . .

Ignatow had his own special form of punishment for perceived misdeeds.

The subject did make demands of the ex-wife for anal sex which was described by the ex-wife as being "used as punishment." When asked what would be the reason for "punishment" the ex-wife's response was for such things as a general argument dealing with money, failure to be home on

time or asking for additional gas money or clothes for the
children.

Mel Ignatow once faked a week-long business trip to Florida, going to great lengths to have postcards mailed from a
Florida hotel. When a relative spotted him in Louisville and
told his wife, Ignatow explained he "needed time on his
own."

He gave his wife a two-carat diamond ring, which she
cherished. Ignatow said it was a token of his sincerity and
love for his wife. He would often use the ring as a weapon
against her complaints that he wouldn't share with his wife
or children.

After their divorce Sharon accidentally dropped the ring,
cracking the stone. A jeweler identified the diamond as paste.

C H A P T E R
9

Mel Ignatow was bawling. The tape recorder had just clicked on in attorney Charlie Ricketts's large office, and Ignatow began sobbing, complaining about shortness of breath, burying his face in his hands.

Jim Wesley was startled. Wesley, FBI agents Maury Berthon and Steve Shiner, and Jeffersontown detective Bob Perkins had just started the interview about 2:40 P.M. Thursday, and immediately Ignatow lost his composure, visibly grieving for Brenda Schaefer.

"I'll give you a few minutes if you need it," said Shiner.

"Just . . . go with it, Steve," Ignatow said.

Wesley suspected that Ricketts, who had represented Ignatow in his IRS pleadings years earlier, had arranged the interview as a way of helping his client rebound from the ugly scene in his kitchen a few days earlier. The officer was working hard at trying to keep an open mind; Ignatow had not been charged with anything and, to be truthful, was only one of a few possible suspects in Brenda Schaefer's disappearance. There was still the possibility Brenda had been abducted; a stranger could have pulled her over, kidnapped her, and driven away. Having the FBI tape Ignatow helped clear the way for possible federal charges.

Ricketts was a voluble man who always left the impression he was addressing a roomful of people even if there weren't two other people around. His convoluted speeches and flattering delivery would wear on Wesley, who found him condescending, questioned his sincerity. Ricketts often let Louisville reporters know that he once worked with a Louisville television station. He continually reminded local police he had worked for the FBI. He had a huge gun collection, occasionally joining FBI agents at the county police firing range. He would become a four-hundred-pound bulldog in his defense of Mel Ignatow. Before this case ended, Wesley would hear a lot of the wit and wisdom of Charlie Ricketts.

"I have counseled with Mel and he knows this is not accusatory in its nature but rather investigatory in its nature and that he wants to cooperate as best he possibly can to the location of his fiancée," Ricketts told Wesley.

"That preamble having been made, why don't you ask . . . why don't you inform us whether you want us to start with the beginning of the relationship or at the time most closely in relationship to the actual loss?"

Ignatow had calmed down, stopped crying. Wesley listened carefully as Shiner questioned him, but there was little new. The one major change Ignatow made in his previous story was that he and Brenda had not driven to a new subdivision the day she disappeared. He was mistaken; they had driven there the previous Saturday. Ignatow's voice was flat, smooth, almost monotone, rising noticeably when he became anxious or talked at length. His hands moved constantly, flopping open to make a point, tugging at his mustache. He had a habit of pulling off his glasses, blowing on the lenses, putting them back on.

Ignatow dropped small pieces of unsubstantiated information into play, always introducing other possible suspects: Brenda had told him Jim Rush was occasionally involved in substance abuse; Pete Van Pelt, although remarried years before, had never fully gotten over Brenda, had even been following her.

"Gosh," said Ignatow, "I hate to say these things about people only on a hearsay basis...."

Wesley looked at Shiner, trying to get some reading on what he was thinking. Ignatow was cool now, answering questions calmly. Ricketts sat nearby, ready to jump in at the first sign of trouble. Shiner had Ignatow again replay his last day with Brenda.

"It's important to try, Mel ... to find out if anybody was following you ... you know we have to figure it that way, too."

Ignatow explained he wouldn't know if they had been followed. He also took great pains to explain that although he was more than a foot taller than Brenda, he hadn't adjusted her car seat or mirrors when he drove her car the previous Saturday.

"I knew that she was going to end up wanting to drive. ... It wasn't too uncomfortable for me ... so I just ... you know, left everything that way."

Mel Ignatow's boyhood friends remembered him as someone who would be thoughtful enough to do that. It was a recurring theme; the young Mel Ignatow was so easygoing and obliging his former high school buddies couldn't imagine him hurting anyone.

Melvin Henry Ignatow was born March 26, 1938, in Philadelphia, the second of three children of David and Virginia Ignatow. David was Jewish, Virginia was Catholic, a very rare union at that time, although the separate faiths did share a similar depth of spirit, ritual, and literature. The Ignatows moved to Louisville in the early 1940s at the urging of David's family. They joined other family members in a city teeming with wartime construction, chemical production, and soldiers from nearby Fort Knox, who made the thirty-mile trip up Dixie Highway by the thousands to bawdy Louisville night spots.

David Ignatow had been a reporter for *The Philadelphia Inquirer,* but tried his hand running a small grocery store at Twenty-second and Cedar streets in an older area of town.

The family lived in the back of the store, which did very poorly, closing in two years. David and Virginia then got into the taxi business, operating Victory Cab, primarily ferrying soldiers between Louisville and Fort Knox. When Melvin was about twelve, the cab business folded. His father bought another grocery store, this one at Twenty-fourth and Cedar, in a slowly decaying neighborhood. Mel Ignatow helped stock shelves, making neighborhood deliveries in a small wagon, always the most helpful of the family.

Within two years that store folded and David Ignatow became involved in a Foodliner grocery store on Poplar Level Road not too far from where Mary Ann Shore would live. Mel clerked in the store, stocked shelves, worked the cash register. The store did well for about four years until other chain competition cut into its profits. David then moved his family to tiny Washington, Indiana, about seventy miles northwest of Louisville, where they ran another small grocery store. Mel worked there as a butcher. The venture was a disaster; the store closed in nine months. The Ignatow family blamed small-town anti-Semitism for its failure. David moved his family back to Louisville, where he worked in a discount store as a carpet and television salesman until his retirement. He had never provided his wife and children with a solid economic base. Along with the numerous moves they involved, David's business failures had twice bankrupted the family.

Virginia Ignatow was a registered nurse at Jewish Hospital for many years, then served as a volunteer in nursing homes and as a counselor for relatives of the critically ill, winning awards for her volunteer work. She was kind, generous, well organized, often serious and strong-willed, a dominant figure in her son's life. She never converted to the Jewish faith.

Mel was raised in the Louisville Jewish community, which in the 1940s and early 1950s was centered near downtown Louisville and its western edges. He joined the Young Men's Hebrew Association and Resnic AZA, an international boys' club that combined social, athletic, and community activities. He attended Hebrew school and Sunday school. He attended the Anshei S'fard synagogue, an Orthodox congregation, but his friends don't remember his being particularly active.

"I was baptized in the Catholic religion, but we really were never raised in any religious sect at all until I was about ten or eleven," he would say.

"My dad came to me and said would you like to be bar mitzvahed? . . . A kid of ten or eleven years old, what do I know? I said 'Okay, sure, why not?'

"So I went to Hebrew school and I studied and became bar mitzvahed and I grew up with a lot of Jewish friends. . . . But I never really felt close in that respect. I always felt like a half-breed."

Resnic AZA was one of several clubs at the Young Men's Hebrew Association, clubs often differentiated by income or social class. Ignatow was picked in part because he was so tall; the basketball team needed him. He proved to be a basketball disappointment. He was painfully thin and clumsy, too easy to push around.

"He was very nonaggressive," said a teammate. "I mean, if you went up for a rebound you could knock him out of the way. Not only because he was on the thin side, but he just wouldn't get in there and fight you. He was just a real easygoing, nice, sweet kid."

Louisville was a changing city in the 1950s. Racial barriers had begun to fall but the city was still highly segregated and smug about it; civic leaders resisted real change. As housing barriers fell, old-time families fled the downtown residential areas and large, lovely homes along West End parks, heading east into the all-white Highlands. The Ignatows would move from south-central Louisville into the Highlands. Mel went to Highland Junior High School, then to Atherton High School, about 10 to 15 percent Jewish.

Family wealth and social status mattered at Atherton. Its students lived with high expectations; college prep was the norm. Many would go on to become Louisville's best surgeons, general practitioners, accountants, lawyers, and business owners. Mel Ignatow did not make a splash in that pool. He was a C student, a follower who would be willing to help clean up after a dance but never be asked to organize one. He ran track, often a gaunt figure in black, high-top shoes near the back of the pack. He had few close friends. He dated a little, taking in movies and a hamburger at The Beast drive-in, the Ranch House, or Mammy's. Many of the girls thought him a little nerdy. You could see that in his 1955 yearbook photo: a shy, pleasant, perfectly groomed kid in glasses, who liked math and chemistry. He talked of being a heart specialist, but was out of his league.

He tinkered with old cars and gasoline engines, would briefly drive a dragster called "Mighty Mouse" on Louisville drag strips. The hobby seemed somewhat out of character with his clean, fastidious ways. His high school nickname became "Ignition." His favorite song was "You'll Never Walk Alone." His favorite saying: "So I'll give you a McCarthy button."

"You have your chiefs and you have your Indians at any high school," one of his friends said. "Melvin was always an Indian."

In the early 1950s, while Mel was at Atherton, his family moved to a house on Spring Drive. It was a prestige address for the Louisville Jewish community, big houses set well back from the road under broad trees, with a large city park just a few minutes away. The Ignatow home came with a fine address, but badly needed painting and repairs. About that time David Ignatow suffered one of his bankruptcies. The family moved to an apartment, then another house. Mel Ignatow's teenage years were badly disrupted by the family's drop in income. He worried about his parents; he felt a little cheated. Someday he would earn a lot of money, drive a nice car, become somebody important.

He went to the University of Louisville, accumulating ninety-seven hours of credit, but never declared a major and cut too many classes to raise his average above a C. He joined Sigma Alpha Mu fraternity, but wasn't very active other than going to a few dances. For many years he kept his fraternity paddle, the Sigma Alpha Mu letters crudely carved into one side, clearly visible in his home. The engraving on the paddle said: TO MEL '59 FROM JIM '59.

Ignatow worked for his father from 1960 to 1963. He then worked for Medco, a jewelry company that leased departments in various stores. Years later Ignatow would brag he paid his way through the University of Louisville by selling pornography—a relatively rare commodity in those days—then got out when a partner was shot. Ignatow would come to say things like that for shock value; people were never quite sure if they should believe him.

He quit college about the time he married Sharon Kippen, who had been a few years behind him at Atherton. It was after their divorce that old friends noticed dramatic changes in Ignatow, an almost complete transformation, although the hedonistic tendencies may have been there all along.

"I don't know if he was so much mad at Sharon as he was pissed off at the world in general," an old friend would say. "His supposed anger toward Sharon might have been a cover-up for his whole attitude.

"He had a good job, big money. He was more cocky, more the debonair, worldly type, or at least trying to act that way. It just wasn't the Melvin I knew in the past."

This Mel Ignatow wore flashy jewelry, drove a Corvette, had his hair dyed and permed, and dated younger women, including Mary Ann Shore. He hung out in single bars, became a regular at happy hours, once went to a party with a lollipop shaped as a dildo and went around asking women to lick it.

"It's a dick on a stick," he told them.

He bought a long-barreled .44 magnum after seeing the movie *Dirty Harry*. He joined Louisville singles clubs such as New Beginnings, where he told one woman he had dated for six months he was in the "smuggling" business. A second woman from the same club said Ignatow once invited her to see his house; he opened a box in his bedroom to get some money and she saw $100 bills in three-inch stacks. Ignatow began bragging to old friends of going to swap parties for group sex. He enjoyed talking about group sex, reveled in it, with no sign of embarrassment.

"I'd heard how he had treated Sharon," a friend said, "about anal sex and all those things. I thought to myself, only a sadistic type of individual would want to do this type of thing."

After Ignatow's interview in Ricketts's office had ended, Ricketts called FBI special agent Steve Shiner to again stress that Ignatow believed Pete Van Pelt should not be overlooked in the investigation. Ricketts told Shiner that Ignatow had again become upset after the interview; teary-eyed, vibrating, at the point of losing control. Ricketts would always say he believed in Ignatow's innocence. He sat Ignatow down and told him he needed to pray.

CHAPTER
10

Tom Schaefer parked his car along Breckenridge Lane and walked out onto the Interstate 64 overpass, staring down at the river of headlights that flowed smoothly beneath him. Schaefer was tired and depressed. He needed to feel as if he was contributing to the investigation. He wanted to know what I-64 traffic was like at 11:30 on a Saturday night, the time Mel Ignatow said Brenda had left his house. Tom was surprised by the volume of cars, the intensity of the headlights as their beams splashed against the gray bridge abutments. It didn't seem possible that an abduction had taken place below him just one week earlier without someone seeing it. Or maybe witnesses just didn't want to get involved.

Schaefer stood there for half an hour, mesmerized by the traffic, staring at the spot where Brenda's car was found, not knowing that within two days he would be deeply involved in the investigation. There was an air of sadness about him, a bone-deep melancholy. Brenda's disappearance was just one of a series of recent tragedies that had hit him, problems that reawakened the black grief he had felt over the loss of Jack.

On August 17, his eighteen-year-old stepdaughter, Jennifer Hayes, was nearly killed in a motorcycle accident in Florida.

Her pelvis was crushed, her hip bones had broken away from her spine, a wrist was broken, and tendons were severed. A vein had broken loose in her leg, causing massive, internal bleeding. Jennifer would be in the hospital six months. For the first three weeks, Schaefer and his ex-wife slept in the hospital waiting room every night.

He stayed another week, then returned to Louisville to read a *Courier-Journal* story that said William Michael Tinsley, one of two brothers sentenced to death for the brutal murder of his brother, Jack, on May 2, 1971, would be paroled on September 16. Tinsley's brother, Narvel, also convicted in the murder, had been recommended for parole by the Kentucky Parole Board and would soon be released to California.

The Schaefer family was stunned, angry, feeling betrayed by the criminal justice system Jack had sworn to uphold. At first, the family and police feared William Michael Tinsley might be involved in Brenda Schaefer's disappearance as a matter of revenge. Police subsequently learned Tinsley had been living with family in western Kentucky.

Seventeen years after the murder, Tom Schaefer was still grieving for his brother; his eyes still teared at the thought of him. Tom had spoken with Jack only a few minutes before he'd been murdered, perhaps even had a chance to alter the path of events that led to his death, a guilt he lived with every day.

Jack, twenty-eight, and his partner, Wilbur Hayes, twenty-six, had pulled up to a Louisville bar called the Recovery Room about 10:00 P.M. that Sunday night. The officers wanted to check on a keg of beer to be picked up later for a shift-change party. Jack had been an officer only eighteen months. He was enjoying it, especially his plainclothes assignment in the new Model Police District, a semi-elite group with some undercover activity. After several false starts, including a stint as an inhalation therapist, it seemed Jack had finally found his niche in life.

Tom Schaefer had stopped by the Recovery Room that

night for a beer. He was leaving as Jack and Wilbur Hayes
pulled up in unit 525, a white unmarked car so nondescript
it had "police" written all over it. Hayes wasn't Jack Schaefer's regular partner; their partnership was to be temporary.
Jack, as he often did, asked Tom to come ride with them for
a few minutes.

"No, thanks, I've got to go to work in the morning," Tom
said.

"You sure?"

"Yeah."

"Okay, we're gonna head on up the street."

Tom watched the police car pull away at 10:10 P.M. A
strange feeling came over him.

"Well, there they go," he said to himself.

Jack Schaefer was wearing a tan nylon jacket, a blue shirt,
and blue jeans, a 9mm Browning automatic in his shoulder
holster. Hayes was wearing a green sweater and slacks. He
carried two .38 revolvers. The officers apparently were on
patrol in Smoketown, a tough, economically depressed
public-housing area with a lot of street crime and racial ten-
sions. At 10:20 P.M. they turned down Waterbury Street,
spotting three people in the shadows at the far end—Narvel
Tinsley, Jr., twenty-two, his brother, Michael, seventeen, and
David White, sixteen. Hayes, a wiry ex-basketball player,
drove the police car down the alley toward them.

Hayes had a reputation for being opinionated, aggressive,
sometimes too aggressive. Just a month earlier he had shot
and killed an eighteen-year-old while investigating a break-
in during which the teenager came at him with a screwdriver.
Hayes had received death threats after the incident. A black
Smoketown community action group had also written a letter
asking that Hayes be reassigned.

The Tinsleys were carrying guns, which they'd dropped
into the tall grass along the alley as the police car came
closer. Hayes shouted at Narvel Tinsley, asking him to approach the car. As Hayes got out of the police car to question
him, the men argued. Hayes pushed Tinsley up against the
police car to subdue him. Michael Tinsley grabbed a gun

from the weeds, firing three shots into Hayes's head and back. Jack Schaefer came around the car to help his partner. As Hayes crumpled to the ground, Narvel Tinsley grabbed his .38 pistol and fired at Schaefer, striking him three times in the back. As he fell to his knees, he was shot twice in the top of his head at close range.

David White, who had no part in the shootings, remembered Narvel Tinsley telling him afterward he "didn't want to shoot Schaefer because he was really a nice one."

Hayes's body was shoved facedown onto the rear floor of the car, legs up in the air. The car was driven about three hundred yards south down the alley, where it was not found for almost eight hours, light on and engine running, a dead police officer in back. Schaefer was apparently placed on an old mattress and dragged almost four hundred feet to an alley off Waterbury. A thin trail of blood led from the shooting location to the mattress.

When his body was found facedown on a concrete slab, his nylon jacket was pulled over his head and he was holding a red cloth over his stomach; Jack Schaefer had not died instantly. His wallet and police badge were discovered in a nearby trash can. His shoulder holster was empty. Tom Schaefer learned of the murder the next morning; a girlfriend brought the news to him at Jeffboat, a Jeffersonville barge-building company where he had worked for twenty-six years.

More than three hundred people, including officers from three states, attended the funeral. The violent thunderstorm that had washed over the city stopped just as the service ended. Church neighbors stood on their front porches and housewives wearing aprons peered through half-open front doors as the procession slowly made its way down wet streets to the grassy slope at Cave Hill Cemetery. At one intersection a man got out of his car, stood erect, and saluted.

An investigation into the shooting showed that although Schaefer and Hayes failed to respond to eleven radio calls over a five-hour period, no search was ever ordered. Louisville police then instituted a new plan requiring plainclothes officers to be in contact every hour. The Tinsley brothers were arrested four days after the shooting, huddled in a small, cramped maintenance chamber alongside a railroad track, about twenty officers surrounding the scene. Two .38 caliber pistols were thrown from the shaft before the men surrendered quietly.

Tom Schaefer was one of the many family members who faithfully attended the trial. There he met Regina Hayes, the widow of Wilbur Hayes. They began dating about eighteen months after the murders, marrying in 1974. They divorced ten years later, but would remain close friends.

On Monday, October 3, two days after Tom walked out onto the Breckenridge Lane overpass, FBI special agent Maury Berthon asked Schaefer if he would wear a hidden microphone and meet Mel Ignatow to talk about Brenda.

Schaefer didn't hesitate. "I'll be glad to."

FBI special agents met Schaefer at his house on Warner Avenue, where family gathered every night. Essie Schaefer had stopped sleeping in her bedroom; she slept on the living-room couch. A half-dozen times a night the sound of a car, the slamming of a door, would send Essie to the front porch, peering down the street.

"I know she's going to come through that front door," Essie would say. "I'm going to go out to the front yard and let her in."

Carolyn Kopp came by every night for a year, Mary Ann and Bernie Hilbert almost every night for three months. Mary Ann, who had always considered Essie and John Schaefer her parents, would sleep on the floor near Essie's couch, getting up to help John when he needed it. In time Essie would come to pray that somebody would at least drop her daughter's broken body on their front lawn.

"Even if her legs and arms are broken we'll get that all fixed," Essie would say. "If they'll just throw her out everything will be okay."

Seeking privacy, Tom Schaefer and the FBI agents climbed the steep stairs off the dining room to the second floor, walking down the narrow hall to Brenda's bedroom at the front of the house. A transmitter the size of a telephone pager was taped to his skin with duct tape just inside his waistband. A loose-fitting shirt hid the bulge.

"Be careful," Schaefer was warned. "If you sweat too much or allow moisture on the transmitter, you'll get a little bit of shock and it will heat up."

Sweat seemed a definite possibility. Schaefer was nervous, unsure of exactly what to ask Ignatow. The FBI didn't want to coach him too much; Schaefer might sound unnatural, more like a policeman than a worried brother.

"Say whatever comes to mind," Schaefer was told. "Anything to get a reaction."

Schaefer arranged to meet Ignatow at the KingFish restaurant on River Road, a brownish-green, two-story building with a terrace and a broad lawn sloping down to sturdy boat docks built into the Ohio River. A police minivan filled with monitoring and taping equipment was parked outside. The two men sat at a table a little away from the other diners, looking out at the pale lights reflecting off the dark water. Ignatow talked mostly of himself and his difficulty dealing with Brenda's disappearance. He said he had gone to his boat once, had pulled off the cover, but couldn't stay long. His voice quivered, moved to a higher, whiny pitch.

"I could see where Brenda would always sit," he told Schaefer. "It tore me up. I could see her sitting there. I can't believe I'm going to go through the rest of my life without her."

Ignatow, leaning a little forward, led the conversation down a familiar path; Pete Van Pelt should be investigated, Dr. Spalding was spreading false rumors, Brenda was feuding with some office help.

The men ordered more drinks. Schaefer insisted on paying. He told Ignatow of walking out onto the Breckenridge Lane overpass at 11:30 the Saturday night after Brenda disappeared. Ignatow misunderstood, thinking Schaefer meant the night Brenda disappeared.

Ignatow's eyes widened. He looked as if he wanted to

jump from his chair: *"You were there? You were there . . . on Breckenridge?"*

"Yes. But it was this past weekend."

Within a few minutes Ignatow became very businesslike. He asked Schaefer if he might someday have all the cards and letters he had sent Brenda. He asked for any old pictures, particularly one of Brenda wearing cutoff shorts. He pulled out a sheet of paper listing Brenda's assets, handing it to Schaefer. It was two columns of forty-two items listed in Ignatow's scratchy handwriting. He began ticking them off in rapid order: $4,500 in one savings account, a $6,000 certificate of deposit that had been a gift from her father, $2,000 in an IRA account, $1,000 in checking, $600 in another savings account, about $20,000 in a profit-sharing plan from Dr. Spalding. The list also included her $36,000 condominium, with a note for $31,500, about $5,000 worth of furniture and another $2,000 in clothes.

Schaefer was becoming irritated; the grieving fiancé had turned accountant. Ignatow knew *everything*; all Brenda's credit cards, even the location of the receipts for her breast and nose surgery. He knew that a $100 payment was due on a $2,300 grandfather clock Brenda had purchased on a trip to Gatlinburg. He knew about her life insurance. Ignatow saved the best items for near the end; Brenda's jewelry and fur coat. Always mentioning "appraised" value, he listed a $500 opal ring, the $5,000 diamond bracelet, the $20,000 engagement ring, and the $5,000 cocktail ring. He added the Silver Shadow fox jacket appraised at $5,000 by Yudofsky Furriers in Louisville, a coat with a receipt from Yudofsky listing its price at $2,304.75. The fur and jewelry had been carried on John Schaefer's homeowner's insurance, for which Brenda paid the $500 annual premium.

Calmly, like a lawyer walking a client through a will, Ignatow told Schaefer where his sister's assets belonged.

"What she told me when she got this list together was that certain things should go to certain people.

"For instance, the various money, the CD, the IRA account, the checking account, the condominium, the car, stuff like that, she would have wanted your mother to have.''

Schaefer was furious, but didn't want to blow his cover. Brenda was missing eight days and her fiancé was allocating her possessions with an unsigned list drawn up in his hand. He stared at Ignatow, guessing what might come next.

''Anything that I had given her, the diamond bracelet, the engagement ring, the cocktail ring . . . the fur coat. Those four things she said she wanted to come back to me.

''Or in the case they never find any of the stuff, whatever funds from the . . .

''. . . insurance,'' said Schaefer, finishing the sentence for him.

''Yeah,'' said Ignatow.

Schaefer couldn't believe it. Ignatow was acting as if the list was a will, with Mel Ignatow the prime beneficiary of Brenda's jewelry. Ignatow hadn't even given Brenda the cocktail ring. Brenda was gone barely a week and Ignatow was trying to cash in. A murderous rage surged through Schaefer's body.

''What kept you from coming across the table and choking the son of a bitch?'' FBI special agent Maury Berthon would ask Schaefer later.

Tom Schaefer's career as a sleuth lasted about five weeks, covering three visits with Mel Ignatow at the KingFish. One of them ended in very difficult fashion; Ignatow's Corvette wouldn't start. Tom had felt duty-bound to offer him a lift in his rattletrap pickup truck.

''I'm sorry, fellas,'' Schaefer spoke into his microphone as he walked across the parking lot. ''Now I've got to give him a ride home.''

It was a miserable ride. Ignatow, already in a foul mood, raged all the way home that Brenda's co-workers, especially Joyce Smallwood, had poisoned the atmosphere toward him in Dr. Spalding's office.

''There's a lot of talk coming out of that office that really makes me mad,'' Ignatow fumed. ''It's just bullshit.''

On the final visit with Ignatow, Schaefer was told to just keep Ignatow busy while his car was bugged. Less than a week after Brenda Schaefer's disappearance, Jefferson County police were in District Court seeking permission to attach a beeper to his car. Ignatow was tracked over a period of weeks, both by county police and FBI agents in cars and in a helicopter. He was followed while shopping, jogging, going out to eat at a Chinese restaurant. Reports indicated that at one time there were six cars and an airplane watching him, but he never led them anywhere vital, even managed to elude his posse on occasion. Ignatow would later say he had found the beeper on his car; he knew he was being followed.

Within a week of Brenda's disappearance, the investigation had assumed a life all its own. County police had begun to suspect the damage done to Schaefer's car came from thieves who broke into it after it had been abandoned along the interstate. Their vandalism—and their bloodstains— made the case that much more difficult.

Detective Dave Wood tracked down Michael Boyd, whose 1983 Dodge had been found along Interstate 64 a little ways west of Brenda Schaefer's car. It also had been vandalized. Boyd, twenty-five, said his car threw a rod about 5:30 P.M. on September 24. He began walking, was picked up by a motorist, then given a ride by a friend. When he went back to check on his car Sunday, it was gone.

"Do you know Brenda Schaefer or Mel Ignatow?" Wood asked.

"No."

"Did you even realize your car was found near Brenda Schaefer's?"

"No."

Police had no reason to suspect Boyd, but he might have known more—or seen more—than he said.

County police and FBI agents carefully searched the 550-acre Seneca Park near where Brenda's car had been found. FBI agents checked the local pawnshops for Brenda's jewelry, and the Goodyear store where Mel Ignatow had his car serviced September 17, a week before his last date with Schaefer. Goodyear mechanic Lee Loveless said Ignatow had a "dismount and mount" done on his 1984 bronze Corvette, but there was no mention of a specific tire problem.

Ignatow was asked to take a county police lie-detector test, but refused; he and Ricketts said the stress might be too much on his heart. Meanwhile, three other men close to Brenda Schaefer were checked out; it was way too soon to eliminate anyone as a suspect.

Pete Van Pelt had worked his regular shift with the Louisville Police Department the night Brenda disappeared, clearing duty at 11:51 P.M. He changed into civilian clothes, then worked a private security job in his marked police car at Louisville's Assumption High School until 6:00 A.M. on the twenty-fifth. An eyewitness and pay documentation could prove he worked that night, but no one could verify all his movements.

Jim Rush, who lost Brenda after eight sometimes difficult years, said he had been home the night of September 24. He found out about Brenda's disappearance when Essie Schaefer called him about 4:30 the next morning. He told police he got dressed and rode around alone for an hour looking for her, spending much of the time in the Florian Road area near Ignatow's house. Given his long history with Brenda, police had to keep Rush high on the suspect list.

Dr. William Spalding had been in North Carolina that night to watch his daughter ride in a horse show. FBI agents had called Budget Rent-A-Car in Greensboro and a Holiday Inn motel in Clemmons to verify that.

Spalding was not a strong suspect, but persistent rumors of romantic attachment had surfaced because of his obvious affection for Brenda. The doctor had remained badly rattled. He started a reward fund to pay for information that could help the police. The fund was boosted by growing radio, television, and newspaper coverage. Within two weeks it had reached $16,000, including $1,000 from the city of Louisville's Crime Stoppers account. Mel Ignatow never contributed a nickel.

Five days after Brenda had disappeared, Jim Wesley met with FBI special agents Maury Berthon, Amy Newton, and Connie Reed at the Oxmoor shopping center in St. Matthews, trying to retrace the trail Ignatow said he and Brenda had taken the Saturday she disappeared. The mall had about 125 stores and almost 5,000 parking places, part of a long shopping strip pointed right at the heart of Jefferson County's high-income district.

Carrying pictures of Schaefer and Ignatow, Wesley and the agents canvassed the mall for 2½ hours, asking store clerks to remember the couple from the thousands of people who tramped through every day. In Embry's, an upscale store featuring designer clothing and furs, clerk Helen Stainback took a look at Schaefer's picture and a memory flashed through her mind.

"Yes," the clerk told Berthon. "I remember her."

"Are you sure it was Brenda Schaefer?" Berthon asked.

"She was similar to your picture," the clerk answered.

Other people would eventually surface with stories about Ignatow and Schaefer's being together that Saturday, stories that would conflict with Ignatow's own tale, stories that would haunt the investigation.

Sharon Stratton, a waitress at Pitts Smokehouse and Grill in Prospect, would say she was almost certain Schaefer and Ignatow were there from 6:00 to 9:00 P.M. on Saturday, September 24. Stratton remembered Schaefer's gold earrings, light-colored sweater, and glossy lipstick.

Scott Pullem, general manager of Kentuckiana Yacht Sales, remembered Ignatow and Schaefer coming onto a boat he had for sale the rainy afternoon of the twenty-fourth, even though Ignatow said they never got out of their car, which was parked on the landing.

Sue McKinney, a waitress at Flaherty's bar for fourteen years, told Detective Dave Wood she knew Ignatow and Schaefer and was fairly certain they had been in the bar that Saturday around 10:00 P.M. McKinney never volunteered that information; she was interviewed several weeks later only after mentioning it in casual conversation with a police officer. When interviewed, McKinney said that at 1:00 A.M. on September 25 she spoke with Brenda Schaefer, who was alone in the rain-slick Flaherty's parking lot, a parking lot

Brenda could have reached on foot from a car abandoned along Interstate 64.

"Can I call AAA or get you a cab?" McKinney said she had asked.

"No" came the answer.

Wesley never gave much credibility to McKinney's story, but it had to be checked out. His commander, Sergeant Lewis Sharber, made that very clear. As much as Wesley hated to hear it, he knew Sharber was right. Wesley liked and respected Sharber. The sergeant looked and acted like a minister's son: soft-spoken, balding, almost professorial. But he had an air of authority about him, an *expectation* of having his orders obeyed, that went beyond his words. Wesley knew he needed to push himself harder. With help, Wesley would talk to more than 170 Jefferson County cab drivers over a six-week period that spring, mostly by telephone, to see if they had picked up Schaefer—or Ignatow—on September 24. The work was tedious, boring. Not one driver had seen them.

At the request of county detectives, Sergeant Malcolm Deuser, commander of the county's K-9 unit, took his bloodhound A.J. out to the site along Interstate 64 where Schaefer's car had been found. A.J. worked hard, circling the car, but was unable to pick up a scent. A.J. seemed perplexed, as did Deuser. The officer had no idea what had happened to Brenda Schaefer, but all his instincts told him she never walked away from her car.

County police received a letter from Smithers Scientific Services, Inc., the Akron, Ohio, company that had analyzed the nail-punctured tire taken from Brenda Schaefer's car. Smithers experts, using a stereo, 70-power microscope, came up with results that seemed curious, almost contradictory.

Its engineers reported that there was no conclusive evidence the nail—a typical drywall nail—had touched the road surface, or had been struck by a hammer. The company concluded the nail had probably been picked up in the roadway or placed in the tire several hundred to several thousand miles before the vehicle was stopped, doing its damage over a long period. It said the tear inside the tire was longer than the external hole, indicating the nail had "worked" back and forth inside the tire. Smithers experts said the tire definitely went flat *after* the car was parked, probably in about thirty-five minutes.

Brenda Schaefer's disappearance struck a community chord in Louisville, a city learning to live with its growing share of puzzling and violent crimes, but still not numb to them. Tom Schaefer made a public plea for help. Mike Schaefer joined his brother in distributing flyers bearing Brenda's picture. The brothers drove along interstate highways in all directions from Louisville, leaving the flyers at truck stops and restaurants, asking anyone who would listen to please help, pointing out the reward—now about $20,000—for the right information.

Tom Schaefer and Linda Love even took some posters the almost three hundred miles to Pigeon Forge, Tennessee, where Brenda had purchased a Howard Miller grandfather clock for $2,300 while on a trip with Ignatow. After she disappeared, Tom had made the $100-a-month payments; he knew how long Brenda had searched for just the right clock; she would still want it if she ever returned. The clerk remembered the clock purchase.

"He said the guy with her was a nut, a screwball," Schaefer would say. " 'I couldn't talk to your sister. He would dominate. I would talk to him or nobody else.' "

Eight members of the Kentucky Rescue Association spent eighty hours in the Ohio River looking for Schaefer's body along the Kentucky shore. On one dive they located a stolen Cadillac upside down in the mud; the trunk contained something that, on first glance, resembled a severed human head. It turned out to be a mud-soaked milk carton.

One of the divers, Milton Hettinger, said a psychic who had been consulted believed Brenda had been murdered, placed inside a plastic bag, then stuffed inside a fifty-five-gallon drum in "some wet place."

On one dive Hettinger found a fifty-five-gallon drum near Twelve Mile Island north of Louisville, an area where Ignatow often went boating. The drum had holes cut in its side, a plastic bag stuffed inside it.

"We've got it," Hettinger thought.

The drum was empty.

Joyce Smallwood, Brenda's co-worker and friend, offered more help. Smallwood knew Lauren Lechleiter, a hair stylist who had known Mary Ann Shore for ten years and also cut Mel Ignatow's hair. Lechleiter met Shore in the late 1970s while working in a downtown office building for the National Conference of Christians and Jews, sometimes going out to dinner or the movies with her. The women had been close. Shore told Lechleiter that Ignatow had come to her Poplar Level Road house for sex several times while dating Brenda. Shore said Ignatow had bullied her into having several abortions during their relationship, taking away her chance at a family; he wasn't going to be trapped into marriage by the threat of children.

Lechleiter was fascinated by that relationship, the tight hold that Ignatow had over Mary Ann. After their final breakup, Shore told Lechleiter she would park outside Ignatow's house early in the morning, knowing he was inside with Brenda. She would follow him to local clubs, waiting silently in the parking lot for him to leave.

"You're not in love with him. You're obsessed with him," Lechleiter told Shore. "If you just loved him, you could let him go."

By mid-November, six weeks after Brenda Schaefer had disappeared, Mel Ignatow was dating again, inviting a woman named Joyce Harper, thirty-six, to his home, aboard his boat, and out to dinner. Harper had met Ignatow eight years before at a Parents Without Partners meeting, but had not seen him while he was dating Brenda Schaefer. By then Ignatow was living off savings, feeling the pressure of a diminished lifestyle. He'd been without steady income for a year, something that ate at his self-image of the high roller. The $48,000 he'd received from Rosalco as a distribution from his pension plan was dwindling.

Ignatow had been pushed out of Rosalco in December

1987, then gone to Boca Raton, Florida, to work in the real estate business with Bob Deatrick, a former Louisville businessman who was building expensive homes. Deatrick was the brother of Marlene Ash, who managed the doctor's office where Brenda worked. Ignatow and Deatrick met in the fall of 1987 at the funeral for Deatrick's mother.

In January 1988, Ignatow and Brenda Schaefer visited Deatrick's huge home. Both were very impressed. Brenda brought back pictures; Ignatow brought back hopes for a huge kill in the treacherous waters of Florida real estate.

In early February, Ignatow moved to Florida, investing about $20,000 in a project with Deatrick. He called Brenda almost every night, talking for hours, trying to persuade her to move to Florida, telling her how lonely he'd become, how much he needed her, working on her guilt.

At one point Brenda told Ash she was going to quit Dr. Spalding, marry Ignatow, and move to Florida. A few days later, with her sick mother very much on her mind, Brenda again went to Ash.

"Marlene, can I have my job back?"

"Brenda, as far as I'm concerned you haven't left. But what happened?"

"I'm not going to Florida and I'm not getting married. I'm afraid if I go down there Mel won't let me come back to visit my family."

By early summer of 1988, Ignatow had moved back to Louisville, his money still tied up in Florida real estate, his savings dwindling. He took the job selling water-softener equipment and began to rely heavily on charge cards, using plastic at every opportunity, always opening new cards, watching his retirement money slip away.

On November 15 he applied for a job with American Family Life Insurance, owned by Diane and Lyndell Whitaker. The Whitakers recognized Ignatow's name from news stories. Ignatow, charming, ingratiating, eased the Whitakers' fears by telling them of his last night with Brenda. He explained he was a gourmet cook; he had prepared a meal for her; they had enjoyed their last night together, spending a quiet evening in his house with his mother. Brenda had left about 11:30 P.M. When he learned she was missing, he and Tom Schaefer had gone out to look for her.

"I was the last person to see Brenda alive," Ignatow told them. He began crying, telling the Whitakers how unfair it was the police had made him a suspect, that he wished he and Tom Schaefer had done more to look for Brenda.

"Mel, I wouldn't worry about that," Diane Whitaker told him. "If you spent the evening with your mother in your house, you've got an alibi."

Ignatow was hired as a contract salesman on November 16. During the company's insurance classes, he began spending a lot of time with another prospective employee, Nancy Treece, a pretty, quiet woman who looked a little like Brenda Schaefer. Ignatow made it a point to sit next to Treece, always being friendly with her, even though she already had a boyfriend.

"Nancy said she felt sorry for Mel," Diane Whitaker would say. "Everyone here felt sorry for him. He was a nice man. Mel just always seemed more comfortable with the girls than the boys."

Ignatow left American Family Life Insurance within two months, telling the Whitakers he wanted to spend more time selling water softeners. He never sold an insurance policy.

CHAPTER
11

When Jim Wesley was finished shouting at Mary Ann Shore, he stared into her face and told her she was as good as dead.

Much of Wesley's shouting had been calculated; a deliberate police show to get the five-month-old Brenda Schaefer case off dead center. But he was also venting a policemen's frustration—and some honest emotion—at being denied the truth.

"Mary Ann," said Wesley, jaw set, his voice measured, "We know Mel killed Brenda. We know you know all about it. What *are* you thinking?

"Brenda Schaefer was beautiful. . . . Brenda Schaefer was beautiful and Mel loved her and he still killed her. You're ugly and Mel doesn't give a shit about you. . . . You're dead!"

Shore was stunned, angry at Wesley, upset about being brought down to the Jefferson County Police Department twice in the same night, the second time in a driving rain.

Shore had something to say. She was very close to saying it. She just couldn't let go. Part of her knew Wesley was right. The other part, the controlling part, knew it would be tougher to face an angry Mel Ignatow than anything Jim Wesley could throw at her.

By February 1989, Wesley and the FBI had decided that Shore was the key to getting to Ignatow. They'd learned Ignatow and Shore had dated for a long time, and suspected they were still entangled in some way; their mutual friends kept linking them. It was time to push Shore as hard as possible; what did they have to lose?

Some of the incentive for that push had come after Wesley interviewed Robert Spoelker, who worked third shift at the huge Ford Motor Company plant in Louisville. Shore had worked for him about a year as a live-in baby-sitter. Spoelker had previously lived at 4921 Poplar Level Road, a house owned by his mother. When Spoelker and his children moved from the Poplar Level Road home in 1987, Shore moved in, paying $125 a month rent. Spoelker's family kept him apprised of Shore's continued meetings with Ignatow.

Spoelker paid Shore $125 a week to baby-sit, extra if she worked weekends. His financial records showed that he, Shore, and his children had visited Mammoth Cave on September 17, 1988, the week before Brenda Schaefer disappeared. But Shore had not worked on September 24.

A routine police check on Shore had turned up five arrest warrants for bad checks, including a $23.27 check to Kmart written December 16, 1987, and a June 26, 1988, check for $18.68 written to Wal-Mart. Wesley, his boss, Lewis Sharber, and FBI special agents Maury Berthon and Amy Newton decided to use those checks as a wedge: first ask Shore if she would talk to them; then, if she refused, threaten her with the bad-check charges.

About 5:30 on Monday, February 13, the four drove to 4921 Poplar Level Road. The evening was cool and gray, typical for early spring in Louisville. Shore wasn't home, so they drove a few miles farther south to Robert Spoelker's home at 6711 Green Manor Drive at the southern end of Jefferson County. The modest brick home was perched at the top of a grassy knoll, a silhouette against the night. A long concrete drive connected the house to the road. Nobody was there. As they discussed leaving, Shore drove up in her gray 1977 Pinto; she had a load of groceries and one of the Spoelker children.

"Can I help?" asked Wesley, placing a grocery bag under each arm.

Shore remembered Wesley; he'd interviewed her at her house, and she'd been at Spoelker's home when Wesley first interviewed him. Shore didn't like Wesley, wasn't happy he was there, but didn't seem surprised. Wesley carried the groceries into the house, making small talk, looking for an opening.

"Mary Ann," he said. "We have some things we'd like to talk to you about. Would you mind coming down to headquarters with us?"

To his surprise, Shore agreed. Wesley hadn't mentioned the bad checks. He wasn't about to mention a lie-detector test. Maybe Amy Newton's presence had helped. Whatever the reason, Shore agreed to be questioned. They took Spoelker's child and the family dog to a relative's house, then headed downtown toward county police headquarters. Wesley was a little anxious, not wanting to push too hard too early. It was about 7:30 P.M. when Mary Ann sat down in his office, still strangely compliant. After some preliminary discussion, Wesley moved in.

"Listen, Mary Ann, we think you know something. The best way to clear yourself is to come clean. Would you be willing to take a polygraph test?"

"Yes."

Wesley was even more surprised, elated. Jefferson County detective Ron Howard, a polygraph expert, was quickly called in, informing Shore of her rights: She could remain silent; she had the right to talk to an attorney; she could stop at any time.

"I understand," she said, signing a waiver of rights, never asking to see an attorney.

Howard knew what he wanted; Sharber had given him a handwritten note asking him to zero in on two areas.

RON,

WE HAVE TWO RUMORS THAT HAVE NOT BEEN CON-
FIRMED. ONE IS THAT MEL IGNATOW PAID FOR HER TO
HAVE TWO ABORTIONS. THE OTHER IS THAT SHE AND
MEL RECENTLY REKINDLED THEIR RELATIONSHIP.

WE BASICALLY NEED TO KNOW TWO THINGS:

1. WAS SHE TRUTHFUL IN HER CHARACTERIZATION
OF MEL IN THE 9-27-88 INTERVIEW?

2. DOES SHE HAVE ANY KNOWLEDGE OF, OR IN-
VOLVEMENT IN, THE DISAPPEARANCE OF BRENDA
SCHAEFER?

Howard gave Shore a series of tests that lasted about 2 ½
hours. Wesley knew no mention of a polygraph test would
be allowed in court; all he could say was "interview specialist" Ron Howard had spoken to her. After talking to
Howard about the results, Wesley confronted Shore.

"Mary Ann, the test indicates you knew more than you
were telling us, that you were not being truthful. In fact, you
flunked the hell out of it."

Shore, growing angry, refused to say anything else. Wesley had no hold on her; she'd never been arrested; the bad
checks had never been mentioned; they could wait until another time.

Shore had two requests: She wanted to make a telephone
call and she wanted to go home. She went into a private
office to make several calls, then asked Amy Newton to take
her home; she wanted nothing more to do with Wesley, Sharber, or Berthon.

It was almost 11:00 P.M. when Newton took Shore back
to Robert Spoelker's home on Green Manor Drive. It was
raining, water gathering in low, grassy spots along the road.
Newton dropped off Shore, watched her go into the house,
then pulled her car about one hundred yards down Green
Manor. She parked, turned off the lights, and waited. She,
along with Wesley and Sharber, suspected Shore might have
called Ignatow from the county police office. Newton had
decided to wait it out and see.

They were right. Close to midnight, not long after Wesley got home, he got a call from Sharber: "Mel's with Mary Ann. They're walking down the street in the rain."

Shore and Ignatow had walked so close to Newton's car she had to duck down, hoping Shore wouldn't recognize it. The special agent couldn't hear any of the conversation, but it was a cinch Ignatow was furious with Shore. Scooting down in her seat, Newton radioed Berthon, who'd called Sharber.

Initially there had been no plans to arrest Shore, just to see what happened. Now an arrest seemed like a good idea, the best possible chance to force the case, to swoop in and frighten the already-nervous Shore into saying something. Within ten minutes Newton, Sharber, and Wesley met at a nearby convenience store, each driving an unmarked car. Newton leading the way, the three drove into a thick, driving rain toward Green Manor. The headlights of all three cars caught Shore and Ignatow at the edge of the street, pinning them in the darkness.

Wesley jumped out of his car.

"Okay, Mary Ann, you're locked up."

Shore froze in place. Ignatow, believing he was safe, remained calm, ingratiating.

"Mary Ann," said Ignatow. "Go with them nicely. Don't give them any trouble."

Wesley's anger flared, but he didn't say anything.

"Shut up, Mel," Sharber fired at him.

Within minutes Shore was in the police car, Wesley was headed back downtown, and Mel Ignatow was left standing on Green Manor Drive in the rain.

Wesley took Shore back downtown, sensing this was his best chance. Shore was developing a hatred of him, that was easy enough to detect. But she was sitting before him like a wet puppy, confused and a little frightened. She had volunteered for the polygraph test. She knew she had flunked it. Maybe she was ready to cave in.

The only trick Wesley had left was to rage at Shore. He went at her for almost ten minutes, screaming that it was obvious she and Mel were working together, that Ignatow was going to fall, that her only hope was to cooperate.

"You could be looking at a year in jail. We may do everything we can to get these charges kicked up to a felony."

Wesley rarely lost that much control, but he wanted to go over the edge, to scream his frustrations. He owed it to himself, the county police, the Schaefer family.

"I'm telling you, Mary Ann, you're dead!"

Mary Ann Shore may have feared that, but whatever Ignatow had told her during their walk in the rain worked. She wouldn't say any more. She signed her rights statement, but requested an attorney. At 12:45 A.M. on February 14, Valentine's Day, she was fingerprinted and lodged in jail on five outstanding warrants, all for bad checks under $100.

Louisville attorney Jack Vittitow received a telephone call at home about 7:00 A.M. from William Shore, Mary Ann's brother. Vittitow did not know Shore; he assumed he got his name from the telephone Yellow Pages. He later learned Ignatow had pushed the Shore family to find an attorney.

"My sister's been arrested on some bad-check charges," said William Shore. "Could you help her out this morning in arraignment court?"

Vittitow, fifty-five, was used to such calls. He'd built up his clientele from sudden, early-morning phone calls. He was a history buff, an old-time, seat-of-the-pants attorney who'd grown up in a Catholic orphanage. As a teenager he would hang out in the old county courthouse, fascinated by lawyers, the legal music of their work. He never wanted corporate or banking law; he best understood the people he'd grown up with.

Mary Ann Shore showed up in his second-floor office at 8:30 A.M. on February 14. She was wearing a trench coat with the collar turned up, gloves, dark sunglasses, and a brightly colored scarf around her neck, not the usual dress of his clientele. Vittitow had never seen her before. He was vaguely aware of the Brenda Schaefer case, but media coverage of it had almost stopped. He made no immediate connection between Shore and Ignatow, and Shore didn't mention any names.

Shore took a seat across from Vittitow's wide desk, its

glass top remarkably clean for a busy lawyer. A photograph of Vittitow's father, who, in a rakish white hat, looked the part of a likable rounder, peered down at her from the wall. The rest of the beige walls were sprinkled with the plaques, certificates, and diplomas lawyers always like for company.

"The police questioned me last night about my boyfriend," she told Vittitow. "His girlfriend is missing and they think he knows something about it."

Shore told Vittitow about the bad checks, the lie-detector test, her wish for him to represent her that morning at arraignment, where a court date would be set on her charges.

"Let's go get this thing over with," said Vittitow, seeing Shore as just another bad-check client.

Vittitow and Shore walked the two blocks to the Hall of Justice. The morning was chilly, the streets still wet from the night's rain. The Hall of Justice was its usual legal zoo, a crush of lawyers and clients meeting in dim, crowded halls, the pungent mix of law and disorder. Vittitow waited his turn in Jefferson District Court, getting Shore's court date set for March 26. As he and his client stepped back into the teeming hallway, he was met by Maury Berthon and Amy Newton.

"We're with the FBI and we'd like to talk to your client," Berthon told Vittitow.

"My God," Vittitow was thinking to himself, "what kind of checks has this woman written?"

Berthon and Newton wanted Shore to come with them, to take an FBI lie-detector test. Vittitow and Shore huddled in the hallway; then Vittitow went back to the two agents.

"She's already taken a test," Vittitow told them, protecting his client.

"The results weren't satisfactory."

"She doesn't want to take another test. That's enough for the time being. Get back with me."

Vittitow handed the agents his business card and led Shore out of the building. Vittitow was barely back in his office when he got calls from Jim Wesley and the FBI. Both told Vittitow the same thing: "Mary Ann Shore is in more danger than she might realize. We want to help her. We need to know what information she has.''

Vittitow was sympathetic. He called Shore, who didn't act concerned, or even interested.

"All right," Vittitow told her, "I'll see you later."

Shore's arrest came near the end of a very busy two days for Lewis Sharber. On February 13, the body of Dr. Jim Rush, Brenda's former boyfriend, had been found facedown in his bed in a downstairs bedroom, a blue sheet pulled up over his body, his clothes on the floor near the foot of the bed.

The night before, Rush had been in TGI Friday's, a Louisville singles bar. He'd had five or six beers and his car wouldn't start, so an old friend, Pat Tedford, gave him a ride home about 10:00 P.M. She came by at 7:40 A.M. the next day to give him a ride to work and couldn't get an answer at the door.

Tedford was concerned. Rush drank too much, was smoking two packages of cigarettes a day, and had complained of a "numbness" in his arms. Tedford genuinely liked Rush. He was opinionated, but good company. Their relationship wasn't serious, they just hung out together for companionship. Only a week earlier she and a female friend held a "pajama party" at Rush's house—an innocent affair, childlike but fun. About 8:10 Tedford called Rush's office. Susan Payne, a receptionist, went to Rush's home, crawled under an overhead garage door, found him in bed, and called for an ambulance. The coroner's report showed Rush, only forty-five, had died of atherosclerotic cardiovascular disease.

As a matter of course, the Jefferson County police Evidence Technician Unit took fingerprints, palm prints, hair and blood samples from Rush's body. Sharber did not seriously believe Rush's death was connected to Brenda Schaefer's disappearance, but he immediately pushed for a search of the doctor's house and office, looking for any evidence. Jim Wesley, feeling miserable about the assignment, was sent to the funeral home to ask the Rush family about the search.

"No" was the answer.

Rush was buried in Cave Hill Cemetery on Thursday, February 16. It was a cold, gray, rainy day, the temperature just a few degrees above freezing. A flat bronze marker was placed at his grave, bronze roses carved at its edges.

In late winter, with the gray limbs of the cemetery shrubbery bare, you could stand at Rush's marker and look up the gentle slope to the gray granite stone where John Schaefer, Jr., had been buried in the family plot. The two plots, by some odd coincidence, were only 150 feet apart in a 350-acre cemetery.

CHAPTER
12

Not long after Brenda Schaefer disappeared, Dr. William Spalding had become so frightened of Mel Ignatow he was instructing his office staff how best to shoot him if he came bursting through the clinic door.

It was a scene that would have been backlit with comic relief had not Spalding, edging ever closer to a mental breakdown, been dead serious. The doctor had organized and contributed heavily to the Brenda Schaefer reward fund, which had now climbed to almost $25,000. His public persona remained that of father figure: kindly, very concerned. Now Spalding, and his staff, frightened of Ignatow, had begun seeing things that may not have been there. Spalding had reported several incidents of someone breaking into his office. The doctor said he saw Ignatow, a tall man, peeping over his back fence. He'd received anonymous letters linking him romantically with Brenda.

He reported being followed by a middle-aged couple, then having his car vandalized. He said three adult men got on the roof of his clinic, screaming and jumping up and down, then pounded on the metal back door. Spalding said members of his staff were getting phone calls every thirty minutes, but no one would speak. Police, knowing Spalding's mental state, tended to discount the stories, but the doctor persisted; he had not fired a gun in more than forty years, but he bought more than $1,000 worth of ammunition and went out to his mother's farm for target practice.

Spalding looked terrible; he had shrunk to five feet nine and about 120 pounds, gaunt, wispy, and gasping for breath. He began to carry a fifteen-shot 9mm Beretta in a shoulder holster while making rounds at St. Anthony's Hospital, where other doctors and some patients got a peek at it. After being reprimanded for his firearm, he kept the gun under his car seat.

"Yes, I had the gun in my office," he would say later, "and we practiced shooting Ignatow. We didn't know what he was doing. All this stuff was happening all the time and nobody's doing a damned thing about it.

"Joyce had a thirty-eight in her desk. If Ignatow comes in the front she was going to hit the floor. I was going to kill him. If he came in the back Joyce was going to try to shoot him.

"I even took my gun out and tried to shoot it. I couldn't lay down and shoot because of my trifocals. So I had to stand up and shoot."

Spalding had done more than prepare for a shootout. He'd also arranged to have a letter sent to Ignatow from Miami, saying Mel would be executed by Cubans unless he sent information about Brenda to a Louisville post-office box within two weeks. The death threat arrived at Ignatow's house by Purolator Courier about 4:30 P.M. on Wednesday, March 22. The two-page letter was single-spaced, neatly typed, but rambling, almost nonsensical; it wasn't until the second page that the execution was mentioned.

The letter had a Ft. Lauderdale postmark. It supposedly came from a Florida multimillionaire named Manuel Perez, an old friend of the Schaefer family who was terminally ill with lung cancer and had nothing to lose by arranging a hit on Ignatow. It said a private investigator had been checking on him, warning:

DO NOT ATTEMPT TO TRACE THIS LETTER, REPORT
TO ANY POLICE AGENCY, OR DISCUSS WITH YOUR AT-
TORNEY, MR. RICKETTS. ANYTHING PERTAINING TO
THIS LETTER AND TRANSACTIONS HAS BEEN DONE IN A
WAY THAT IT CANNOT BE TRACED TO ME OR MY PRI-
VATE INVESTIGATOR. HOWEVER, IF IT IS TRACED IN
ANY WAY THE CONTRACT WITH THE CUBANS IS SET UP
TO BE EXECUTED EVEN IF HER BODY IS FOUND.

I HAVE ARRANGED FOR THE CUBANS TO ARRIVE IN
LOUISVILLE 1 WEEK PRIOR TO TERMINATION OF DATE
OF DISCOVERY OF HER BODY AND REMAIN IN LOUIS-
VILLE UNTIL CONTRACT IS COMPLETED. UPON PROOF
OF YOUR EXECUTION, THEY WILL RECEIVE REMAINDER
OF THIS $15,000 PLUS $5,000 EXPENSE MONEY IF THAT
AMOUNT IS NEEDED.

A closing paragraph was strangely conciliatory, bottom-
line businesslike:

UNDERSTAND, I HAVE NO DESIRE TO HARM YOU OR
SEE YOU PROSECUTED, AND UPON HER BODY RECOV-
ERY THE CUBANS WILL RETURN TO MIAMI, FLORIDA
AND WILL NOT BOTHER YOU FURTHER. IT WOULD BE
HELPFUL AND LESS EXPENSIVE TO ME IF THIS IS DONE
IN 1ST WEEK SO THEY WON'T HAVE TO GO TO LOUIS-
VILLE THE 2ND WEEK OF OUR CONTRACT.

A FAMILY FRIEND RETURNING
A FAVOR YEARS OVERDUE.

Incredibly, county police already knew about the letter.
Weeks earlier Sergeant Lewis Sharber and Lieutenant Don-
nie Kirgan had interviewed Spalding in his large, comfortable home on Briar Hill Road. Sitting in his maple-paneled
family room, Spalding unloaded a string of wild theories and
stories, including having five people approach him to kill
Ignatow. Spalding concluded the interview by reading the

officers a copy of a letter he was contemplating sending to Ignatow about a squad of Cuban assassins.

"I could send it in a way that could never be traced back to me," he told Sharber. "What would you do to me if I sent the letter?"

"I'd lock you up," Sharber answered.

"What's the fine?"

"A five-thousand-dollar fine and a year in jail."

"I wouldn't mind going to jail for a year. I need the rest, but I sure as hell hate to pay you five thousand dollars."

Sharber repeatedly advised Spalding not to send the letter. He also told him it was illegal to carry a concealed deadly weapon; he should be very careful with his gun.

Spalding would later say his problems were caused by giving himself too much cortisone to control his disabling asthma, which was compounded by the stress of Brenda's disappearance. He was also having trouble remembering things.

"I'm not excusing what I did," he would say later, "but cortisone made me hyper as hell."

Spalding's death-threat letter had not placed Mel Ignatow in a forgiving mood. March 1989 had been a difficult month. *Courier-Journal* reporter Elinor J. Brecher had written a long, detailed article about Brenda Schaefer's disappearance, a story that angered Ignatow because it portrayed him as the logical suspect. The story had also angered the Schaefer family; it quoted Frank Prell, a man who dated her only briefly. It used the loaded phrase "gold digger" in connection with Schaefer, but only in the context of having ex-husband Pete Van Pelt deny that it fit Brenda. The Schaefer family considered Van Pelt, who did characterize Brenda as being interested in men with money, to be a very poor source. Van Pelt had not spoken to Brenda in many years; their divorce had not been a pleasant experience.

The article also said one of the men she dated paid for her cosmetic surgery; in fact, Brenda had borrowed the money from family. The story generally left the impression Brenda was much more materialistic and status-conscious than her family knew her to be: Brenda was working sixty hours a week for Dr. Spalding, trimmed toenails in nursing homes on some evenings, and was living at home to be with her sick mother.

The *Courier-Journal* story was widely read and discussed. It created lasting impressions and reawakened interest in Schaefer's disappearance, making Ignatow's life as a home-water-softener salesman that much more difficult. Ignatow also was upset over an exchange of letters between his mother and Schaefer's parents. Virginia Ignatow had sent John and Essie Schaefer an Easter card in March, writing across the top, "I think of you often and pray daily that this nightmare will be over very soon for all of us. Fondly, Virginia Ignatow."

The note was in character; everyone who knew Virginia Ignatow found her thoughtful and sincere. John Schaefer, Brenda's father, accepted her wishes in good faith but did not apply them to her son. He wrote back on March 22, apparently basing some of his letter on information received from a psychic:

DEAR MRS. IGNATOW,

WE RECEIVED YOUR NICE CARD AND GOOD TO HEAR FROM YOU. THE NIGHTMARE YOU WROTE OF WILL NEVER GO AWAY TILL SHE IS FOUND.

WE HAVE INFORMATION THAT SHE IS ALIVE, BUT NERVOUS AND WORRIED. SHE IS HELD CAPTIVE BY TWO PEOPLE. THEY LOOK LIKE MEN. HOWEVER ONE COULD BE A WOMAN. WE KNOW MORE, BUT CANNOT SAY AT THIS TIME.

IF MEL WISHES TO TALK ABOUT THIS WE FEEL IT WOULD BE BEST FOR HIM, MAYBE WE COULD HELP HIM.

THE WAY WE FEEL ABOUT HIM NOW, IF SHE IS HARMED IN ANY WAY, HE WILL BE RESPONSIBLE.

Ignatow called Charlie Ricketts, telling him he believed the death-threat letter had come from Jim Wesley, who had been in Florida on vacation. According to Sharber, Ricketts then told the FBI the Jefferson County police might have been involved in the death threat, severing what little remained of any goodwill between Ricketts and Wesley, if not also his superiors.

At 5:45 P.M. on Thursday, March 23, Sharber, Kirgan, and Berthon met with Ignatow in Ricketts's office to discuss the death threat. At the insistence of Ricketts and Ignatow, arrangements were made to have a Jefferson County police SWAT team guard Ignatow.

At 10:15 P.M., Sharber and Berthon went to St. Anthony's Hospital to confront Spalding, who was making rounds in the coronary care unit. Sharber, of course, already knew the truth; he'd read the letter in Spalding's home. Sharber didn't really want to prosecute Spalding, nor did Berthon. The letter was a hoax; Spalding was a sick man under great stress, consumed by a need to help Brenda. Sitting in the doctors' lounge, Spalding briefly denied any involvement, then changed his story.

"Yeah, I wrote the letter," he said.

The doctor had asked Molly Henley, the secretary of his stockbroker, to type the letter. He paid her $100, which she donated to the Brenda Schaefer fund. He'd asked Carl Markwell, a friend in Miami, to forward the letter to Ignatow.

"I didn't give a shit if they put me in jail or not," Spalding would say later. "I was worn out. I was tired of fooling with all this . . . carrying a gun and constantly hearing footsteps."

Berthon and Sharber drove to Ignatow's home, explaining to Ignatow, his mother, and Ricketts that Spalding admitted writing the letter; there was no death plot. Berthon and Sharber told Ignatow any prosecution was up to him, and his SWAT team protection would be terminated. There was never any doubt Ignatow was going to sign a warrant for Spalding's arrest. But he had one other item of business to take care of first.

Ignatow had been dating Barbara McGee, forty-five, a state clerical worker. They had first dated three years earlier, but that relationship had deteriorated because Ignatow had been pushy about sex; it fell apart the day Ignatow refused to let McGee set a birthday cake in his Corvette because it might spill crumbs.

They met again at Flaherty's, the singles bar, in February 1989, five months after Brenda's disappearance. McGee knew about Brenda Schaefer, but Ignatow was kind. He seemed sympathetic, sensitive to her needs, understanding of her longtime co-dependence with others.

"Mel liked to have fun and was adventurous," she would say later. "He liked to drive fast and so did I."

They dated for five months. She went to Sanibel Island, Florida, with him. She was convinced he knew nothing about Brenda's disappearance. Ignatow called McGee every day. He began pressuring her to invest in National Safety Associates, sell water softeners with him, form a partnership. McGee had little money, but Ignatow pressured her to invest $3,000, most of which she would lose.

One night in late March, soon after receiving the death-threat letter, Ignatow showed up at McGee's apartment with a brown bag containing a dildo, K-Y jelly, and condoms. He said he feared the police might soon be searching his house.

"The police wouldn't want me to have this," she remembered him saying. "I just don't think it would look good."

McGee was surprised. She had no reason to see any link between the dildo, the jelly, and condoms and the disappearance of Brenda Schaefer. Her immediate thought was "Well, I wouldn't want anybody to find anything like that in my house, either."

A month later she threw the dildo into a Dumpster.

At 8:35 P.M. on Friday, March 24, Ignatow went to the Hall of Justice to sign a criminal warrant against Spalding for terroristic threatening, a misdemeanor. He also was thinking of a civil suit against Spalding; he'd already promised Mary Ann Shore a piece of that financial pie to keep her from talking to police.

Ignatow went directly from the Hall of Justice to the Jewish Hospital emergency room, complaining he had suffered a heart attack. He was admitted for three days of tests and observation. Sharber arrested Spalding at his home about 10:30. He was immediately released on his own recognizance and pleaded innocent in Jefferson District Court the next day. On March 27 Spalding wrote a letter to Sharber saying, ''I want to convey to you my sincerest appreciation for the respect and courteous treatment that I received from you the night I was arrested.''

On March 29 he admitted himself to the psychiatric ward of St. Joseph Hospital in Lexington, Kentucky, seventy miles east of the county police and Louisville media, which often led newscasts with the story. In Lexington, Spalding insisted he be allowed to make a telephone call to cancel a death threat on Ignatow.

Ricketts sought to have police security given Ignatow in Jewish Hospital. Jefferson County police sought to have a mental-inquest warrant served on Spalding, but were denied because he already was in a hospital getting required treatment. Spalding's preliminary diagnosis was ''bipolar disorder, manic type.''

CHAPTER
13

It was August 8, 1989, before Dr. William Spalding's terroristic-threatening case went to Jefferson District Court—but it was Mel Ignatow who would be on trial.

Almost a year had passed since Brenda Schaefer's car had been found along Interstate 64, and county police were no closer to an arrest than they were the day she disappeared. Jim Wesley tried to stay with the case, but all his leads had melted away; his failed confrontation with Mary Ann Shore was still bothering him six months later. Much of his time was occupied by a new murder. Michael Mark Morgan, a Louisville restaurant manager, was charged with brutally stabbing his wife, Gretchen, twenty-four times in the back with a knife. The murder took place in April, but hadn't yet gone to trial.

Wesley had seen the scrawly, four-page letter Ignatow had written Tom Schaefer after Brenda's disappearance. It pretended to offer sympathy to the family, but was mostly filled with grinding self-pity, the usual Ignatow litany of his personal gloom and depression, his increasing dependence on alcohol and drugs. The letter infuriated the Schaefers and Wesley, whose frustration and rage mirrored the family's. But he was too busy with other cases to drop in on the Spalding trial, missing a chance to watch Ignatow.

Ignatow had forced the trial by signing the warrant, putting himself in the witness box, with dreams of a civil-suit payday to follow. Spalding remained a mostly sympathetic figure in Louisville, a man driven over the edge by the loss of Brenda Schaefer. The doctor had spent about a month in the Lexington hospital, being released in April. In July he sold his practice for $250,000, staying home to rest and putter around the house. He was on the road to recovery, eventually to practice medicine again in a Jefferson County health clinic.

Spalding's trial drew heavy media attention, plus police, FBI agents, and two assistant U.S. attorneys, John Caudill and Scott Cox, all eager to watch Ignatow in the witness box. The terroristic-threatening case was only the backdrop to the larger drama. Spalding still looked frail, almost brittle. He was defended by Tim McCall, a veteran Louisville defense attorney who had been one of the court-appointed attorneys for Michael Tinsley in the 1971 Jack Schaefer murder trial. McCall had become so well known for his tearful closing arguments that playful prosecutors would occasionally bring Kleenex into court.

The aggressive, emotional McCall went after Ignatow with a vengeance; his only hope was that the jury might forgive Spalding's actions if Ignatow was shown to be the only logical suspect in Brenda Schaefer's disappearance. McCall stared at Ignatow, who looked confident, smug, ready to begin the duel. McCall asked Ignatow if there was any "bad blood" between himself and Spalding.

"Nothing I know of."

"You were the last one to see Brenda Schaefer alive?" McCall asked.

"I assume so," Ignatow answered, staying calm.

McCall hammered at Ignatow's relationship with Schaefer. He questioned Ignatow about the death-threat package from Florida:

"Didn't you consider the letter an attempt to find Brenda Schaefer's body?"

"No. I considered it an attempt to kill me," said Ignatow,

an earnest look on his face. "... It scared the living daylights out of me."

McCall raised his voice, asking Ignatow about his refusal to take a lie-detector test, his relationship with Brenda and her family, the possibility of Brenda's moving to Florida.

"I did not want Brenda to come down to Florida because of her mom's condition," Ignatow said. "We were both afraid something would happen.

"Mrs. Schaefer and I are still on very good terms. We talk to each other once in a while. I talk to Tom all the time. We're still very good friends."

When asking Ignatow why he took the threatening letter to Charlie Ricketts instead of the police, McCall began shouting at Ignatow, his voice filling the courtroom.

"Didn't the police have to come out and meet with you . . . ?"

Ignatow used the question to his advantage:

"I can hear you very well. You don't have to scream."

McCall came on even stronger in his closing argument to the jury, saying of Ignatow: "He's a liar. You know he's a liar. He said his relationship with Brenda Schaefer was good and loving, but I'm telling you it wasn't. It was just the opposite.

"This man thinks he can fool everyone all the time, but he can't. He's a convicted felon not worthy of belief. He's lied to you, and he's lied to police officers."

Tears trickling down his cheeks, his voice cracking, McCall added, "I hope all citizens who are affected by crime will do what Dr. Spalding has done . . . work with the police to help them."

The closing was powerful, but Spalding had already testified he'd arranged to send the letter. Ignatow had testified it had caused a heart attack. Lewis Sharber had testified that "the totality of Spalding's efforts were a hindrance."

Prosecutor Bob Webb reminded the jury that Spalding, not Ignatow, was on trial, but he added a curious afterthought.

"I don't know if he did anything to Brenda Schaefer. If he did, I hope he's caught someday."

McCall had already tossed in the towel.

"Doctor," he said to Spalding right after his closing argument, "we're going to lose this case."

"Tim," said Spalding. "I'd lose faith in the judicial system if they didn't convict me."

Spalding was quickly found guilty and fined $300. He said he wasn't unhappy with the verdict, defiantly calling the fine "a pittance." John Schaefer, Brenda's father, was more upset than Spalding.

"What he did wasn't wrong at all," Schaefer said. "It was for the benefit of Brenda."

Legal niceties aside, Schaefer's attitude was mirrored by many of the police and attorneys in the courtroom, including Assistant U.S. Attorney Scott Cox, who had been silently rooting for Spalding. Cox had developed an interest in Mel Ignatow beyond that expected in his particular job, an interest that would finally lead the case in a direction not even he could have imagined.

Cox, twenty-nine, a Louisville native, was appointed an assistant U.S. attorney for the Western District of Kentucky in 1987. He had been doing mostly civil work, defending federal employees involved in lawsuits, when he inherited a case load from another attorney. The new case load included the Brenda Schaefer file. Cox was new, generally unaware it was the FBI's job to actively investigate and his job to give agents advice when asked.

Cox was a solid man, about six feet tall and weighing 200 pounds, with a soft, almost muted voice. He was ambitious and aggressive, occasionally to the point of irritating the FBI supervisors. He had been intrigued by Elinor Brecher's story about Ignatow. He began calling FBI agent Maury Berthon, asking about the case, working on background. Berthon, as frustrated as everyone else, was all but convinced Ignatow had killed her. He told Cox of the FBI's criminal sexual sadist profile, saying it seemed a perfect description of Ignatow.

"According to our behavioral sciences people," Cox remembered Berthon telling him, "Mel wants to be caught. He has a subconscious desire to be caught. He just needs to be pressured and he'll spill the beans.''

Cox went to the Spalding trial partly to represent Berthon, who was also testifying and might require legal advice. Ironically, while Cox was rooting for acquittal, he ended up providing information that helped the prosecution solve a legal point: At the judge's request Cox provided case law saying it had been legal for police to question Spalding in the hospital lounge. Mostly Cox was there to watch Ignatow, to see if he looked like a man who could be pressured. Cox was generally impressed with what he saw.

''Mel did a pretty good job,'' Cox would say. ''He held his own. He did not become flustered. It's clear to me from watching him testify that he's a bright guy and he basically puts himself well.''

Cox wasn't going to quit there. During the trial he met Charlie Ricketts, who was there to help Ignatow if needed. Cox had never met Ricketts, who effusively greeted him like a long-lost relative.

''Hey, Scott. Good to see you again. How are you doing?''

Cox admired Ricketts's abilities as a legal marketer, a man who knew how to develop a huge private practice. Ricketts had his clients establish ''trust accounts'' that would serve as a reservoir for legal fees. He knew Ricketts to be a competent, very thorough attorney, a man who would cover all legal bases and back up many conversations and interviews with long, detailed summary letters. Cox knew he would have to go through Ricketts to reach Ignatow.

''We need to talk about this sometime,'' Cox told Ricketts as they stood in the dim, crowded hall.

''Fine,'' Ricketts said, staying noncommittal.

For two weeks Cox mulled over what he had seen at Spalding's trial. Berthon seemed confident of Ignatow's guilt, but Cox hadn't been *that* close to the case. Cox was certain that if Ignatow had been involved, he had to have a partner; he would not have walked away from Brenda Schaefer's abandoned car by himself.

Assistant U.S. attorneys were given a lot of leeway on

their cases, and Cox wanted to push it a little more. He asked Berthon what he thought of asking Ricketts if Ignatow would volunteer to testify before a federal grand jury. Cox liked to use the grand jury. It was a big club. Grand jury witnesses were not allowed to have an attorney present; they could be intimidated. They were under oath, liable for federal perjury charges if they lied.

Berthon called back the next day: "We want you to do it."

Even though it was his idea, Cox had little confidence in the plan; any lawyer's general legal rule of thumb was never to let a client voluntarily go before a grand jury. The automatic response was that a client would take the Fifth Amendment, refusing to say anything self-incriminating, unless full immunity was granted. In fact the U.S. attorney's manual discouraged the subpoenaing of suspects because they always pleaded the Fifth Amendment; it was a waste of time and money.

"I knew Ricketts would say no," Cox said later. "I told Maury we'd try, but don't count on anything."

Cox called Ricketts.

"Charlie, your client did a really good job at the trial. I believed him. I think he's probably innocent. He came across that way to me.

"We're going to open up a full-blown federal grand jury investigation on this and we'd like your client to come down and make a statement."

Ricketts's first impulse was to refuse the offer.

"Why in the world would I want to do that?" Cox remembered him saying.

Cox had an answer prepared.

"Two reasons. One, if Mel does as good a job in the grand jury as he did in the Spalding trial, he can redirect the focus of the grand jury investigation and get them to look at other suspects.

"Two, grand jury proceedings are secret and I can't talk about them. But you're not bound by that rule and you can have a press conference.

"After the Ellie Brecher article, Mel's just been smeared. You can stand on the courthouse steps and say Mel volunteered to come down, that he wants to help in this investigation. That will help him in the eyes of the community."

Cox remembered Ricketts being interested, but he wanted to talk to Ignatow. About a week later, Ricketts and his assistant, Valerie Herbert, met in Cox's office to fine-tune the idea. Ricketts seemed convinced of Ignatow's innocence. He told Cox that Ignatow was lost, confused, a man with a Jewish father and Catholic mother, who had never quite belonged.

"I've represented Mel for years and he's a good man," Ricketts said.

Cox, still doubtful Ignatow might actually testify, told Ricketts: "Charlie, I'm willing to come meet Mel in your office to discuss this with him. If he's not comfortable he can get up and leave the grand jury anytime he wants. There's nothing I can do about it.

"Not only that, I'll let him make a statement after we're finished where he can say anything he wants. It seems to me he has nothing to lose."

Ricketts seemed more interested. On October 6 he wrote a letter to Ignatow outlining his meeting with Cox, suggesting they get together to discuss a grand jury appearance, which was tentatively scheduled for October 16, 1989. Ricketts would later say he then advised Ignatow not to testify before the grand jury, but was willing to meet with Ignatow to give him the "ground rules" of what to expect.

In mid-October, Cox met with Ignatow in Ricketts's office. Ignatow was in tears, keeping Cox a little off stride.

"The goddamned *Courier-Journal* has slandered me," he told Cox. "They've done a job on me. I can't even go out and shop. I feel like I can't live my life."

Cox repeated his grand jury offer, complete with press conference.

"I want to do it," Ignatow said.

October 16 dawned warm but cloudy, with the threat of rain, which could have dampened the media parade. The grand jury room was on the third floor of the massive federal courthouse, a block-long stone building fronted by Greek columns across Sixth Street from the *Courier-Journal* building. Entrance to the room was clandestine, almost spooky: twisting metal stairs that led up one flight to a narrow hall with a bare, hardwood floor, then into the room.

Federal prosecutors often used the grand jury as an investigative tool; once in the room, witnesses were often reluctant to leave; they might appear guilty of something. Prosecutors took great delight in shouting down from the top of the stairs for their next witness, their voices echoing ominously around the marble and steel.

Cox led Ignatow into the grand jury room. He sat behind a small, worn, oak desk facing the twenty-one grand jurors, who were seated in horseshoe fashion in front of him. A bookcase filled with legal tomes ran along the left wall. Looking out the back windows, Ignatow could see the Federal Building, headquarters for the Louisville FBI branch.

Ignatow was wearing a light gray suit, a white shirt, and a dark blue tie with red stripes. He looked tired, thin, a little uneasy. Watching Ignatow climb the stairs and walk toward his chair, Cox had been struck by how gangly he looked, clumsy, skinny, all elbows and knees. The Louisville media, tipped off about the testimony, set up a Mel Ignatow watch at the building. Louisville attorney Frank Haddad, long considered one of Kentucky's best defense attorneys, happened to be in the building.

"What's going on, Charlie?" Haddad asked.

"Mel Ignatow is testifying before the federal grand jury." Haddad couldn't believe it.

"Are you out of your mind?"

"Mel said he hadn't done anything and he wants to testify."

"Since when does that make a difference?"

Ignatow testified for almost four hours, producing 220 transcript pages of testimony. Cox's game plan was to proceed as if he were taking a civil deposition: ask lots of questions about family and work history, then hit Ignatow with

questions about Brenda, his sex life, the police investigation.
Cox had also been fed some questions from Jim Wesley.
"Mel has suddenly turned very religious," Wesley clued
him. "Ask him some questions about God and Brenda."

Cox delighted in asking personal questions, sexual questions, things Ignatow would never discuss during police in-
terrogation, or with an attorney present. Cox knew very little
about Mary Ann Shore's relationship with Ignatow, so he
tried the direct approach.

"Have you all had sex this year?" he asked Ignatow.

"Yeah."

The answer surprised Cox; Brenda Schaefer's grieving fiancé had quickly found solace in Shore?

"How many months from the time Ms. Schaefer disappeared in September of 1988 until you were sleeping with
Ms. Shore?"

"Gosh . . . I don't know . . . it was after the first of the
year. I can't remember exactly when. . . . Not on a regular
basis. We'd just see each other once in a while. I think it
was more a need on my part than anything else . . . an emotional and physical supportive type of thing."

Ignatow was on a mission of his own, to sell the grand
jury on his innocence. He depended on that ability to sell,
often by seamlessly mixing fact and fiction. His grand jury
testimony was seasoned with personal financial tidbits and
medical reports, most designed to ingratiate:

He was a ruined man; he had $26,000 worth of credit-card
bills, no income, first and second mortgages on his home, a
$1,192-a-month house payment, and no hope for a job. He
was taking three different heart medicines for blocked arter-
ies, blood pressure, and high cholesterol. The police had
done a terrible job; why hadn't they gone harder after other
suspects—Jim Rush or Pete Van Pelt. Brenda's engagement
ring, appraised for $20,000, had actually been purchased for
$7,500 on one of his overseas trips; he couldn't remember
exactly where.

"You can get things a lot cheaper in some places overseas."

Cox asked if Mel had ever put a rag soaked with chloroform over Brenda's mouth while she was sleeping.

"... I have bad allergies and I take shots for it ... you know, I get stopped up at night and I take a handkerchief or a Kleenex to bed with me quite often, and Brenda gets stopped up occasionally ..."

"Did you all put it on each other's faces, or did you put it on your own?"

"Oh, no, just use it ourselves if we needed to. But, I mean, you know how you'll be playful sometimes. ..."

Ignatow testified he had been drinking too much since Brenda disappeared, mixing vodka and Valium, the latter having been prescribed for his mother's heart condition. He said he considered suicide, then began to recover, joining a Christian church where he had found help.

"Do you think God knows what happened to Brenda Schaefer?" Cox asked him.

"God knows everything. He doesn't necessarily tell us everything, but yes."

"Did you kill her, Mel?"

"No. Absolutely not. I did not kill her. I would not have laid a finger on that woman."

Afterward, Ignatow and Ricketts held their press conference. Louisville television reporters, photographers, and a *Courier-Journal* reporter had waited for hours in the cavernous courthouse hallway. The media moved outside to the courthouse steps, a light rain falling on the street. Ricketts, in a dark gray suit and red tie, said Ignatow was a volunteer and not necessarily a target of the investigation. Ignatow stood with his hands folded behind his back, his head bobbing. He looked sincere, *sounded* sincere, an anxious, hurt look on his face, the picture of a wronged man. Speaking as if from a prepared statement, he looked into the television camera.

"I hope that in some way this will help the investigative officers involved to redirect their case in an effort to try to find my fiancée and find out what happened and who was involved.

"This has certainly been a nightmare for me for well over a year, and I'm very exhausted from it."

He thanked the grand jury for being "very congenial." Then he and Ricketts walked off into a gentle rain, striding side by side, Ricketts holding a black umbrella over his client's head.

Scott Cox wasn't happy. The whole plan had been to pressure Ignatow, find an opening in the case. Now Ignatow and Ricketts were out on the front steps making a mockery of the grand jury.

"They had a trained circus out there," Cox would later say. "Four television stations and I mean I have mud on my face. This guy is abusing us. He's making fun of the grand jury system. And *that* was a mistake."

In the following weeks Cox mentally replayed the grand jury events. The one thing that stood out in Ignatow's testimony was sex; he and Mary Ann Shore had been intimate just a few months after Brenda had disappeared.

"That just stuck out like a sore thumb to me," Cox would say. "There had to be some kind of connection with those two and Brenda's disappearance."

Cox wanted to bring Shore before the grand jury. He and Berthon agreed to have her subpoenaed. Cox knew the county police had pushed Shore pretty hard with no success; he didn't expect too much. It just seemed like the next logical step, but it wasn't easily taken.

"Maury gets Mary Ann Shore served," Cox would say. "We have a meeting and the whole criminal staff is there. They ask: 'What is Mary Ann Shore doing on the grand jury list? . . . We're sick of you wasting the grand jury's time.' "

Cox knew he was being kidded, but with an underlying seriousness; Ignatow had embarrassed them. What was Shore going to do to them?

"Mary Ann apparently had sex with Mel," explained Cox, desperate for a one-liner, "and I want to hear about sex."

Everybody laughed. Mary Ann Shore stayed on the grand jury list.

CHAPTER
14

Attorney Jack Vittitow hadn't heard from Mary Ann Shore for eight months when she called him in late November to say she had been subpoenaed to appear before the January 3, 1990, federal grand jury.

"You probably don't remember me," she said to Vittitow.

Vittitow did remember Shore—the bad-check charges; the FBI's asking her to take a lie-detector test; the disposition of her case: restitution with probation until 1990. Beyond that there was only a general awareness of the Brenda Schaefer case, intermittent flashes of television and newspaper stories.

"Come to my office beforehand," Vittitow told her. "I'll go with you."

Shore arrived at Vittitow's office wearing jeans and a jacket; Vittitow would never again see her as well dressed as the first day they met. Vittitow sensed Shore's uneasiness; she would begin to laugh at something, then nervously cut it off. She was cool, diffident, but a little frightened.

"I don't know what the grand jury wants with me," she said. "I've already told the police everything I know."

Vittitow explained how grand juries worked, what to expect, what to avoid, her Fifth Amendment rights.

"I can't be with you in the room. The main thing you

don't want to do is lie. Don't ever perjure yourself. If you have any doubts about a question, you can come outside and talk to me.''

Shore said very little about Mel Ignatow. Vittitow did not ask.

Ignatow had been dealing with his own private demons. A few weeks after his grand jury testimony and press conference, he'd received a letter from Charlie Ricketts proposing an even broader public-relations coup. Ricketts wrote to Ignatow that he initiated a conversation with John McGrath of WHAS-TV on Monday, October 30, after McGrath had reported on a murder trial that had produced a lot of news attention. Ricketts said he'd suggested McGrath do a story on Mel's life, the damage caused to his reputation and income. By then Ignatow had no income; he'd left National Safety Associates after six months; his co-workers were finding his presence had hurt sales. John R. Michael, who leased Ignatow office space, said he had been friendly, reliable, a good businessman.

''Frankly,'' Michael would say, ''some people in his group might be regarded as fly-by-night. Mel was the guy to go to if there were any problems. He was very professional.''

On August 27 Ignatow's life took another turn; after counseling with one of its ministers, he joined the booming Southeast Christian Church. The church had become a religious force, the fastest-growing ministry in Kentucky, if not the entire South. Its leader was senior minister Bob Russell, a charismatic, personable man who mixed devotion to strong basic values with insightful humor. His Sunday-morning show heard on the 50,000-watt WHAS radio had a tremendous following, both inside and outside his church.

Ignatow would become active in the church's singles group, BYKOTA (Be Ye Kind One To Another). He dated or made friends with several women, all of them professionals. Ignatow was not just another lonely single; his appearance created a dilemma. A basic tenet of the Southeast Christian faith was not to judge, but to love and accept. Ignatow's notoriety preceded him; some members were uneasy, talked about dropping out. Several would leave a singles party if he appeared, convinced he was cynically using their faith to cover his sins. They were not alone.

"The day Mel came forward and said he wanted to be a part of the fellowship of the church was the first day I met him," Russell would say later. "We just met briefly when he came down the aisle.

"Immediately that same day a policeman and an FBI spokesman came to me and said, 'We want you to know who that is. That's Mel Ignatow ... we know he killed Brenda Schaefer.'

" 'Our psychological profile on this guy suggested he would do something within a year to absolve his guilt. We really suspect his motives for coming forward saying he wants to accept Jesus Christ and begin all over again. We think you ought to watch out for him.' "

Russell spoke with Ross Brodfuehrer, the minister who worked with the singles group, who spoke to Ignatow.

"Mel," Brodfuehrer said, "if you are guilty of this murder, part of your obligation if you're genuine in accepting Christ is to tell the truth."

"I did not do it," Ignatow answered.

Southeast Christian had no choice but to accept him; he was baptized into the church. Ignatow had found a haven; given time, he would convince many church members of his innocence.

"I didn't know what he did or didn't do," said one woman who befriended Ignatow soon after he joined. "If the FBI, the state police, the local police, and all the other agencies that are trying to nail him can't do it, who am I?

"Even if he's guilty, that doesn't mean we treat him ugly, or we don't treat him with love."

The woman, open, friendly, a Christian, refused to judge. Ignatow spent hours sitting in her living room telling his side of the story. He was sincere, convincing, always the perfect gentleman. Over the next few weeks Ignatow talked to her almost daily, hours at a time, always carrying his little gifts of guilt and flattery.

"You are an angel God has brought into my life," he told her.

Ignatow overdid it. He did not wear well. He talked of nothing but himself, his problems. The woman, who never actually dated Ignatow, tried to break away.

"Believe me, the last thing I need to be is somebody's angel," she would say. "I didn't like him and I still believed he was innocent."

Ignatow wouldn't let her go. He called incessantly:

"Mel, I'm busy now. I can't talk to you."

"What's the matter? I thought you were my friend."

Ignatow called her again, asking questions about the meaning of baptism, what it meant to be saved, to be forgiven. He had convinced himself that to be baptized was to be absolved of all sin. A cold chill came over the woman; she sensed where Ignatow was leading.

"The blood of Christ covers our sins," she told him. "The scriptures say he forgives us our sins, casts them into the sea of forgiveness, and he'll never bring them up again. That's the end of it."

"Well, if that's true . . ." Ignatow began.

"It *is* true . . ."

"Well," Ignatow continued, "then if Christ has forgiven me my sins, if a sin will never be remembered, then should that apply to everybody?"

"Mel, what do you mean?"

"I didn't do it, but let's just say I killed Brenda Schaefer. If Christ has forgiven me my sins and cast them into a sea of forgiveness, why wouldn't the state do the same thing? Why should I ever have to answer to the state if God has forgiven me?"

The woman was stunned.

"Mel, if all it took was a conversion to Christianity for the state to give up their right to prosecute, we wouldn't even need locks on the jail cells because who in the hell wouldn't want to make a quick conversion? I'd confess anything to get out of jail, wouldn't you?''

Ignatow didn't answer.

''The Bible also teaches us the laws of the land, and that's what we have to answer to on this earth. While you can live with the peace of forgiveness of Christ, it doesn't mean you don't have to pay the price of sin here on earth.''

Ignatow wasn't satisfied with that answer, wouldn't accept it; he knew God would forgive him.

The conversation jolted the woman, opening a wide door of doubt about Ignatow. He hadn't confessed to anything. Their discussion had been personal, religious, probably too general to mean anything in a court of law where a good lawyer could pick it apart. The conversation bothered her— she could never get it fully out of her mind. She never talked to Ignatow again.

Not all church members felt that way. Dr. William Spalding's conviction and the grand jury press conference had given Ignatow credibility at Southeast Christian. More members began to warm to him, convinced of his innocence. He began seriously dating another singles-club member, talking marriage after only a few weeks. She broke away in early December; Ignatow was desperate to get her back, calling other people to intercede.

About 1:00 P.M., December 14, a few weeks before Mary Ann Shore was to appear before the federal grand jury, the Jeffersontown police got a frantic phone call from Virginia Ignatow; her son had locked himself in the bathroom, had taken a large amount of Valium on top of vodka, and dropped to the floor. To police, it sounded like a suicide attempt.

Emergency Medical Services technician John Layman found Ignatow on the floor, crying, complaining about the recent breakup with a woman, apparently from Southeast Christian Church. Ignatow seemed groggy but never lost consciousness. He was taken by ambulance to Humana Hospital University. A little more than two weeks later, he appeared at a New Year's Eve party of a church member who had an indoor swimming pool. Ignatow, wearing a diaper over his swimsuit, briefly played the New Year baby.

The New Year blew in cold, a low of 19 degrees. The cold snap was brief, the temperature into the mid-fifties by January 3 as Mary Ann Shore settled into Jack Vittitow's office, the federal grand jury on her mind.

She was accompanied by a new companion: live-in boyfriend Charles "Butch" Inlow, fifty. In September, Shore had moved from the small frame home at 4921 Poplar Level Road; she'd not gotten along with the landlady and the house was up for sale.

Shore moved a few miles north to a small, second-floor apartment at 329 Huntington Park Drive off Poplar Level Road. She was still doing part-time work for Manpower Temporaries. She didn't mention her relationship with Inlow to the lawyer, explaining his presence by saying, "I just got a ride with him."

Vittitow noticed Shore had gained a lot of weight, seemed unconcerned about her personal appearance. Vittitow was more fascinated with Inlow; he carried a paperback book he would stare at but seemed never to read.

Inlow was recently divorced from his wife of thirty years. They had six children. Inlow's mother lived next door to Shore on Poplar Level Road; Shore had met Butch in 1988 while he was painting his mother's house and mowing her grass. They became friendly, eventually intimate. Inlow often visited his mother driving a truck from the Black Mudd Volunteer Fire Department, where he'd been a member for many years.

Scott Cox met Shore, Inlow, and Vittitow outside the grand jury room. There was little discussion before Shore went into the room, no attempt by Vittitow to work a deal; at that point there was nothing to deal about.

"Tell the truth and nothing but the truth," Vittitow told Shore. "I'll be out here if you need me."

As with Ignatow, Cox first went into broad relationships.

Had Shore ever met Brenda Schaefer, spoken with her, talked to Ignatow about her?

No was the answer on all counts, except one time when Mel borrowed a photo album of trips he and Shore had taken together to show to Brenda.

Cox thought Shore looked nervous, ill at ease.

"You knew he was dating Brenda?"

"Yes."

"How did you know that?"

"He told me."

Cox kept pushing Shore about meetings with Ignatow since September 1988, when Brenda disappeared. She admitted to four, most very brief, including their walk in the rain.

"Have you had sex with Mel since Brenda Schaefer disappeared?"

"Yes."

"When?"

"In November 1989."

"Did he spend the night?"

"No."

"How long was he there?"

"I'd say forty-five minutes to an hour."

"Has it not been your intent then to try to rekindle this romance with Mel?"

"No. At present I'm engaged to be married, June sixteenth."

"To whom?"

"To the man sitting out in the hall, Charles Inlow."

"How long have you been dating him?"

"Since June 1989."

"So you had sex with Mr. Ignatow after you started dating this gentleman?"

"Uh-huh."

"Don't you think that's unusual?"

"No."

"To be engaged to someone . . . ?"

"Well, I just now got engaged Christmas."

Cox kept moving, looking for openings, steering the conversation into seemingly innocent territory. Shore testified she had seen Ignatow and Schaefer together only once, at a 1987 New Year's Eve party at a Louisville night spot called Jim Porter's Good Time Emporium.

"Describe Miss Schaefer," asked Cox, just keeping conversation going.

"Pardon?"

"Describe Miss Schaefer for the grand jury."

"What do you mean, describe her?"

"Describe her physical appearance."

"When I saw her in the bar?"

"Did you ever see her again other than that?"

"No."

"Then describe her from then."

Shore froze, unable to talk. Her face whitened. Sixteen months of guilt, fear, and pressure had worked to the surface, triggered by an image that would not be repressed; *describe* Brenda Schaefer?

Shore couldn't do it.

"Can I see my attorney?"

Vittitow was waiting downstairs in the marbled hallway, mostly watching Inlow, who was still staring at the same page. Shore, tightlipped, walked past Vittitow.

"Give me a cigarette," she demanded of Inlow.

She looked frightened, trapped.

"Mary Ann," asked Vittitow. "What happened?"

"They asked me a question?"

"Fine. What was it?"

"What did Brenda look like the last time I saw her?"

Shore leaned against a window, looking out at the yellow brick walls. Inlow didn't say anything.

"What's the problem with that?" asked Vittitow. "Where did you see her last?"

"Jim Porter's."

"Then what's the problem?"

Shore didn't want to answer. She stared out the window, puffing furiously on her cigarette.

"Let me finish my cigarette and I'll go back."

Inlow, saying nothing, went back to his book. Shore returned to the grand jury with a very brief description of Brenda Schaefer: "She had short, dark hair."

"Why are you uncomfortable answering questions describing Brenda Schaefer?" asked Cox.

"Because . . . I don't know . . . all I know is she had dark hair. . . . I don't know how to describe her."

Cox and Hancy Jones, another assistant U.S. attorney, who was helping him interrogate Shore, turned up the heat, firing questions in bursts. Shore's sexual encounters with Ignatow became a central theme. The questions approached voyeurism; anything was allowed inside the secrecy of the grand jury. Shore could have refused to answer any question, plead the Fifth Amendment; Vittitow told her that. She could have walked away anytime.

"Do you consider Mel a good lover?"

"Yes."

"Better than your fiancé?"

"No."

Shore had regained her composure; she toughed it out.

"Did you assist Mel Ignatow in killing Brenda Schaefer?"

"No."

"Do you think Mel Ignatow killed her?"

"No."

"Why?"

"Because he wouldn't do anything like that. He's a very nice person."

Cox was convinced Shore was lying; *something* had caused her to flee the room. The day after her testimony, he began calling Vittitow.

"Jack, that woman is a liar. She's going to be prosecuted. I think we've got her on perjury. She's eventually going to get the death penalty. Why don't we cut a deal now and make it easy on her?"

Vittitow was cagey, noncommittal; he had a lot more to learn himself.

"Let me talk to her. I'll talk to you later."

Cox kept calling Vittitow, eager to deal. Vittitow was walking a legal tightrope; his first obligation was to his client, but he didn't know what she'd told the grand jury. What if the feds did have something on her? He knew clients rarely told their lawyers everything. He called Shore:

"Mary Ann, they feel like they have something on you. If you want my advice, if you know anything at all, you better meet with me. Let's get this thing straightened out. Let's get up there and talk about it."

"I don't know if I should," Shore answered.

"You don't have to. But the best thing to do is get it over with now before something pops up, if there is anything. If they're going to indict you on charges of lying, then maybe it's already too late."

Vittitow knew what was at stake. He'd been filled in on Shore's past relationship with Ignatow, and he knew that Ignatow was the prime suspect. He pushed Shore to meet with Cox, to have everyone sit in the same room and talk it out. Cox sweetened the pot by offering an off-the-record meeting.

"Shore can say whatever the hell she wants," he told Vittitow. "If we can't work out a deal, then she can walk out of the office. There's nothing we can do."

Early in the afternoon of Tuesday, January 9, 1990, Shore and Vittitow walked into the U.S. Attorney's office. Vittitow had always found Shore cold, distant. He couldn't tell what she was thinking. He had no idea where the meeting might lead.

Scott Cox didn't either, but January 9 had already been an interesting day for him. A few days earlier, he had called Charlie Ricketts to tell him he had heard something about Mel Ignatow's trying to commit suicide and wanted to ask about his condition. Ricketts had followed that conversation with a letter to Cox, which arrived January 9. The letter thanked Cox for being the one person in law enforcement who cared about Mel Ignatow.

Cox led Shore and Vittitow into the office of First Assistant Cleve Gambill, who occupied a huge, comfortable room where conversation would seem easier. Waiting for them was FBI special agent Deirdre Fike, a pretty, friendly, dark-haired woman who'd been working in Louisville since April 1989.

Fike's appearance was no accident. Her partner, Maury Berthon, Lewis Sharber, and Jim Wesley had all angered Shore; she would never talk to them. Fike would eventually become the Schaefer case agent for the FBI. Right now she was vital in establishing a new link, a friendly face in a hostile environment, but she expected nothing more than a brief meeting.

Fike had grown up in Peru, Nebraska, a farm town of about one thousand people. A graduate of Omaha County High School, she attended college at Peru State for two years, then dropped out to work in retail management. While there she met two FBI agents on an investigation. Fascinated, she went to the University of Nebraska-Omaha with FBI as a goal. After the normal year of background checks and psychological testing, she was accepted into the FBI Academy in January 1989.

Louisville was her first assignment. She had worked some with Sharber on the Brenda Schaefer case but had never before met Shore. Gender arguments aside, Fike was professional enough to accept the fact there are times when it helps to have another woman in the room.

"I think it is an advantage in a lot of cases," she would say, "and I think this probably was one of them."

Fike, Shore, and Vittitow sat on the couch, with Shore in the middle. Assistant U.S. Attorney Hancy Jones and Duane Schwartz, the head of the criminal division, were also in the room. Gambill was in charge, but Cox would do most of the talking. He sat in a chair off to one side, looking at Shore, trying to read her face. He didn't know what to expect but was ready to push, to bluff as much as possible to get the Schaefer case off dead center.

"Mary Ann, we need to talk. This is off the record but I'm going to tell you the facts. The main thing you need to know is, if that body ever turns up, you'll be facing the electric chair. If you come clean, we'll help you."

Tears formed in Shore's eyes. Fike took her hands, held them.

"I'm afraid of Mel," she said.

Cox had his answer:

"If you come forward and help us, Mel will be in jail before the sun goes down. You won't have to worry anymore. Deirdre can give you twenty-four-hour around-the-clock protection. You'll have no fear of being harmed. Everything will be fine.

"I don't know what happened to Brenda Schaefer. I don't know what your role was. But if you'll take the time to talk to your lawyer today, we're willing to deal with you."

Vittitow led Shore down the hall into Hancy Jones's office. They sat in front of a window, the growing Louisville skyline in the distance, the low Indiana hills a green smudge behind them.

"Mary Ann," said Vittitow, "these people are here to help you. I don't know what you know, but somehow you know that they know. Mary Ann, I want to help you."

They sat there, avoiding eye contact, looking out the window. Vittitow took her hand.

"Mary Ann. Please. For God's sake. This is your chance."

"You don't know Mel," said Shore.

"Mary Ann, if you've got any reason to fear this guy, tell me now. If you walk out of here and something happens to you, then nobody will ever know anything."

Shore considered the logic of that, then avoided it.

"Let's just get out of here," she said. "Let's come back another time."

"Mary Ann, there is no other time. This is now. This is your chance. You have to begin someplace. Tell me something."

Shore said she didn't know anything. Vittitow suggested they leave. Shore hesitated; her moment of truth. She was tired of the hassle, of the guilt. Ever since Ignatow had been baptized into Southeast Christian Church, he'd been acting as if God had forgiven him; the burden was now on her. She wanted to marry Butch Inlow, begin her new life.

"Well, what if I did know something?" she asked Vittitow. "Suppose I know where she is?"

Vittitow played his remaining cards.

"Then you've got to tell them where she is."

Shore was silent, her body trembling.

"Suppose I know where she's buried."

C H A P T E R
15

As Mary Ann Shore said "buried," Jack Vittitow felt the air rush from his lungs. His shoulders sagged. He finally knew what everyone had suspected for almost sixteen months: Brenda Schaefer was dead.

Vittitow blinked his eyes, regained his composure. Shore was trembling, tension ebbing from her body. Vittitow took both her hands, held them. Shore was frightened of what she had said, but she was more frightened of Mel Ignatow.

"If I tell the others, then Mel will know."

Vittitow was careful; he still had no idea what had happened to Brenda.

"Mary Ann, if he knows you have this knowledge, you're already a danger to him . . . if he's responsible."

"He's responsible."

Vittitow felt his tension returning; he'd never expected anything this dramatic.

"Then these people are willing to protect you. This is the FBI trying to protect you, not trying to harm you."

"What will they do to me?"

"I'll work something out. Just hold off. Before you give a complete statement, we'll see what we can work out."

Vittitow and Shore went back to the others. Shore went

with Deirdre Fike. Vittitow signaled to Scott Cox he wanted
to talk. The two, along with Duane Schwartz and First Assistant U.S. Attorney Cleve Gambill, walked into Schwartz's
office. Vittitow quickly came to the point:

"Suppose she knows where the body is?"

Cox felt a jolt of excitement. Most of the U.S. attorney's
work involved thefts, drugs, bank robberies. Suddenly, he
had a murder on his hands, a murder in the most highly
publicized abduction case in Louisville in years.

"What do you mean?"

Vittitow repeated himself: "What if she knows where the
body is?"

"Let's hear it," Cox said. "What does she know?"

The more experienced Gambill urged a little caution. He
wanted to call the Department of Justice, get something
down on paper. Cox was anxious, eager to push.

"Come on, Jack, tell us something."

"She knows where the body is. Can we work something
out?"

"We got to hear it first."

The men walked back into Gambill's office. Mary Ann
Shore and Deirdre Fike were sitting together on the couch,
the agent holding Shore's hand. All eyes focused on Shore;
she was now someone to be sized up, measured for a prison
sentence.

At Vittitow's urging, she briefly told her story: Mel Ignatow brought Brenda Schaefer to her house, sexually tortured and murdered her, then buried the body in a grave in
the woods behind her house. Shore was nervous, dwarfed by
her surroundings, the moment. Under questioning by Cox,
Shore said she was in her kitchen when Brenda died, but she
did help carry the body to the woods. She gave few details
beyond that.

"I'm scared to death Mel's going to kill me."

Cox upped the ante. He'd recently been badly stung in a
case where he failed to record an incriminating conversation
between a murderer and a witness. He vowed if the situation

ever came up again, the witness would be wired for a recording. Mary Ann Shore was that witness.

"Mary Ann," he told her. "You had just as much motive
to kill Brenda as Mel did. Your story isn't going to hold up.
You've got to meet with him and you've got to have your
conversation recorded."

Shore agreed to do it.

Her surprise confession, the sudden flow of events, gal-
vanized everyone, and presented some immediate legal problems. Brenda's body apparently was in Jefferson County; the
county police and Commonwealth's Attorney Ernie Jasmin
had to be called in on any deal. Cox called the commonwealth attorney's office; Jasmin was out. Cox called four
assistants, one of them a man named Jim Lesousky; all were
out. Cox went back to Jasmin's secretary, Cherry Trumbo,
and quickly explained the situation.

"I gotta talk to somebody right now."

Trumbo found First Assistant Commonwealth's Attorney
John Stewart, who got on the phone with Cox.

"We've got a major break in the Ignatow case. We need
Ernie, or somebody from the office, right away."

Stewart knew Jasmin was at a conference in downtown
Louisville and couldn't get away. Stewart called Jasmin, told
him what little he knew of Shore's confession.

"Go down there," Jasmin told him, "but keep me
posted."

Stewart was a gregarious man, a good student; quick on
his feet. He looked for Lesousky, a friend and steady hand,
but couldn't find him. Stewart felt the excitement the moment he stepped into the federal prosecutor's office. It was
thick with county police, FBI agents, assistant U.S. attorneys,
and a lot of their top brass, including Jefferson County police
detective Lewis Sharber and Joe Whittle, U.S. attorney for
the Western District of Kentucky, as well as Duane
Schwartz, head of its criminal division.

Jack Vittitow also felt the sense of urgency.

"This was it," he would say. "It was just a matter of
reaching in, making the drawing, finding the magic spot for

Brenda's body. Nobody knew for sure where it was, but they knew things were going to be resolved. I wanted to make sure I had a good deal for Mary Ann.''

Stewart had walked into a whirlwind. He later remembered being briefed by Cox, Vittitow, county police brass, the top people in the U.S. Attorney's office, and the FBI. Their sense of urgency was unmistakable.

"We were all moving around real quick,'' Stewart would say. "From what they could piece together it sounded like all Mary Ann Shore had done was assist in burying the body. There was no evidence to suggest she was involved in the homicide.''

The pressure of the moment was heightened by another problem: Mel Ignatow was expecting a phone call from Shore around 4:00 P.M. It was his daily check to keep her in line. If Shore was to be wired for a recording and arrange a meeting with Ignatow during the call, a deal had to be cut soon.

"The window had cracked open a little bit and we had to get through it,'' Stewart would say.

Stewart called Jasmin, telling him what he knew; Shore was ready to lead them to the body, had agreed to be wired, and as far as anyone knew, hadn't participated in the murder.

"Ernie, it sounds to me like all we've got is tampering with evidence.''

Anyone who knew Ernie Jasmin, who watched him prosecute, knew he had a warehouse of standard phrases he would use, pulling them out at specific moments. He urged Stewart to be careful, to get all the facts first, but left the final decision on the charge against Shore to his first assistant, advising him, "Sometimes it takes the little devil to get the big devil.''

Vittitow and Stewart walked across the hall to another room and shut the door. It would be a very brief conversation. Vittitow knew he had the advantage. Stewart was in unfamiliar surroundings; the pressure was all on him. Vittitow felt so confident he first mentioned only a misdemeanor charge against Shore.

Stewart ignored that. He offered the tampering-with-evidence charge, a Class D felony, the lowest possible, with a sentence of one to five years. Shore would not be immediately arrested; her case would be presented to the state grand jury for indictment. Shore would be allowed to go back before the federal grand jury and recant earlier testimony, freeing her of perjury charges. The commonwealth would take no stand on probation; the judge would decide that, depending on Shore's full cooperation. There was no discussion of a possible joint trial with Ignatow, or what might happen if Ignatow was never convicted.

"If she doesn't level with us one hundred percent, all deals are off," Stewart said. "She has to testify. She has to testify fully and completely."

"It's a deal," said Vittitow.

Jasmin would later rip into Stewart—privately and publicly—for offering Shore a Class D felony charge instead of pushing for a stronger charge, even murder. Stewart believed—would always believe—that given the moment, and the briefing he'd received from a half-dozen high-level law-enforcement people, he had done the right thing.

"At the time everybody felt like it was a hell of a deal," he would say. "You have to go with your gut. My gut was I had a U.S. Attorney's office who felt things were copacetic. The FBI felt comfortable. I had the lead police unit in the county and the state comfortable with it. We don't find there's any reason to disbelieve her at the time.

"This is the break we've needed. If she could deliver the body, we could figure out a cause of death, charge Mel. Hopefully when she was wired he would make some incriminating statements which would just put icing on the cake. If she's lying, we can come back and nail her."

The person everyone wanted to nail was Mel Ignatow. His arrogance, his lies, his smug smile and pious demeanor had infuriated every officer who went near the case; retribution was at hand.

"This was like crash-bam, let's get on with this," Vittitow remembered. " 'Let's get Mel now.' It wasn't like 'Settle

down, we've got a day, we've got a week.' It was 'Go drag
him in here.' "

There were huddled meetings and hasty decisions. The
first idea was to have Mary Ann Shore call Mel from the
office; cooler heads prevailed. Mel wasn't stupid; he'd hang
up, call back, and get the U.S. Attorney's office. The second
plan was that Shore's apartment would be bugged. She'd ask
Ignatow to come over, get him to talk about Brenda and the
murder, then they could nail him. Nor was there any legal
reason to warn Charlie Ricketts of possible entrapment; the
law as they read it said defense counsel didn't have to be
notified in such a situation.

One late arrival on this frantic scene was Deirdre Fike's
supervisor, FBI special agent Mike Griffin, who'd been notified soon after Shore's confession. Griffin was an amiable
bear of a man—six feet three and 225 pounds—with a deep
voice and a passion for all things John Wayne. He'd been a
high school basketball coach in Corvalis, Montana, in 1970
when a man walked into the gym unannounced. Griffin
thought he was a spy; the man was a recruiter looking for
high school students with a career interest in the FBI. The
recruiter ended up with a basketball coach. Griffin was put
in charge of the Louisville FBI unit handling the Schaefer
case in the late summer of 1989. Ignatow had frustrated Griffin as much as anyone else. Even though it appeared he no
longer had jurisdiction, Griffin wanted Ignatow too badly to
bail out immediately.

"What do you need from us?" Griffin asked the county
police supervisors.

"Will you wire Mary Ann Shore's apartment?"

"We can do that."

The crowded bedlam of the U.S. Attorney's office was
soon repeated at Shore's second-floor apartment, a typical
suburban building built of orange brick and gray mansard
shingles, each apartment with a little balcony, often with a
black barbecue grill sitting out twelve months a year.

It was midafternoon, about 2:40 P.M., as Gambill,
Schwartz, Cox, Vittitow, Sharber, and Shore crowded into

her one-bedroom apartment. Someone else drove Shore's car back to the apartment; Ignatow would be sure to notice if it was missing. FBI surveillance experts dressed as repairmen began removing big tool chests from a white van parked out front, carrying them up the apartment stairs, taking a left at the landing.

Neighbors, if they noticed, must have thought every faucet in the complex was under repair. The agents were silent, saying nothing to anyone. A round, black lamp with a grayish shade was placed on a table near Shore's living-room couch. A video camera and audio transmitter built into the lamp's onyx-looking base would transmit to high-tech receivers in the bedroom. As they worked in the living room, the agents and police had to walk around a sturdy, glass-topped coffee table. They placed their receiving equipment under the queen-sized bed.

Shore was standing at the front window looking out over the small balcony waiting for Butch Inlow to come home; he was the last person anyone wanted to see. When he did arrive, Shore walked outside, leaned against his car, said something to Inlow while staring up at her apartment window. She spoke to Inlow just a few minutes before he drove away.

"He's not going to be coming up," Shore said.

About 3:00 P.M. Shore agreed to lead investigators to Brenda's body while the FBI technicians finished wiring her apartment. Vittitow, Shore, Berthon, Cox, and Fike rode together, another police car behind them. Shore guided the mini-parade south on Poplar Level Road. They passed her old house, turned left on Rangeland Road, then took another left into the asphalt parking lot of Thomas Jefferson Middle School, a slate-front building with a robin's-egg-blue walkway connecting outside doors.

There was little conversation; the whole afternoon had been a ride on a high-speed train, events passing in a blur. Shore directed them down a gravel road that skirted the west side of the school property, past an open gate, then down another gravel road. Several baseball diamonds protected by a low Cyclone fence stood on the right, a thick grove of leafless trees on the left.

"You see that building?" said Shore, pointing to a small shed behind one diamond. "That's where we're going to stop."

They stopped at a point more than two hundred yards directly behind Shore's old house, its white exterior barely visible through the thicket of second-growth white oaks, red oaks, and greenbriers. The ground was swampy, coated in gray, moldy leaves, soft and wet to the touch. Shore was confident she could find the grave.

"It's right over here," she said, pointing west toward her house.

The party, also including John Stewart and Jim Lesousky, got out of their cars. They had to jump a shallow ditch. The rotting body of a dead dog met them at the edge of the woods. Guided by Shore, the party waded through the leaves and debris to a place near a large fallen tree. The ground was littered with jagged pieces of rusted metal, the pitted hulls of discarded appliances, and lidless paint cans.

"The adrenaline was really flowing," Vittitow remembered. "The whole atmosphere was one of elation, anticipation, excitement. They were all part of something that was going to be big news."

Shore paused, looking at her old house to get her bearings. She scratched through the leaves trying to find a depression wide enough to hide a human body. She had finally come full circle.

"I think this is the spot."

Sharber picked up a big white, bullet-riddled can with the word CONOCO on it. He walked to the spot Shore had indicated and set the can down in the decaying leaves as a marker. Yellow police tape marked CRIME SCENE DO NOT CROSS was strung through adjoining trees, sealing the area.

Within hours the site would be teeming with county police evidence technicians and a medical examiner, all bearing new shovels. Spotlights would add drama to the wooded scene. But Shore and the four men had to get back to her apartment.

"Let's go call Mel," one of them said.

CHAPTER 16

Jim Wesley could feel the elation in Lewis Sharber's voice:

"Jimmy," his commander told him, "this is it."

Sharber had called Wesley at home about 1:00 P.M. on January 9, 1990, a day Wesley would remember as vividly as any in his police career. Sharber was at the U.S. Attorney's office, where Mary Ann Shore had just told her story. He wanted to spread the word to the officer who most needed to hear it.

To Wesley's disappointment, Sharber asked him to go down to headquarters and stand by; it was already too crowded at the U.S. Attorney's office. Wesley waited more than two hours. He was almost out of his mind with suspense when Sharber called after 3:00 P.M. with a few details.

"We're going to put a tail on Mel," Sharber told Wesley. "We don't want him running now. I need you to get a package of photographs of Mel to Sergeant Janice Reed at Vice and Intelligence to help with the tail."

Wesley met Reed at the county police garage on Newburg Road at 3:45 P.M. He gave her a copy of the same picture of Mel Ignatow and Brenda that would be flashed hundreds of times on Louisville television screens: Ignatow in a tan knit shirt, grinning broadly, his arm around Brenda. Her dark brown hair was dangling loosely on a white turtleneck sweater, her smile just a little forced, her brown eyes pensive, uncertain.

After dropping off the pictures, Wesley was directed a mile north to Shore's place at 329 Huntington Park. He had not seen or spoken to her since the infamous walk in the rain on Valentine's Day eleven months earlier. Absence had not made his heart grow fonder.

"I'm on a high," Wesley would say. "It's a real high, but it's met with mixed feelings and anxiety because I'm supposed to go to Mary Ann Shore's apartment.

"I walk in there and I see Mary Ann Shore and my gut feeling is to grab her by the throat and let her have it: 'Why didn't you tell me this eleven months ago, sixteen months ago?' And she knew. Our eyes met when I walked into that apartment and she knew I was pissed at her."

The day was hurtling toward a climax. Shore's telephone line was bugged. The FBI camera hidden inside the black lamp was tested; it worked fine. Everything was in place; Jim Wesley was thinking that if Mel said enough to fully incriminate himself, he might be arrested in the apartment. FBI agents believed it might be best to first review the videotape, to be sure Mel had incriminated himself, then move; he was being tailed all day anyway. Scott Cox vividly remembered what Maury Berthon told Shore to give her a sense of security:

"I'm going to be in a closet here. There are going to be agents in the bedroom closet and another across the hall. If he so much as lays a finger on you, dive on the floor and we're going to come out firing."

At 4:05 P.M., right on schedule, Shore called Ignatow at his home.

"I need to talk to you," she said.

Then Shore panicked. Ignatow's mastery of her was total. He didn't want to meet at her apartment. He wanted to meet at their "usual place," an Ehrler's ice-cream bar at 3231 Poplar Level Road, a few miles north of her apartment. He certainly didn't want to talk on the phone. The nervous Shore automatically agreed to Ehrler's, where Ignatow often went for ice cream. In seconds she destroyed hours of planning; there would be no apartment videotape, no special agents hidden in closets, no immediate protection. A new plan had to be devised, and quickly; Ignatow was already on his way to Ehrler's.

"There was a wild scramble, a *wild* scramble," Wesley would remember. "We had to put a body mike on her, and that's where we had trouble, too, because obviously we wanted her to talk about the murder, to get Mel to talk about it."

Berthon had already given Shore a story to use at her apartment: Tell him the woods behind her house had been sold; it might be dug up as part of a shopping center; Brenda's body might be found. Shore had been coached to mention Brenda's name, something about the grave in the woods, perhaps an FBI lie-detector test, but it was always dangerous to overcoach—the questioning could sound rote; the always suspicious Ignatow might figure something out.

"Let Mel do most of the talking," Berthon told Shore. "Just be sure he mentions her name and the burial spot."

"He talks about it all the time," Shore answered. "That's no problem. That will happen."

Scott Cox wasn't around for Shore's phone call. He had been pushing hard all day. While inside Shore's apartment, he was still attempting to direct some of the investigation even though he was outranked and had little jurisdiction. His actions irritated FBI special agent Mike Griffin, who asked Cleve Gambill to have Cox back off. Cox, along with Duane Schwartz, was sent back downtown to the office to wait.

About 4:40 P.M. Ignatow wheeled his Corvette into Ehrler's, a large, orange-brick building fronted with broad glass windows. A Jefferson County police surveillance unit was not far away, watching him. Shore drove her silver Pinto into the lot moments later. Her microphone, hidden near her waist, had been tested at her apartment; it worked well. She parked next to Ignatow. He quickly moved from his Corvette into Shore's car, ready to calm her fears one more time.

The new game plan was to have Lewis Sharber and Maury Berthon, a county policeman and an FBI agent, stay in the FBI van to monitor the conversation. The recording device was attached to the FBI radio; the conversation could be heard while it was being recorded. In the rush of events, Griffin and Berthon both ended up in another FBI vehicle, Griffin's 1989 Chevrolet Caprice. The special agents had been about 150 yards behind Shore as she drove down Poplar Level Road. When they arrived at Ehrler's, they were amazed to see Ignatow's Corvette already there.

"He must have flown over here," Griffin was thinking. "He had a lot longer drive than Shore."

Ignatow's incredible luck was holding. His presence meant the agents didn't have time to select the perfect spot to observe him, or to record something on their tape as a preface to eavesdropping on the conversation. The agents eased past Ehrler's, turned around, and pulled into Nightingale Road, across the street and a little south of the ice-cream parlor. Griffin edged his car out just enough to see Ignatow's car.

"We really can't visually see them," Griffin would say, "but we can see his car and we can see what's going on."

Meanwhile, Wesley and Sharber were sitting in their unmarked county car at the corner of Whippoorwill Road and Quarry Hill Road about seventy-five yards south of Ehrler's. They were separated from the store by a wide, grassy field and a few leafless trees; they could see both vehicles. The officers, along with their brethren in the county surveillance units, were ready to move in on signal from the FBI unit.

"Obviously they're listening for Mel to say, 'What if I killed the bitch?,' or 'I'll kill you if you don't shut up,' " Wesley would say. "We're going to nail him right there in the parking lot. That was our hope."

Griffin flipped on his cassette recorder at the moment he heard Ignatow greet Shore. He missed perhaps one or two seconds of their initial conversation, a moment clouded when an emergency vehicle—an ambulance or fire truck—drove past with its siren blaring. The immediate problem was that

the county police cars—including that of Wesley and Sharber—were not equipped to pick up the FBI frequency; the
officers couldn't hear the conversation. The FBI unit did
have RF3, the county police frequency, and could talk to
county units. Berthon would step from Griffin's car with a
hand-held radio to transmit.

The FBI agents needed to keep county units apprised, but
every time the FBI transmitted to the county, it would break
into the signal from Shore's body transmitter, briefly dis-
rupting their recording. Those disruptions would come to
haunt everything that had been accomplished that day.

"The continuity of the conversation was not being interrupted," Griffin would say later. "Anybody with any sense
could tell that."

Mary Ann Shore didn't help. Had she been given a full
day to plan a conversation with Ignatow that would be ambiguous, unclear, and largely irrelevant to the Brenda Schaefer murder, she couldn't have done a better job. Nervous,
cowed by Ignatow, she blew her assignment.

Ignatow did 98 percent of the talking during their thirteen-
minute conversation, mostly ranting and raving at her to stay
calm. Shore never once mentioned Brenda Schaefer by name,
never directly mentioned a grave site, never connected any
crucial dots linking Ignatow, Schaefer, and the night of September 24, 1988.

The first few minutes, they talked about an FBI lie-
detector test, with Shore complaining about FBI harassment.
Berthon and Griffin, huddled in their vehicle, peering
through the windshield, could hear every word.

"Wait a minute!" Ignatow told Shore. "You talked to
who today?"

"The FBI. That Maury guy."

"OK. So for one thing, what did you tell him?"

"I would have to talk to my attorney."

Ignatow went ballistic.

"No. No. Just tell him you're not taking the test. Period.
Tell him you're not taking the test. They can't. They've been
pressuring me and pressuring me to take the test. . . ."

Twice in the next few minutes, the recording of the conversation was very briefly interrupted, apparently as FBI agents checked with county police. Very little was lost; Ignatow was berating Shore the entire time.

"Where is it written that you have to do anything? What are they going to do, tie you up and make you take the test? They cannot do anything to you, Mary Ann. Don't you understand that? Don't you understand it's a goddamn pressure game.

". . . Why do you keep aggravating yourself with this stuff? It isn't necessary."

Shore was frightened. She feared Ignatow might reach over, touch her, feel the transmitter. She abruptly changed the subject:

"Plus the property has been sold."

"Fine," Ignatow said. "It's been sold. Who'd they sell it to?"

"I don't know who it's been sold to."

"So let it be sold."

"Yeah, but what are you going to do when they go back . . ."

Ignatow leaped back into the conversation, not letting Shore finish. He spoke very slowly, very clearly, enunciating each word.

"Will . . . you . . . let . . . me . . . handle . . . it?"

He followed that up with some real concern:

"What am I going to do when who goes where?"

This was Shore's big opportunity, the time to say "When contractors dig at Brenda's gave site" or "That spot where we buried the body." Shore didn't do it. She couldn't fully commit, perhaps out of nerves, perhaps fearing that if Ignatow did talk it would only drag her deeper into the case; at this point she was facing only one to five years on a charge of tampering with evidence.

"But . . . what if they clear that?" was all Shore would say about the woods.

Ignatow unloaded again.

"Get serious. Don't worry about what they do, or what

they don't do. Okay. They're not gonna do anything about it until there's good weather. . . . And even if they do clear it, then what are they gonna put on it? A parking lot . . . a warehouse . . . something like that.''

Shore went on:

''I worry about the property back there.''

''Does it do you any good to worry about that property? All you gotta do is just keep your eye on things. . . . Don't make a spectacle of yourself, and don't make an issue of it. . . . How'd you know it was sold?''

''Butch's mother told him Sunday. . . . It's in the works and it's probably sold.''

Ignatow almost screamed at Shore, his words unconvincing, even to himself.

''. . . You do not have to talk to them. Now you're just plain fucking afraid to stand up in the face of authority. . . . You're letting them intimidate you and they know it. . . .''

But Ignatow *was* worried. He told Shore to get back to Butch Inlow, ask some causal questions, try to find out what kind of development might go in the woods.

''. . . And don't get rattled. I don't give a shit if he tells you they're going to dig down eight feet the whole damn length of the property. . . . And they're not going to do anything like that so stop worrying about it. I know what type of structures they've built out there. . . . They build slab structures. And even if they clear the damn thing, they clear the top part of it and that's it. And that's no big deal. It isn't going to stir anything up.''

Ignatow had talked nonstop for almost five minutes, an exasperated, almost hysterical edge to his voice. No one with the FBI or the county police believed that he knew Shore was bugged, but he had done a masterful job of avoiding self-incrimination.

It was Ignatow's final words that would eventually get the most airtime, produce the most print news, cause the most controversy. Because of the quality of the tape, the breaks in communication, the general hustle of the day, people would be arguing over their meaning for a long time. To the casual listener, it sounded as if Ignatow had said:

"Believe me, that's not shallow. That place we dug is not shallow, so don't let it get you rattled. Besides that one area right by where the safe is does not have any trees by it. The trees are down, if you remember, so it's not a big deal. . . . If worse comes to worse and something needs to be done, I'll handle it. . . ."

In time, county police, FBI agents, electronics experts, attorneys, and jurors would debate whether Ignatow had actually said "that place we *dug!*" or "that place we *got!*" More puzzling was his phrase "that one area right by where the safe is." What safe? No one had ever mentioned a safe. Was he referring to one of the old rusted appliances or containers in the woods near the grave? Did he mean to say Brenda's body was in a safe place? Was it just a slip of the tongue?

Many police and government officials and some in the news media would come to think Ignatow actually said—or meant to say—"that one area right by where the *site* is"— meaning the site of Brenda's body. What really would matter was the interpretation attorney Charlie Ricketts and a dozen jurors would put on the word.

Shore's conversation ended about 4:53 P.M. Berthon and Griffin hadn't heard a thing to bring the county police out of hiding.

"We'll have to let them go," Griffin radioed the waiting units.

Ignatow slipped into his Corvette and left, the county police surveillance team close behind. He arrived home at 5:20 P.M., pulled into his rear garage, and disappeared. Shore drove back to her apartment. At 5:00 P.M. Wesley and Sharber met with Griffin and Berthon at an Arby's restaurant, 4322 Poplar Level Road. The mood was somber; no one was happy with Shore's performance.

"It's a tragedy," Wesley would say.

Wesley and Sharber went back to Shore's apartment. Jack Vittitow would join them, along with county police detective William Hickerson and FBI agent Deirdre Fike. They were preparing to take a statement from Mary Ann Shore, her first detailed report of the murder. Hickerson, Vittitow, and Fike quickly learned that Shore was more of an accomplice than had been realized; Ignatow had planned his crimes against Brenda Schaefer for months, calling Shore two or three times a week to discuss them.

"Mel said . . . that his relationship, sex-wise, with Brenda was not very good," Shore told the officers. "She was a very cold person and he wanted to bring her over and maybe bring her out of that. . . . He called it sex-therapy class."

Shore said Brenda's grave had been dug in August, long before her September 24 murder, and she had helped Ignatow dig it. Ignatow wanted to use Shore's dislike of Schaefer to fuel his sadistic fantasy, to get Shore involved in the sexual torture. The ever-compliant Shore had been willing to go along, even left an impression she might have enjoyed it.

"He wanted to perform sexual things on her and he wanted me to get involved with it," Shore said. . . . "At first I was going to, and then the more I thought about it, I didn't want to get involved at all. . . . I didn't even want to be there."

The more Vittitow listened to Shore, the more convinced he became she was still protecting herself, holding back some details about her strange relationship with Ignatow. As she gave the details of Brenda's long torture, her rape while tied facedown on a coffee table, Shore often used the phrase "annual sex" for "anal sex," a bizarre if not interesting ignorance.

The attorney was amazed at how cool Shore could be at times, detached from reality. He would remember a police officer sitting on the bed in Shore's bedroom asking her what happened to the bed on which Brenda was murdered.

"This *is* the bed," Shore told him.

"The coffee table was right out front," Vittitow would say. "We were sitting there eating chocolates off it when the officer asked if that was the one. . . .

"We quit eating chocolates. That's the thing about Mary Ann. She just matter-of-factly let you in on these details."

CHAPTER
17

After two hours of deliberation and worry, Lieutenant Lewis Sharber decided to arrest Melvin Henry Ignatow for the murder of Brenda Schaefer.

Using the Thomas Jefferson Middle School parking lot as a rendezvous point, Sharber consulted with Assistant Commonwealth's Attorneys John Stewart and Jim Lesousky, who were in contact with their boss, Ernie Jasmin. Sharber also spoke with FBI special agents, as well as Jim Wesley and other county officers.

The situation was complicated because the county police were preparing to name a new command staff; Sharber had to keep all parties posted. Sharber would say he couldn't remember hearing the full tape before making his decision, but he and the FBI's Maury Berthon went over parts of it several times. Sharber was not happy, but believed the tape might be enough. Mel Ignatow had certainly made general references to a place being got, or dug; what else could it be but Brenda's grave? Mary Ann Shore had agreed to back the tape up by testifying in court; what could be more powerful for the prosecution than a live witness?

Ignatow's cunning also worried Sharber. Mel might suspect something, try to run, destroy evidence, perhaps even intimidate Shore into recanting her confession.

"I'd hoped the tape would be more explicit," Sharber would say. "I've replayed that decision many times in my mind, but as dumb as Mary Ann Shore was, I didn't believe that sending her back would be any more productive, and it could be less productive.

"We also had to consider the fact that if Mel did suspect something, he might try to harm Mary Ann the second time. We thought we had taken Mary Ann Shore as far as we could. . . ."

Although he did not strongly argue the point at the time, FBI special agent Mike Griffin, the head of its investigative team, would later say he disagreed with the decision:

"If that were our case, if that were a bureau case we were working, after we reviewed the tape we would have had her call again.

"I don't tell Ernie what to do. I don't tell the county police what to do. But there was some conversation about the fact Mary Ann Shore never said the magic words."

Griffin knew the county police thought there was enough on the tape to support their case, and he let it go at that.

"If they're satisfied, I'm satisfied. But for my own sake, it would not have hurt to have Mary Ann call Mel back and say, 'Hey, Mel. I was thinking about this. If they find Brenda buried out there, that's right in my backyard. . . . What am I going to do when they find her?' "

Finding Brenda Schaefer's body was the next logical step. All the county police had at this point was the word of Mary Ann Shore that it had been buried, and a white paint can sitting in the middle of acres of swampy woods. At 6:10 P.M. Jim Wesley, Lewis Sharber, and Major Charles Topp, their commander, went back to the woods to put together enough information for a search warrant. Using a flashlight to guide his way through the dark swamp of trees and discarded appliances, Topp paced off 134 steps from the back of Mary Ann Shore's house to the place where she said Brenda was buried. Topp paced off another 115 yards to the baseball field at Thomas Jefferson Middle School.

Minutes later Wesley met with prosecutors John Stewart and Jim Lesousky; the three men drove to the home of Circuit Court Judge Olga Peers, who signed the warrant. The crime scene was like an archaeological site; digging couldn't begin until the area was carefully marked, photographed, and videotaped. It would be 10:00 P.M. before seven men entered the site where Lewis Sharber had set the white paint can. Wesley had to stay outside the immediate area, again watching from a distance.

The black woods were illuminated with generator-powered lights provided by the Black Mudd Volunteer Fire Department. The scene was eerie, almost a science-fiction setting; the men bathed in artificial light, the steady putter of a gasoline generator, the whole area defined by yellow crime-scene tape flapping in a steady wind. Lewis Sharber figured reporters from Louisville television stations would gather enough information monitoring police broadcasts to know something big was happening.

"We tried to suppress it," Sharber would say. "We asked that they not give too much detail about the location and we would give them the full information later."

WLKY-32 reporter-anchorman Bruce Dunbar, acting on a tip from reporter Steve Burgin, had phoned in a brief story from the scene, but there was neither enough time nor material for live video. The newscast worried Sharber; what if Ignatow was watching the news? Maury Berthon would later tell Scott Cox that apparently Ignatow *was* watching the news.

"Berthon told me they've got agents all around Mel's house," Cox would say. "They're watching Mel like crazy. When the television news comes on, the lights go on in Mel's house, the garage light in particular. Mel is seen through the window with a bag, some kind of bag.

"They're thinking he's going to try to run. . . ."

Sharber had already decided to arrest Ignatow, but the specter of media coverage added to his worries. Brenda Schaefer's body had not been found. What if Mel were arrested and Brenda's body wasn't there? What kind of press conference could he hold then? On the other hand, what if Ignatow did try to flee the state, or the country? He had a lot of overseas contacts.

"We had a lot of concerns," Sharber would say.

Detective William Hickerson had gone downtown to the Jefferson District Court office about 10:00 P.M. to prepare an affidavit for an arrest warrant for Ignatow. Meanwhile, the search for Brenda Schaefer's body was going slowly. It had become obvious Mary Ann Shore was wrong, or lying; there was no body at the place she picked. County police, evidence technicians, and the state medical examiner tried a second site.

The working conditions were difficult, the possibilities for error endless. It was night, the ground was gooey, swampy, crisscrossed with acres of gnarly tree roots. At 11:30 P.M. the search was called off. The whole complicated operation still hinged on the word of a woman who had been steadily lying to police for sixteen months.

"We had full confidence Mary Ann Shore was telling the truth," Sharber would say. "We were still going to arrest Mel Ignatow."

That job would go to Jim Wesley. After the search was called off, he returned to the violent-crimes unit where John Stewart had been working on a search warrant for Mel Ignatow's house. They were joined by Hickerson, who'd finished preparing an arrest warrant. At 2:00 A.M. on Wednesday, January 10, the three men went to Judge Peers's house.

"You know I'm retiring soon," Peers told the men. "You'll not be getting me out of the bed in the future."

Wesley was excited. Arrest and search warrants in hand, he went to the parking lot of the Plainview Center Kroger store near Ignatow's house for a final, prearrest meeting. The nine officers and special agents on hand were a roll call of men and women with a strong vested interest in the case— among them Wesley, Maury Berthon, William Hickerson, and Lewis Sharber. The Jeffersontown police were also notified.

The Schaefer family had been told by county police earlier in the day they were close to finding Brenda's body, and that Mel might be arrested. Late that night Mike called Tom.

"The police want us at Mom and Dad's right away," he said.

They gathered again in the Warner Avenue home, waiting anxiously, another vigil long into the morning. Mike later learned police wanted the brothers at the house because Ignatow hadn't yet been arrested and he feared the Schaefers might go looking for him. There was some reason for that. With rare exceptions, the Schaefer family had been incredibly patient, stoic, helpful. They suffered in silence, but they suffered.

Tom Schaefer had recently bought a fifty-acre farm in the country, a lovely place with a house perched on a crest, a view for miles, an old well. At night he would lie awake, thinking of Ignatow, wondering about dropping him into the well, holding him there until he confessed.

WHAS-TV reporter John McGrath was part of the media vigil. He had joined other television reporters at the woods behind Mary Ann Shore's house; then he and a photographer slipped over to a spot near Ignatow's house on Florian Road. He suspected—correctly—other television crews also lurked in the area, with several of the cars silently parked in a designated "block watch" area.

"After about ninety minutes of waiting at least six police cars went by," McGrath would say. "I figured this was the arrest or a low-key Shriners parade."

Quickly joined by other reporters and photographers, McGrath swung in behind the police parade. It was 2:30 A.M. Ignatow's house was dark as Wesley walked toward the door. He felt good, on a high. A strong, almost eerie gust of wind blew up as Wesley approached the house, tearing at his blue sport coat, kicking his red tie sideways. Wesley knocked loudly on the door. In a few seconds he heard Ignatow on the other side.

"Who is it?"

"The county police. Open the door!"

The door swung open. Mel Ignatow, sleepy, unshaven, wearing only shorts, looked balefully at Wesley.

"Mel, you're under arrest."

Wesley was familiar enough with Ignatow's house to know he wanted to move him into the kitchen, where there was more room to handcuff him, read him his rights. In his excitement, Wesley forgot about a· step leading into the kitchen. He tripped badly, almost going to his knees, barely catching himself, the drama of the moment seriously compromised by his near fall. His partners held back laughter; Ignatow looked at Wesley in astonishment. Wesley glared at him.

"You're under arrest for the murder of Brenda Schaefer."

Virginia Ignatow came downstairs wearing a light blue robe. Wesley made it a point to keep mother and son apart.

"I'll call Charlie Ricketts," she repeated again and again. "I'll call Charlie Ricketts."

Wesley thought Ignatow looked more deflated than shocked or surprised. He got dressed in the dining room, under police eye, as television reporters peered in through the windows. As Ignatow sat down on a chair, his mother bent over him, patting him on the cheek. Within twenty minutes Wesley and Maury Berthon were leading Ignatow out his front door, where they were pinned briefly in the white glare of television lights. Ignatow, wearing a brown leather jacket, white shirt, blue slacks, and casual shoes, looked more sleepy than concerned.

"Mel, do you have any comment?" a reporter shouted.

His answer was muted, blown away in the wind.

Eight Jefferson County police officers then went through Ignatow's house to search it for evidence, mostly looking for photographs Shore said had been taken during the torture and murder. Sharber didn't think the photographs would be in the house—Mel had to be smarter than to leave them there— but the officers were as thorough as possible. For 2½ hours the officers went through every room, every drawer, looked behind every book, searched every closet and appliance, examined every shelf. Ignatow's basement was totally empty, clean as freshly poured cement; officers poked in the ceiling insulation but found nothing. Ignatow's car was searched; his mother's car was searched; his boat would later be carefully searched.

The garage yielded three finds: a short, red-handled spade with streaks of dried dirt across its flat blade; four trays of nails in a small plastic container; and a box containing several trophies from automobile races and a wooden University of Louisville fraternity paddle with a leather strap. The Greek letters Sigma Alpha Mu were engraved into the handle, along with the inscription TO MEL '59 FROM JIM '59. Officers also found a small beige Sentry combination safe rolled against a wall, its door locked.

In the top center drawer of a dresser in Ignatow's master bedroom, the officers found a big Oster vibrator-massager and a plastic container stuffed with drug paraphernalia: marijuana rolling papers, a smoking pipe, a paper-rolling device, and an "alligator" clip used to hold a joint. Officers also found an Olympus 35mm camera loaded with film.

Digging around in Ignatow's closet and office, police also found many of Ignatow's financial records, personal and business letters, and a collection of newspaper articles on the disappearance of Brenda Schaefer. Near the bottom of the mix was a small black 1988 pocket calendar, a giveaway from Hasenour's, a popular Louisville restaurant. Ignatow, the compulsive organizer and note taker, made entries for almost every day of the year. Most had later been heavily crossed out with black ink, especially the dates in late September when Brenda Schaefer disappeared. Police leafed through the notebook, hoping for a clue, but the notations of September 23 and 24 looked to be obliterated. The notebook was added to the pile of other possible evidence.

Each item was photographed, then taken to county police headquarters to be processed, analyzed, and fingerprinted. The dirty spade, fraternity paddle, and camera—especially with film in it—seemed the most promising direct links to the murder, even if it had occurred sixteen months earlier. So did the safe; maybe some pictures or jewelry was hidden inside. Police drilled it open the next day. The safe was empty.

Ignatow's arrest would lead all the television news shows and the *Courier-Journal*. Ignatow would plead innocent in Jefferson District Court to charges of murder, sodomy, sexual abuse, and unlawful imprisonment. A cash bond was eventually set at $500,000. He also faced federal charges of obstruction of justice and perjury, the latter for lying before the federal grand jury.

Attorney Charlie Ricketts was at the Hall of Justice with Ignatow, pleading his case.

"The county, quite frankly, is out to get this man at any cost," said Ricketts, his head swiveling around to face each in a cluster of television cameras. "Regardless of the fact they don't have any evidence save this barefaced affidavit by Mary Ann Shore." Ricketts also told the *Courier-Journal* he had asked Ignatow to keep the file of newspaper clippings about Brenda; he added that the "drug paraphernalia" found at Ignatow's house were a couple of bottles of prescription drugs.

Ignatow—and Ricketts—were careful men. Two days after Ignatow was arrested, he deeded all equity in his Florian Road home to his mother for "$100, love and acknowledgment by the party of the second part" that she would henceforth make all mortgage payments. If the Schaefers pursued a wrongful-death suit against Ignatow, his assets would not include the house. The quit-claim deed was handled by Ricketts and his assistant, Valerie Herbert, who served as notary public. The home's value was listed at $158,000.

Police had notified the Schaefer family of Ignatow's arrest soon after it happened, ending their vigil. Tom and Mike went out to the front porch, briefly considered going to the woods behind Mary Ann Shore's house to watch the search for their sister's body, but decided against it.

CHAPTER
18

Kentucky's chief medical examiner, Dr. George Nichols II, was never a man to suffer fools gladly. Nor was he ever too far away from his next opinion. That became even more evident when Nichols first became involved in the Brenda Schaefer case. In September 1988, Jefferson County police evidence technicians brought the flat tire from Brenda Schaefer's car to Humana Hospital University to have it X-rayed for nail damage.

One of the officers wheeled the car tire into Nichols's office, along with the X rays.

"What do you think, Doc?" the officer asked.

"It looks like there's a nail in a tire. Now take this someplace other than me to get a determination of that."

The veteran Nichols, forty-one, was affectionately nicknamed Dr. Death. With curly dark hair, a mustache, deep voice, and quick delivery, he always presented an interesting figure. He collected art, plants, off-the-wall postcards, pictures, hats, and T-shirts. The son of a doctor who had an office in Louisville's working-class West End more than thirty years, Nichols was helping his father even before going to medical school. He once told a *Courier-Journal* reporter he didn't want to be a "regular" doctor:

"I didn't like telling people about dying. I didn't like telling the victim's family. The active process of dying is very difficult."

Besides teaching at the University of Louisville and lecturing around the country, Nichols performed—or supervised—hundreds of autopsies each year, many of them in cases where homicide was a possibility.

"You don't have a homicide unless I say it's a homicide," he said.

Lewis Sharber knew he had a homicide. He'd called Nichols early in the afternoon of January 9 to tell him Brenda Schaefer's body might be found soon. By the time Sharber called Nichols again, it was already dark, with only the Black Mudd Volunteer Fire department portable lights to show the way.

Nichols arrived at the woods behind Mary Ann Shore's house about 9:40 P.M. wearing his insulated boots, blue jeans, a beige insulated jacket, and bright red ski gloves. He was not happy about the working conditions. Nor were the members of the Jefferson County police Evidence Technician Unit who met him, Detectives Mickey Owen, Joe Hash, Don Taylor, Bob Stein, and Sergeant R. D. Jones.

"The evidence cops are looking at me," Nichols would say. "They know this is not the time to be doing it. What they should have done was just leave a unit out there to watch over the scene until the state police cadaver-sniffing dog could get there.

"The body was supposed to be buried near either an abandoned refrigerator or near a large can. There were multiple large cans at the site. Somebody had decided there was a depression and that was surely the site.

"I was highly skeptical of this being it . . . it's dark, it's cold, in the middle of forested swamp. It was stupid. You can't get any deader than a skeleton. . . . But they were hot to prove Brenda was there."

The dig had to be done carefully; no evidence should be moved, or damaged. Using long-handled shovels with pointed blades, Nichols and the officers dug methodically, the damp, mucky soil clinging to the blades. They soon struck a tree root about 1½ inches thick.

"It's not here, guys," Nichols said.

The men looked around, trying to find another body-sized depression in the dead brown leaves and debris. Their working area was covered in a bubble of portable light, every move casting thin shadows on the whitish tree bark. When they found a likely depression, Nichols—a totally spontaneous man—lay down in it to check its length, his feet straddling a small tree.

"This is why I spent four years in medical school," Nichols announced.

"Trust us," answered one of the detectives.

The officers again hit roots with their shovels.

Nichols was becoming exasperated. Although he didn't know it at the time, he'd picked up some poison ivy. He tried one more depression, again lying down in it. Their shovels hit tree roots soon afterward.

"That's it," Nichols announced. "I'm not coming back until the fucking dog gets here."

The dog was Bingo, a four-year-old German shepherd trained by Kentucky State Police Sergeant Fred Davidson, who was stationed in Harlan deep in the Eastern Kentucky mountains. Davidson arrived about nine o'clock the next morning, driving up from Harlan with Bingo in his gray state police car. He parked it on the gravel road between the woods and Thomas Jefferson Middle School.

Bingo had been born in Germany; he'd learned some obedience commands in German, then was trained to find bodies in Kentucky. Davidson would put a few drops of Caverdine, a chemical that smelled like a decaying body, on a ball, then have Bingo chase it. Davidson would bury the ball; Bingo would track it down on command. In time Bingo didn't care if he was hunting a ball or a body; the work was identical to him. He'd already found bodies under two feet of dirt, would go on to find almost thirty bodies.

"I had seen Bingo in action before," Nichols would say. "Bingo has a wonderful nose. The really funny thing is you've got a Harlan state police detective talking German to Bingo the dog.''

As everyone grew increasingly impatient, Bingo sniffed and pawed through the big woods for almost two hours. Mary Ann Shore was brought back to the woods to narrow the focus. Shore walked around a little more, then pointed out another area about 135 behind her house, but about 200 feet from the first area. Within fifteen minutes, Bingo was tearing at a muddy, slightly depressed piece of ground, tossing dirt and leaves behind him.

County police evidence technicians cleaned the area with rakes, then began digging with shovels, stopping briefly to let Bingo work a little more. Bingo tore eagerly into the loose ground. At 1:56 P.M. the men's shovels struck a piece of black plastic garbage bag. Davidson, more than anybody else, felt a sense of relief.

"I was tickled to death," he would say. "There was a lot of pressure on me. They'd already made an arrest. . . . Everybody in Jefferson County was there asking, 'Where's the body?' ''

Nichols, who was performing routine autopsies, got a call late Wednesday morning that Bingo might have found the body, but he wasn't going back to the woods until it was confirmed. A little later the call came: Bingo had done his job.

Jim Wesley got the phone call at home about 2:00 P.M. Wednesday. He'd worked fifteen hours the day before; he didn't finish getting Mel Ignatow booked, fingerprinted, and jailed until 4:20 A.M. Wesley hustled out to the woods, joining a crowd of spectators that included a half-dozen evidence and medical technicians, Nichols, FBI agents Deirdre Fike and Maury Berthon, county prosecutor Ernie Jasmin, and two of his assistants, John Stewart and Jim Lesousky.

The mood was somber; it was obvious the plastic package was going to contain the body of Brenda Schaefer. With Nichols in charge, the men carefully dug around the body, using their sharp shovels to widen the hole, then broken tree limbs to etch around the outside of the plastic. Nichols bent down to the hole, touching the plastic; he could feel a body, the ropes that had bound it so tightly.

The finished hole was four feet three inches long, three feet seven inches wide, tapering down at the sides toward the black plastic. The hole was sloped; nineteen inches down to the top of the body at one end, thirty-four inches at the other. Nichols took a piece of nylon rope, carefully looped it around one end of the corpse, then repeated the process at the other end. He and an officer then lifted Brenda Schaefer's body from the muddy ground, gently setting it onto an opened body bag on one side of the hole. It was 3:42 P.M.

The package was incredibly small, barely fourteen inches thick, about the size of a soft-sided suitcase. It had been taped shut, with rope carefully looped around it. The officers dug a little deeper and found another package, apparently containing Brenda's clothes. Everyone stood silently, staring at the packages.

"We were really down," Wesley would say. "I mean the elation was gone because of the reality of her suffering. . . ."

Four men, one at each corner, lifted the body bag and carried it slowly from the woods. That grim picture, coupled with the arrest of Mel Ignatow, would lead the news for all Louisville television stations. The body was taken to the autopsy room in the basement of Humana Hospital University. Certain he had Brenda Schaefer's remains, Nichols had two forensic pathologists, Greg Davis and L. C. McCloud, join him. Dr. Mark Bernstein, a professor at the University of Louisville School of Dentistry and state forensic odontologist, was called to help identify Brenda through her teeth. Many of the FBI and county police evidence technicians joined them. So did Sharber and Wesley.

As the body was being X-rayed, Nichols received a phone call from an old friend, Dr. Larry Lewman, chief medical examiner for Oregon, who had just arrived to teach a class at the Southern Police Institute in Louisville.

Nichols immediately invited Lewman to join them, sending a county police officer to pick him up at Louisville's Galt House hotel.

"I can assure you," Nichols would say, "that Brenda Sue Schaefer is the only person in the history of the United States to be simultaneously autopsied by two state chief medical examiners."

Lewman entered the room just as the body was being unwrapped, filling the room with the smell of gaseous flesh, a terrible, overpowering odor that Lewman—cut from the same gallows-humor mold as Nichols—tried to lighten with a joke:

"Jesus Christ, whatever happened to Southern hospitality?"

Nichols began by removing Brenda's clothes from the second package, holding up each item to be videotaped. The yellow rain slicker, her sweater, jeans, nylons, socks, and undergarments, were soiled, yellow, pitted with what looked like rust. There was no sign of her jewelry or her purse.

Nichols turned to the larger package. The body, wrapped in four overlapping black plastic bags sealed with tan plastic mailing tape, had been buried in cool, soggy ground for almost sixteen months. It had undergone a decomposition called adipocere, turning soft tissue into fat. The outer layer of the yellowing skin had dissolved; facial features were gone; most body hair had fallen off; the rest would fall off at a touch. The body tissues were all distorted. Not only did the decomposition make the autopsy more difficult, it made the gathering of vital crime information almost impossible.

The body was bound so tightly with cotton clothesline rope that Brenda's heels were pressed against her buttocks, her head against her knees. Her arms had been wrapped around her legs and tied near her ankles.

Nichols was wearing a standard blue hospital gown, white apron, and white gloves. He spoke into a small tape recorder, automatically recording every move, cut, and inspection. The rope's loops and knots were so intricate, so interwoven that Nichols at first thought it was one long piece of cord twisted as if trying to bundle a soft package. As he slowly unwrapped the body, stretching it out on the table, he saw there were four very intricately tied ropes, bound in complex knots that a boater might use. The ropes varied in length from about three feet to almost thirteen feet. Each of the cut ends of the ropes was sealed with either silver duct tape or black electrician's tape.

The first rope encircled Brenda's head, went around her knees, and then her ankles, where it was knotted with a series of other ropes, then back around the head.

The second rope circled her abdomen, then looped around her ankles, where it was tied in a complex series of knots. The third rope was a series of interconnected loops around the lower chest and her knees, then looped around her right leg, then tied around her right knee. The fourth rope was wrapped seven times around the right wrist, then around Brenda's ankles. The free end of the rope bound her left wrist and right ankle together.

"I had never seen anybody tied with that many different types of knots," Nichols would say. "I thought, clearly if the killer spent that much time packaging the body, then the packaging meant a lot to the killer."

Because of body deterioration, Nichols could find no evidence of trauma, no evidence of a rope being tightened around Brenda's neck, no body tears or bruises. Bernstein, the dental expert, was able to verify Brenda's identity through her teeth. Nichols cut off her hands, placed them in white, snap-lid containers filled with formaldehyde, and had them sent to the FBI laboratory in Washington, D.C. The laboratory, by injecting chemicals into the skin, might be able to puff them up enough to develop a working fingerprint of her hand.

"We did not have any of Brenda's fingerprints to work with," Nichols would say.

The surprise came near the end of the autopsy; Nichols, and the other doctors, noticed Brenda had recently had a hysterectomy; her uterus, ovaries, and Fallopian tubes had been removed. Nichols could not tell how recently, but a suture line indicated it was fairly recent.

The Schaefer family would be shocked at that news, even to the point of believing the body might not be Brenda. No one—her mother, her brothers and sisters, her co-workers—knew anything about it. Brenda had always had severe menstrual problems, terrible cramps, even in high school, but no one could remember her taking off enough time from work for an operation, and a detailed check of her medical and insurance records didn't indicate any procedures. Her gynecologist would say that as of January 1988 there had been no operation. Linda Love remembered a conversation with Brenda the summer before she died when she was complaining of cramps.

Nichols could say only that the particular scars associated with her surgery could be consistent with a sexual disease of the Fallopian tubes—cancer, some type of internal hemorrhage or reproductive problem—but there was no way of knowing, and speculation was dangerous, unprofessional.

"All I know is that the hysterectomy happened," he would say, "and there were three other sets of eyes there to witness the evidence of it."

The autopsy lasted almost four hours. Nichols listed his most important finding in four words: "Homicide by undetermined means." There was enough of the body left to identify it, but not enough to say how Brenda died; there would be no hard physical evidence linking Mel Ignatow, Mary Ann Shore—or anyone else—to the murder:

"We could never have proved chloroform was used because chloroform is a volatile substance," Nichols would say. "If you pour a coffee cup half full, place it on a sink edge, and come back the next day, it's going to be gone.

"We knew who Brenda was. I didn't know how she was killed."

Brenda Schaefer's sealed casket was displayed in the same room at the Ratterman Funeral Home as that of her brother, Jack, nearly twenty years before. An eight-by-ten photograph of Brenda rested on the casket.

Before she disappeared, Brenda was to have been in the wedding of her niece, Cindy Kopp. Her bridesmaid's dress was a dusty rose, a color Brenda loved. Tom, Mike, Carolyn, and Mary Ann Hilbert found a large spray and two side ar-

rangements of roses of that shade for her casket. The casket
was made of polished poplar, chosen because it was very
similar to the wood of the grandfather clock Brenda had liked
so much. Brenda was buried in one of her nightgowns; her
mother picked it for her so she could stay warm.

The funeral service at Our Lady of Lourdes was as sad as
anyone could remember. The priest, Father Osborne, had to
stop in the middle to collect himself; all the mourners wept
openly, sharing the unspeakable grief of the Schaefer family,
the pain softened only by the knowledge the long wait was
over. John Schaefer took his wife's arm as they left the
church to go bury their daughter. His head was bowed; Essie
Schaefer was crying.

Tom and Mike Schaefer had wanted to be pallbearers, to
be with Brenda. They changed their minds; their place was
with their parents and their sisters. With television cameras
at a discreet distance down the hillside, Brenda Schaefer was
laid to rest on January 13, 1990, in the family plot at Cave
Hill Cemetery. As the ceremony ended, family members
were given a rose from the casket.

CHAPTER
19

Suddenly—more suddenly than anyone ever expected—the Brenda Schaefer case would move from an unsolved mystery to courtroom drama, if not theater. Mary Ann Shore made her surprise confession in the afternoon of January 9; Mel Ignatow was arrested soon afterward. Within another fourteen hours Brenda Schaefer's body had been found and an autopsy performed; Jefferson County police had a good idea of the strength—and weakness—of their case.

Outside of possible courtroom testimony and the processing of some evidence found at Ignatow's house, the U.S. Attorney's office and the FBI were now out of the picture. Both offices had provided invaluable help. Assistant U.S. Attorney Scott Cox had pushed hard at just the right time; the FBI had provided surveillance, expertise, an investigator-confidant for Shore, and a general profile of things to look for while pursuing Ignatow.

Both federal agencies would watch the state case closely. Ignatow also had a federal perjury charge hanging against him; the agencies could be needed in a more forceful fashion if the case fell through; both had more ammunition to use.

The state case against Ignatow moved to the office of Commonwealth's Attorney Ernie Jasmin. On January 11 a county grand jury had indicted Ignatow on charges of murder, kidnapping, sodomy, sexual abuse, robbery, and tampering with physical evidence. Mary Ann Shore was indicted only on a charge of tampering with evidence. Jasmin's office was to prosecute both, seeking the death penalty for Ignatow. The indictments were announced at a major news conference at which Jasmin publicly suggested authorities had made a deal with Shore to get to Ignatow.

Five days later—with Jim Wesley seated beside him as lead investigator—Jasmin appeared at a pretrial hearing before Jefferson Circuit Judge Martin E. Johnstone in the Hall of Justice. Ignatow was represented by Charlie Ricketts. The men were about to begin a legal fight that would last longer, become more bitter, and take more strange turns than anyone could imagine.

Ricketts led it off with a motion that Johnstone could not remember ever seeing before: Ricketts wanted the judge to enter an order prohibiting Ignatow from appearing before the court's motion hearings "unshaven, unkempt and dressed in jail clothing." Ricketts argued the motion by saying his "esteemed opponent" Ernie Jasmin had publicly referred to Ignatow as a "big devil." Ricketts argued that such a characterization, along with the wearing of regular jail clothing—an orange jumpsuit with an open collar and the inscription JEFF CO JAIL in large white letters on the back—would poison the minds of potential jurors.

"All the jurors will bring with them," Ricketts would say, "will be the experience to which they have been exposed. That exposure, I submit, Judge, will predispose them to the feeling this man must be guilty. Else he would not be dressed in prison garb. Else he would not be wearing the shackles he is wearing today. . . ."

Jasmin argued that any case law he was aware of involved defendant dress during a trial, not during a hearing, but he did not push the point beyond that.

"As long as he is incarcerated," Jasmin said of Ignatow, "I don't care what he wears."

Johnstone would eventually rule that Ignatow could appear

in court in a suit and tie if arrangements could be made with the Jefferson County Jail personnel, but he would never *order* such an arrangement.

"You know as well as I do no court in the land has ruled on this," he told Ricketts.

Jasmin, Ricketts, and Johnstone had one thing in common: All were graduates of the University of Louisville School of Law. Beyond that, they had little in common. Their differences—the personality clashes between the attorneys with Johnstone serving as judicial referee—would become increasingly obvious, even dominate the news.

Ernest A. Jasmin, fifty-six, was flamboyant, tough-minded, occasionally bombastic. Nicknamed "Preacher for the Prosecution," he had a courtroom voice that would rise and fall like a gospel choir, his hands making precise, chopping motions in the air. He would cup his hands, fold his fingers together as if in prayer, stab a forefinger into his palm to make a point, each movement precisely timed to each word like a metronome.

The prosecutor would linger over sentences, each syllable given emphasis in a key phrase; the word *ev-vi-dence* never sounded more accusatory than when Ernie Jasmin spat it out one syllable at a time. In heated moments, he would fling his arms toward the heavens. Sometimes, when disagreeing with a defense attorney, he would lay his head on the desk and cover it with his arms, as if unable to take any more.

Jasmin grew up in Florida in the Old South; he never *saw* an attorney, black or white, as a child. He graduated from Florida A&M in 1956 with a degree in business administration and economics. He'd come to Kentucky as a Fort Knox tank officer, enrolled in the University of Louisville Law School, and graduated in 1967. Along with schoolwork he juggled three jobs: full-time post-office clerk, substitute post-office clerk, and headquarters commander in the Army Reserve. He retained his military ties, becoming a lieutenant colonel in the Army Reserve before his military retirement in 1984.

Along with "Preacher for the Prosecution," the other

phrase inevitably linked to Jasmin was "the first black commonwealth's attorney elected in Kentucky." He was elected in November 1987, with 70 percent of the vote after serving eleven successful and productive years as assistant prosecutor. No stranger to death-penalty work, Jasmin earned a lot of preelection support with his successful 1986 prosecution of two black males in the brutal murders of two white Louisville high school students.

Charles E. Ricketts, forty-eight, erect, silver-haired, perfectly groomed, was a member of Ricketts and Travis, a five-lawyer firm in St. Matthews, the largest suburb of Louisville. A lifelong Republican, Ricketts graduated from Louisville's Bellarmine College in 1965 with a degree in psychology, then from the University of Louisville Law School in 1968. He'd worked four years as a radio and television reporter at Louisville's WAVE, and then three years as an FBI agent in Minnesota, South Dakota, and Washington, D.C. He'd been a lawyer for the city of Jeffersontown, an assistant commonwealth's attorney in Jefferson County, former president of the Louisville Bar Association, and a member of the Kentucky Bar Association's board of governors.

His courtroom style was aggressive, effusive, dogged; he would eventually file every motion imaginable in defense of Ignatow. Ricketts was prone to dropping little salutations into conversations, addressing other lawyers in court as "my esteemed colleague" or "my learned opponent." His sentences were exceptionally elaborate; phrases would run on at great length. He had a very successful private practice, but didn't do a lot of defense work; the Ignatow case was the most high-profile case he'd ever handled.

Martin E. Johnstone, forty-one, was one of the most respected and best-liked judges in Jefferson County. A Louisville Bar Association poll gave him a 99 percent favorable rating. He was awarded the Henry V. Pennington Outstanding Trial Award by the Kentucky Academy of Trial Lawyers, who judged his fairness, qualifications, and service.

Johnstone's father had been an elementary school principal in Fairdale, a blue-collar community in southern Jefferson

County. Johnstone had planned on a career in education, but was sidetracked in high school when he traveled to Frankfort to watch the Kentucky legislature.

"I was enamored with law ever after that," he would say.

He graduated from Western Kentucky University in 1971, University of Louisville Law School in 1975. Reluctantly— after a lot of prodding and wheedling from local Democratic leaders—he ran for county magistrate in 1976. His dry sense of humor—a staple in his court—was already at work.

"I told them I was flattered to be asked," Johnstone would say, "but I was still trying to figure out where all the court-rooms were."

He was elected magistrate, then two years later was elected district court judge. In 1983 he won a circuit-court seat. He served as chief judge in both district and circuit courts. He got the Ignatow case from what he would joke was a "bad draw"; the case was pulled for his court at random from the hundreds placed in a circuit-court "drum."

"This was a case that started off high-profile and just continued that way," Johnstone would say. "I think both Ernie and Charlie wanted to put their best foot forward.

"From the first hearing, you could cut the tension with a knife every time you walked into the courtroom. There was a clear personality clash between Charlie Ricketts and Ernie Jasmin. They had an apparent distaste and dislike for each other. Sometimes I thought they carried the art of advocacy to its ultimate extreme. . . ."

Along with prison garb, the initial two hearings on the case included motions by Ricketts to get Ignatow's bond reduced. They were accompanied by some preliminary discussion in the judge's chambers about a change of venue— moving the trial to another Kentucky city because impartial jurors could never be found in Jefferson County. That specter would hang over Johnstone a long time.

"The whole thing was a chess game between the prosecution and the defense," Johnstone would say. "With all the pretrial publicity I said there was a very good possibility that there were going to be problems. I kept waiting for a motion from the defense for a change of venue.''

Arguments about the bond reduction became complex because Jasmin suggested he wanted to play at least part of the FBI tape of the conversation between Ignatow and Mary Ann Shore. Ricketts had heard the tape that day as part of the ''discovery'' process: his right to hear evidence against his client. He quickly objected: ''If you play that tape in the presence of the press, it will seriously prejudice the case.''

Johnstone was in a bind. He'd not heard the tape. His courtroom was thick with reporters and photographers. The tape might be prejudicial. He set a January 31 date for a further hearing on the matter—along with Ignatow's bond reduction. Meanwhile Mary Ann Shore had been released on her own recognizance after pleading not guilty to the charge of tampering with physical evidence. A trial date had been set for May 30, 1990.

Shore had gone into hiding, staying with Alice Bymaster, a friend who lived in a small frame house in Clarksville, Indiana, just across the Ohio River from Louisville.

Bymaster had met Shore several years earlier. Both were single; Bymaster was working at the Indiana Employment Office, going to school at night and raising her daughter. Shore was baby-sitting for the Spoelker children for a living. The women would do mutual things with the children— cookouts, visiting parks. At night the women would occasionally go to night spots, or to Louisville Redbirds baseball games.

Bymaster often visited Shore at her Poplar Level Road home before and after Brenda Schaefer disappeared, sometimes spending the night there, occasionally walking in the woods behind her house. Bymaster liked Shore, found her engaging company but very manipulative:

''She was the type that wanted to control things. When I first met her she'd been on a temporary job and I always felt, 'Why doesn't she get a good job? . . . She's single . . . she doesn't have any kids . . . and she ends up baby-sitting.' ''

Bymaster said Shore would talk about Brenda Schaefer, would even speculate what might have happened to her, never revealing her part.

"Mary Ann came over to my work during the Spalding trial," Bymaster would say. "She told me Mel was going to sue the doctor and she was going to get some money and we're going to do all this stuff. . . ."

Bymaster was shocked when Brenda Schaefer's body was found behind Shore's house. A day later she got a phone call from Shore asking if she could come over for a few days to get away from the media. Bymaster agreed. To Bymaster's surprise, Shore brought Butch Inlow with her.

"She treated him like a dog most of the time," Bymaster would say. "She was always interested in what he could get for her, what he could do for her. At that point he was the only thing she had going for her."

Bymaster believed Shore and Ignatow were a lot alike, manipulative, with mean streaks. At that point Shore would tell Bymaster much more than she ever told the police or FBI agents, even talking about the night Brenda was murdered.

"Mary Ann told me, or made me think," said Bymaster, "that Mel came in, locked the dead bolt, and she couldn't get out. Like they were all prisoners in the house.

"And the way I thought was that he just had them all prisoners in the house. I always thought Mel made her do it. Then a week or two later it came out they had predug the grave. I never did confront Mary Ann with that . . . I just quit talking to her.

"She did say that Mel was only going to scare Brenda. I always wanted to believe that Mary Ann didn't realize what they were going to do."

Shore told Bymaster she never expected any jail time; she'd cut a deal with the commonwealth's attorney to avoid it. Shore, in fact, would become indignant with Bymaster about serving time, as if her confession, her willingness to talk, had absolved her of any guilt.

Shore talked to Bymaster about the pictures she had taken

of Brenda's murder—and of the paddle being used to beat her—but never with any sense of guilt; Shore felt no responsibility for what had happened. Shore insinuated that with Brenda gone, she could get back with Mel.

"After the body was found she kept saying, 'Those pictures. We've got to find those pictures of the crime.' She knew that Mel had them. She just knew that would tell all."

Neither police nor FBI agents ever found Bymaster, ever interviewed her. Bymaster said she never really put all the pieces together in her mind until about a month after Shore left. But a phone conversation she'd had with Shore just before Brenda Schaefer's disappearance would bother her for a long time. Had she gone to the police, it might have made a difference:

"Mary Ann called me a month or two before the murder and said Mel had suggested that we capture Brenda Schaefer and blindfold her as some kind of joke. I just kind of laughed it off and said 'no way.' "

On January 18, 1990, Jim Wesley and Detective Dave Wood—with permission from Butch Inlow and Shore—went to Shore's apartment to photograph the glass-topped coffee table, which was roughly fifty inches long, twenty-one inches wide, and fourteen inches high. They also photographed Shore's queen-size bed. Later that night the officers taped a more-than-two-hour conversation with Mary Ann Shore in county police headquarters, part of which focused on Shore's sexual relationship with Mel Ignatow.

Shore said they had been very sexually active, especially on weekends, and that Ignatow had tied her up at least twice. Wesley, a little apologetically, pursued that line of questioning.

Wesley: "Can you describe the . . . bondage events?"

Shore: "Ah . . . he tied me to the bed, this was at his house . . . my arms and my legs."

"When he tied you, was this something you submitted to?"

"Yes, but I didn't know what he was going to do."

"Okay ... what do you think his state of mind was ... when he was tying you to the bed?"

"What do you mean state of mind ... ?"

"Well, was this for pleasure purposes ... for sexual purposes ... or what? ... Why did he tie you to the bed ... ?"

"He wasn't angry ... it's more like I'm-going-to-get-even type thing."

Wesley again asked Shore why Ignatow might have tied her up.

"Well ... if I did something like this, then we would stay together ... it was to straighten me up."

Shore said Ignatow tied her up once in his bedroom on Thames, another time at her apartment.

"Your hands and feet were tied?"

"Yes."

"And you were on your stomach, on the bed?"

"Yes, but he had a pillow under my stomach."

"Okay ... as tactfully as you want to say, tell us what he did."

"Ah ... he did annual sex on me."

"Anal sex?"

"Uh huh ... and then he took a paddle out and hit me with a paddle."

Shore told Wesley the paddle was brown, with a leather strap and the inscription "To Mel from Jim." She identified the Jim as Ignatow's brother.

Wesley continued the questioning:

"When he performed anal sex, was there always ejaculation?"

"I don't know if it was or not ... all's I know I was screaming at the time."

"Did he use any kind of lubricant?"

"Yes, K-Y jelly ... and he told me to be calm and just relax and it wouldn't hurt as much."

"What about the paddling? Did he tell you to be calm during the paddling?"

"No, he just kept hitting me."

Shore told Wesley that she was certain Ignatow still had

the pictures taken the night Brenda was murdered, that the film was undeveloped, even sixteen months later. Shore just didn't know where the film had been hidden. Wesley found it hard to believe the film might still be in Ignatow's house, especially since eight police officers had spent hours in the home looking for it. But it was possible; Ignatow had been under investigation—with some surveillance—almost since the minute Brenda Schaefer had disappeared. It wasn't the type of film you could get developed at Walgreen's, and Ignatow hadn't been overseas since Schaefer disappeared.

Commonwealth's Attorney Ernie Jasmin also was certain the photographs existed. He'd worked with the FBI a little on the Schaefer case; he'd also once been a guest at the FBI Academy in Quantico and was aware of the profile of sexual sadists.

"I knew it fit Ignatow to a T," he would say.

A little past noon on Tuesday, January 23, armed with a search warrant signed by Judge Olga Peers, Wesley and ten other county police, Jeffersontown police, and FBI agents again visited Ignatow's house. Their explicit mission was to find small, black, plastic canisters of 35mm color-print film.

"We wanted to concentrate on the basement," Wesley would say. "We thought about the duct work, the insulation."

The second search was so thorough that Detective Eddie Robinson removed some of the furnace covering and duct work and crawled up as far as he could. The men double-checked the entire house and garage, removing cover plates from light switches, picking their way through every closet, drawer, cupboard, cabinet, and jewelry box. Eleven trained, highly motivated law-enforcement officers searched hard for more than two hours and found nothing.

1960-1961

Brenda Sue Schaefer

LEFT: Brenda Schaefer was barely out of high school when she married Pete Van Pelt, a dispatcher with the Louisville police. Van Pelt was the first person Brenda had seriously dated. Their brief marriage ended in anger, bitterness, and disappointment. *(Courtesy of the Shaefer family)*

RIGHT: Brenda Shaefer dated Louisville dentist Jim Rush for about eight years before she began going out with Mel Ignatow. *(Courtesy of the Schaefer family)*

BELOW: The tall, genial Mel Ignatow and beautiful Brenda Schaefer made a handsome couple while they were dating. This photograph appeared on Louisville television hundreds of times after Brenda disappeared. *(Courtesy of the Schaefer family)*

FACING PAGE, BOTTOM: The lives of the surviving Schaefer children—Mike, Carolyn Kopp, and Tom—were forever changed by the murder of their brother Jack, a Louisville policeman, and then Brenda. *(Robb Hill Photo)*

ABOVE: John and Essie Schaefer at the dedication of the Louisville police substation named in honor of their murdered son, Jack, and his partner. Jack Schaefer's photo is on the wall behind them, to the left.
(Courtesy of the Schaefer family)

RIGHT: This picture was taken of Brenda Schaefer just about the time she disappeared.
(Courtesy of the Schaefer family)

$25,000 REWARD

BRENDA SUE SCHAEFER

Missing since Saturday Evening,
September 24, 1988
Age 36 years   Height 5'4"   Weight 110 Lbs.
Eyes Brown   Hair Brown
Last seen wearing a Light colored short sleeve
sweater, blue jeans and red shoes.

$ 5,000. for information leading to her whereabouts, &
$20,000. for information leading to the arrest &
conviction of person or persons responsible
for her disappearance.

Information about the case can be sent to
P. O. Box 91344, Louisville, Ky. 40291-0344
Calls with information, but not wanting their name
known will be given an identifying number, for reward.

CALL

(502) 588-2105   (502) 581-9247
Jefferson County Police   F.B.I.

The Schaefer family drove thousands of miles across Kentucky,
Indiana, and Tennessee to pass
out reward posters at truck stops
and police stations.
*(Courtesy of the
Schaefer family)*

Jefferson County Police Sergeant
Jim Wesley was the lead officer
in the Mel Ignatow investigation,
the most frustrating of the officer's career. *(Robb Hill Photo)*

LEFT: It was Steve Slyter, a Louisville handwriting analyst, who first read the scratchings on Mel Ignatow's pocket calendar after local police and FBI efforts had failed. *(Robb Hill Photo)*

ABOVE: FBI criminal sexual sadist expert Roy Hazelwood tutored Louisville FBI agents and first developed a psychological profile of Mel Ignatow. *(Robb Hill Photo)*

LEFT: Dr. George Nichols, Kentucky's chief medical examiner, helped find Brenda Schaefer's body, then untied the ropes that bound her while performing the autopsy. *(Robb Hill Photo)*

FACING PAGE BOTTOM: Alan Sears, Jim Lesousky, and Scott Cox were three assistant U.S. attorneys instrumental in the murder case. It was Cox who got Mel Ignatow to testify before a federal grand jury. *(Robb Hill Photo)*

Mary Ann Shore's testimony at the Brenda Schaefer murder trial was key to the prosecution's case, but her dress, crossed legs, and demeanor on the witness stand led to a deep division among the jurors, some of whom thought her capable of murder. *(Permission of Louisville* Courier-Journal/ *Photo by Mike Hayman)*

Defense attorney Charlie Ricketts at a Louisville pretrial hearing. Ricketts and prosecutor Ernie Jasmin clashed publicly and privately for almost three years during the legal course of the murder investigation and trial. *(Permission of Louisville* Courier-Journal*)*

Pastor Bob Russell of Southeast Christian Church, where Ignatow sought refuge in a singles club after Brenda Schaefer disappeared. Russell met with Ignatow once in a Louisville jail after his arrest. *(Permission of Louisville* Courier-Journal)

A smug, smiling Mel Ignatow being led away by federal marshals after his final court appearance in Louisville
(Photograph by Bud Kraft)

Mary Ann Shore Residence

Drawing of the area around Mary Ann Shore's house, including the woods where the body was found 135 yards from her back door
(Court discovery files)

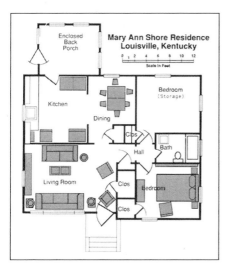

Mary Ann Shore Residence
Louisville, Kentucky

A scale drawing of Mary Ann Shore's house on Poplar Level Road, where Shore said Brenda Schaefer was murdered by Mel Ignatow in the back bedroom
(Court discovery files)

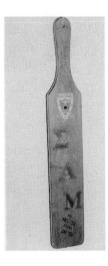

The University of Louisville fraternity paddle that Mary Ann Shore said was used to beat Brenda Schaefer *(Court discovery files)*

Diagram of the hallway of the Mel Ignatow home where the photographs of Brenda Schaefer's sexual abuse were found in a heat duct hidden beneath a carpet. With hallway doors left open, the heat duct was impossible to discover until the carpet was changed.

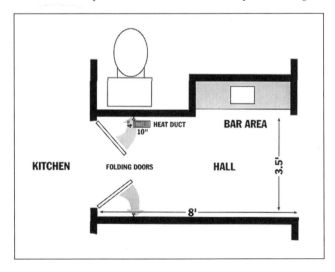

CHAPTER
20

What little hope there had been for a peaceful—and speedy—disposition of the Brenda Schaefer murder case evaporated on January 31 when Commonwealth's Attorney Ernie Jasmin placed the thirteen-minute Ignatow-Shore tape into the circuit-court case file, where the Louisville media had access to it as a matter of public record.

The tape would bob through the judicial proceedings for years like a cork in a stormy sea, surfacing, reappearing, disappearing again, but often the focal point of all legal arguments and motions. WLKY-32 reporter Steve Burgin was the first to air part of the tape on Friday, February 2. It would soon be broadcast—in part—on all Louisville television stations and many radio stations and be reprinted in the *Courier-Journal*.

Suddenly a prime section of prosecution evidence was being heard, seen, or read by hundreds of thousands of Jefferson Countians. The worry in Shore's voice, the rising anger of Ignatow's replies, could be heard as if the audience were sitting in Shore's car with them outside Ehrler's. Like the police and attorneys before them, reporters and editors who listened to the recording dozens of times would have trouble deciphering exactly what Ignatow was saying. Almost all news reports, and the *Courier-Journal's* version, would repeatedly have Ignatow using the word "dug" instead of "got":

"That's no big deal. That isn't going to stir up anything. Believe me, that place we *dug*, that's not shallow."

Most television reports, including WLKY-32, also used the word "site" instead of "safe" near the end of Ignatow's warning to Shore—if they used that section at all.

"Besides, that one area right by where that *site* is does not have any trees by it," Ignatow was quoted on WLKY-32. "The trees are down, if you remember, so it's not a big deal."

The word "safe"—which would become so important later—was never even a part of the consciousness of the Louisville news audience. As the audio portion ran, several of the television news broadcasts showed pictures of Brenda Schaefer's grave coupled with photographs of Ignatow and Shore, forever linking the three together.

Charlie Ricketts said he was "appalled" by the tapes, complaining Jasmin "has polluted and contaminated the mind-set of the public." Jasmin called a press conference to refute the charges, saying he had placed the tape in the public court file as a routine response to a January 16 ruling by Judge Martin Johnstone that required all appropriate evidence given to Ricketts as part of legal "discovery."

Jasmin also said the judge made his ruling following a discovery request by Ricketts; Ignatow's attorney should have requested all records be sealed if he wanted it that way. Jasmin complained he believed the media would use more discretion in airing the tape. No one, including Johnstone, could ever remember an audiotape of such a sensitive nature in a major murder trial being put in the public record, then used by the media—which had a perfect right to use it.

"I did not anticipate anybody really doing that kind of number," an irritated Jasmin would say.

Johnstone had been irritated because the tape had ended up in the public record the same day Jasmin had decided not to place it into evidence during a tape-suppression hearing, partly because of its inflammatory nature.

"We came back to start the hearing on the suppression of the tape and both of the attorneys came up to tell me that they've both decided [that] to prevent any further pretrial publicity they were going to forgo a suppression-of-the-tape hearing. . . .

"Then it was that very afternoon or evening that the tape mysteriously ends up in the public record. . . ."

Once the tape was public, Ricketts bored in on Jasmin—and the state's case—with a blizzard of legal objections and strange, time-consuming motions. He filed an affidavit asking that the state be barred from seeking the death penalty in the case because Jasmin had acted improperly. He charged that Jasmin had violated the state bar's Rules of Professional Responsibility; he should be barred from prosecuting Ignatow, and a special prosecutor should be appointed. Ricketts asked that the commonwealth be ordered to take a public-opinion poll to "study the pervasive impact" of the tape. He filed a motion asking the state to pay the defense attorney's fees since the tape made Ignatow's defense so expensive.

"What made it upsetting," Johnstone would later say, "was that Ricketts would be in the courtroom with the cameras rolling, demagoguing about what a vendetta the commonwealth had, and how they were perpetuating all this publicity when I know who's making the motions, who's setting the arguments on the motions, and who's really perpetuating the publicity.

"Instead of listening to arguments I was just refereeing all the time."

Even the *Courier-Journal* editorial writers got into the act; a Friday, February 9, 1990, editorial headlined FINDING UN-BIASED JURORS bit into Ricketts with a lead that began: "The lawyer for accused murderer Melvin H. Ignatow doth protest too much. . . ."

Intense media interest was again fanned on January 13 when the *Courier-Journal* ran a detailed account of Brenda Schaefer's sexual torture and murder, all of it taken from the county police reports, investigations, and interviews with Mary Ann Shore. These files, hundreds of pages in five volumes, had been placed in open court by Jasmin in response to the court order to provide Ricketts with details of the prosecution's case. Such a procedure was normal, done in thousands of criminal cases every year. Soon after the documents were filed, Ricketts objected to the filings of those volumes, too.

Johnstone brought the Ricketts-Jasmin arguments somewhat under control during a Friday, February 16, motion hearing during which the two men again bickered over the filing of evidence—and who had returned whose phone calls when.

Staring at the attorneys from the bench, anger in his voice, Johnstone told them, "We can spend the next six months trying the *Ricketts* v. *Jasmin, Jasmin* v. *Ricketts* case. . . . And we're not going to do it."

Johnstone resolved the problem by ordering Jasmin to give Ricketts five days to review any new information before it was filed in court. If Ricketts thought the material should be kept out of public view, a hearing would be called.

As the defense motions and affidavits piled up, the trial date kept getting pushed back. Johnstone suggested August 20, but Jasmin had other commitments; Labor Day weekend might interfere. Johnstone asked about July; Ricketts feared the "pollution" from the tape release might not have settled. The men finally agreed on a new, tentative trial date, September 10, 1990, seven months away.

Johnstone would eventually set Ignatow's bond at $375,000 cash or $750,000 property. If Ignatow posted the bond, he would have to surrender his passport and could not leave Jefferson County.

Over the next sixteen months Johnstone's court would become a battleground for a bizarre variety of medical, ethical, and constitutional questions, one kicked up to the Kentucky Supreme Court. The delays were painful for all the families involved; Ignatow's mother would die in the interim, as would both Essie and John Schaefer, who wouldn't live long enough to see their daughter's accused murderer in court.

It was July 24, 1991, before Mary Ann Shore would appear in court to testify in a hearing on a Charlie Ricketts motion to suppress the thirteen-minute tape from the trial. Shore was supposed to have testified more than a year earlier, on June 8, 1990. In late May 1990, Shore's attorney, Jack Vittitow, told Johnstone it appeared his client would not be able to testify.

"She can't talk," Vittitow said. "She has a condition called Bell's palsy. There's no feeling in the side of her face. She's very uncommunicative."

Shore appeared briefly in Johnstone's court on June 7, walking gingerly, as if in pain. She was wearing a bright red baseball cap over closely cropped hair and a gaudy black, pink, and green flower-print shirt. Her left eye was covered by a huge white patch, her black-rimmed glasses over that.

Johnstone attempted to question her, but her answers were as strange as her appearance—a muffled series of vibrating "favh, favh, favh" sounds that could not be understood.

Shore had a letter from her doctor, a general practitioner named Paul R. Pollitt, who said as of May 23 Shore had developed Bell's palsy, a sudden, mostly painless swelling of the motor nerve on one side of the face, causing one side to droop.

"How long will it be until you get your feeling back?" Johnstone asked.

"Favh, favh, favh," answered Shore.

Johnstone asked Vittitow if Shore might be examined by a neurologist, to report back to the court with the findings. The judge set another hearing date for July 23, still hoping to begin the trial by September 10. Ricketts did not trust Shore, suspecting she might be faking her Bell's palsy to avoid testifying. He hired Sam Hicks, a retired Louisville police lieutenant colonel, to spy on Shore. On June 22 Hicks was sitting in his car in the parking lot outside Shore's apartment when Shore walked to a nearby laundry room carrying a basket, then spoke to someone.

"Her walk and speech appeared to be perfectly normal,"

Hicks told Ricketts, "and Ms. Shore's eyes was not covered with any type of patch or bandage. In fact, there was no evidence Ms. Shore's face was distorted in any way."

Shore returned to court July 23 in a brightly colored print dress, a mix of pinks, blues, and blacks. Her hair, which had been long, dark, and frizzy in earlier testimony, and then short enough to hide under a baseball cap, was now a shaggy blond, dark at the roots. She had a huge white medical patch over her left eye, with dark sunglasses over that.

Again Vittitow had to escort her to the stand. She appeared wobbly, uncertain where to sit. After a long legal fight, Ricketts had been given approval to ask her 114 specific questions.

Johnstone began the day by asking Shore about her condition.

"Favh, favh, favh . . ." came the answers in a curious, almost humming pitch.

"Miss Shore," the judge asked, "would it be possible for you to type out your answers?"

"Favh. Favh, favh . . ."

Johnstone called for a conference of the attorneys at his bench, irritated that a key witness was again delaying the highly publicized murder trial. He ordered a court-appointed neurologist to examine Shore.

"I'm sort of shocked that she has not seen a neurologist and has not been referred to a neurologist," he told the lawyers.

Johnstone excused Shore from testifying, setting a date for another hearing in August. No one now believed the case could go to trial by September 10; a new date was set for December 4, 1990.

On August 15, Dr. William H. Olson, chairman of the neurology department at the University of Louisville School of Medicine, testified that Shore did have Bell's palsy, but the condition does not cause the slurred speech and halting walk Shore had displayed.

"I've seen hundreds of patients with Bell's palsy and their speech is perfectly understandable," the doctor testified. He could find no physical reasons for her speech or walk; her symptoms could be caused at some "unconscious level" or Shore might have been purposely lying "for some kind of gain."

"I do not know which," the doctor said.

The Ignatow case had also developed serious legal maladies. On Tuesday, August 14, at Jasmin's request, Kentucky State Court of Appeals Justice John P. Hayes had issued a temporary stay to block Shore from testifying. That stay came as a result of Johnstone's ruling that Jasmin could not specifically object to Ricketts's lengthy list of questions. On October 18, 1990, Jasmin's appeal of that decision went from the Court of Appeals of Kentucky to the Supreme Court of Kentucky. It wouldn't be until March 14, 1991, that the Supreme Court would issue an order dismissing the appeal, basically on the grounds it didn't think Johnstone would really stop the commonwealth from objecting to questions. Johnstone placed the case back on his docket for July 15.

Much had happened in the interim between Shore's incoherent court appearances, much of it behind the scenes:

Dozens of motions were filed, amended, argued, accepted, and rejected; Johnstone would ultimately side with Jasmin in most areas. Ricketts and Jasmin continued to fire often angry letters at each other over lack of evidence received, poor communication.

Ricketts would make the FBI's use of Mary Ann Shore to tape Ignatow without first notifying his attorney an ethical battlefield, with Ricketts bringing in Monroe Freedman, former dean of law at Hofstra, to defend his position that Shore was unethically acting "as an agent for the government."

Mary Ann Shore married Butch Inlow on August 26, 1990, adopting the name Mary Ann Shore-Inlow. The couple also managed to work in a Caribbean cruise, although Shore never told police or Jack Vittitow she was leaving the country.

Shore-Inlow finally took the witness stand on Wednesday, July 24, 1991. She had gained weight, but without her glasses, her blond hair almost touching her shoulders, her tough edge had softened; she looked as attractive as she ever had.

Ignatow, seated at the table next to Ricketts, stared at Shore-Inlow, occasionally taking notes on a legal pad. Ricketts maneuvered Shore-Inlow through the January 9, 1990, meeting with Ignatow.

"They didn't make me do it," Shore said of the FBI. "I wanted to do it."

Ricketts asked her a question on everyone's minds—why Brenda Schaefer's name was never once used in the entire tape.

"I don't know. I just didn't mention her name."

"Weren't you supposed to ask if Mel killed her?"

"I don't recall."

Ricketts stared at her incredulously. "Didn't the cops tell you to ask Mel why did he do it? Wasn't that what this whole case was about?"

"He wouldn't discuss all that stuff. He'd get upset when I said anything about it.

"I just wanted him to say where the body was in the ground. He never did say it. . . ."

Ignatow's mother, Virginia, had died of cancer on May 13, 1990, at age eighty-one. Johnstone had given Mel permission to be released to see his mother before cremation and then visit his father's grave in Cave Hill Cemetery.

Richard Frey, director of the Department of Corrections, didn't want Ignatow out of jail, fearing he had some "rabbit" in him. Ignatow went to his mother's funeral at the Herman Meyer & Son Funeral Home in handcuffs and leg irons, the irons being released on his arrival. Frey was taking security very seriously; he sent half a dozen guards with Ignatow, an unarmed guard near the prisoner, officers with shotguns at a distance.

Frey grabbed an AR16 with a 10-power scope from his armory and followed his guards, positioning himself on a hill above the funeral home. His biggest worry was at Cave Hill Cemetery, a bushy, hilly place, where Ignatow would visit his father's grave. Ignatow had spotted Frey with his rifle at Cave Hill. He questioned him about it when they returned to the jail.

"Was that necessary?" Ignatow asked.

"Goddamn right it was, Mel!"

Frey would remain a controversial man in the judicial system. He was subsequently fired after becoming an FBI target in a bribery investigation that had nothing to do with Ignatow.

Virginia Ignatow's ashes would be buried next to those of her husband, David, in Cave Hill's Lot 33, a flat, well-kept plot backed by Foster holly and green ivy. Her grave site was barely one hundred yards from the hillside stone where Brenda Schaefer and her brother Jack lay buried.

Ignatow had deeded his share of their Florian Road house to his mother two days after he was arrested. In Virginia Ignatow's will, dated July 19, 1984, she had agreed to leave the house to Mel's children only if he died before her. On April 23, 1990, two weeks before she died, she wrote a codicil to her will leaving the Florian Road property to Mel's three children. She left the rest of her estate—including about $7,700 in coins and savings and her old home at 3741 Avon Court valued at $64,440—to Mel's brother, Jim, and his sister, Natalie Lisanby.

Ricketts prepared all the legal documents. Virginia Ignatow left nothing to Mel.

Essie Schaefer, long suffering with lupus, died on July 13, 1990, at age seventy-four of a cerebral hemorrhage. Her life had slipped away in the seven months after Brenda's funeral; she rarely left her house. Tom Schaefer had come downstairs one morning and seen the back of his mother's head over the top of her chair, the television set on. He walked into the kitchen, looking for the pot of coffee his mother always prepared. It wasn't there; his mother was in a coma. She died the next morning in Baptist Hospital East.

Essie Schaefer's casket and dusty-rose flowers were identical to Brenda's. She was buried in a dark blue suit with an off-white blouse. Linda Love styled her hair, did her makeup.

Mike Schaefer's two sons brought flowers and an old-fashioned Depression doll to the funeral home. Mike placed the doll at his mother's side just before the casket was closed.

John Schaefer died February 6, 1991, in Baptist Hospital East at age seventy-seven. He, too, had become more withdrawn, spending most of his time in his TV room. Tom Schaefer would find him there staring at the wall, the television set on, an empty coffeepot glowing dangerously in the kitchen.

He developed a continual coronary cough, filling the house with it at night. He'd gotten so weak that Tom, Carolyn, and Mike were convinced he should be in the hospital. He was taken by ambulance to Baptist East. The family learned he apparently had suffered a heart attack in December 1989, but he didn't complain about being sick or feeling bad until after Brenda's funeral. His heart stopped beating while his children had gone out into the hall to give him a rest.

John Schaefer didn't like wooden caskets, so he was buried in a copper one. His flowers were the same arrangement as his wife's and daughter's, only with dark red roses. For the third time in thirteen months, a hearse made its way from Our Lady of Lourdes to a green slope at Cave Hill Cemetery, where John Schaefer joined his wife, a daughter, and a son.

As far as the Schaefer family was concerned, Mel Ignatow had to account for three deaths.

CHAPTER
21

Mel Ignatow was in the Jefferson County Jail only a few months before several of the inmates began referring to him as "Reverend," a title he seemed to accept with pride.

Sanctimony had suited Ignatow before his arrest. In jail, he portrayed the role of a Christian with equal resolve. He quickly joined the jail's Faith and Hope Ministry, a group of nondenominational volunteers who met on Tuesdays. On Sundays Ignatow would go to church services in the jail's fifth-floor gymnasium, a small, hollow room with a worn cement floor and basketball goals at each end, one dedicated to the University of Louisville, the other to the University of Kentucky.

Ignatow would become active in services, would read scripture in his cell daily, sometimes quoting it to other inmates or to corrections officer Joe Riggs. The officer, twenty-two, small and soft-spoken, prided himself on a knack for being able to see through people. He and other officers joked constantly about inmates who turned to Jesus soon after the jail key turned behind them.

"Mel professed to being a Christian," Riggs would say. "That was a soft spot with me because I'm a Christian."

Riggs paused a long time before finishing his thought: ". . . Yeah, I guess I did believe him."

Ignatow was assigned to the fifth-floor psychiatric unit in South One, an area of ten one-room cells strung against one wall like a row of empty ammunition boxes. The hallway outside the cells was painted a cream color, trimmed in ocean blue.

Ignatow was in cell 10, closest to a guard station. His cell was about eight feet by six feet, its walls painted peach with a row of bars slatted across opaque windows. His bed was a wide slab of welded steel bolted to one wall. The bed was attached to a slab-metal table supported by painted cinder blocks. A poured-cement sitting stool with a metal cap rose from the cell floor like a stubby pier. A stainless-steel commode was bolted to the wall across from the bed. For a man who prided himself on bathroom elegance, this was a long comedown. The cramped cell lacked any immediate bathroom privacy; only the guards could shut the slablike metal doors.

South One was an area for prisoners with prior mental problems or prisoners with high-ticket charges against them. Ignatow's neighbors included men charged with murder, robbery, and rape, many of them on prescription medicine to help moderate paranoid, manic, or depressive behavior. When on proper medication, these men were not considered especially dangerous; they had full use of a narrow sixty-foot "walk" that ran in front of their cells. At the end of the walk was the "day room," a roughly fifteen-foot-square room painted cream and ocean blue with shower facilities and a more private commode off to one side.

The bunkerlike day room had long tables bolted to the walls, a half dozen poured-cement stools, coffeepot, telephone, and cable television; the inmates picked what to watch. A huge, somber mural of a lighthouse on an ocean coast done in gray, black, and white dominated one wall. The whole area—the prisoner walk and the day room—resonated with institutional noises, the slam of metal and echo of feet, the intrusive arguing and bored laughter of trapped men.

To change from his orange prison jumpsuit into the three-piece suits he wore at court hearings, Ignatow would leave civilian clothing in the basement "intake" room. He was allowed only one suit at a time, changing before and after each court appearance, occasionally waiting in a basement cell for hours while wearing a suit if his court appearance was delayed.

Ignatow maintained all his civilian habits in jail. While other inmates kept their books and magazines under their beds, allowing their thick, gray wool blankets to flop over far enough to hide them, Ignatow's wool blanket was always neatly tucked under the mattress military style, his books stacked as evenly as a row of bricks, his cell floor constantly swept and mopped. He was a model prisoner, never far from his Bible, rarely arguing with anyone unless his medicine was late or he got the wrong pill—and he was taking ten pills a day for heart and stress problems. Ignatow checked all his medicine with the intensity of a paranoid man; he would quickly correct a nurse who made a mistake.

He willingly did small custodial jobs in his area, volunteered to deliver meals on metal carts to other inmates, which often meant he would get "work-aid status": a little more to eat, a little more freedom to move around. Working the jail system as well as it could be worked, he was soon trusted to make "suicide walks"—covering the outer perimeter of the entire fifth floor with its forty cells checking on self-destructive inmates. There was something about him that made jail supervisors nervous—"I just never liked that son of a bitch," one of them would say—but the officers who had contact with him every day had few complaints and seemed to like him.

Ignatow once told one of them, corrections officer Glynis Baines, "It's not over until the fat lady sings or I run out of money, whichever comes first."

Living in a prison culture that most honored its own disturbed values, Ignatow also had a lot going for him with other inmates; high-profile notoriety in a murder case; a tall physical presence; money to spend in the commissary so he could buy them coffee, candy bars, peanuts, or crackers. He had a habit of standing close to other inmates, making them feel smaller. He enjoyed telling stories of his sexual conquests. Combined with his intelligence, his ability to manipulate, and a certain mystique, he became a leader, easily dominating the others.

"He would never try to overly manipulate," Riggs would say. "He would do the little things, body language, gestures, mostly speech. . . . As good as he was it was hard to see them."

Ignatow often wanted to talk to Riggs about his case, the unfairness of the charges against him. He would sit in the day room with other inmates, watching himself on the nightly news, pointing out the lies and misinterpretations, as the others gloried in knowing him. Ignatow talked often of a change of venue.

"That's my ace in the hole," Ignatow told Riggs one day. "I don't think there's a way I can lose if I get a change of venue."

From January 29, 1990, until March 4, 1991, Ignatow wrote twenty-six letters to a woman named Linda Brooks, whom he'd met at BYKOTA meetings at Southeast Christian Church. Brooks, a Blue Cross service representative, was divorced and raising a daughter when she met Ignatow in July 1989. Their relationship stayed within group gatherings, but Brooks would become friends with Ignatow's mother and sister, eventually buying his 1984 Corvette for $10,000, well down from the $16,000 Ignatow had first wanted.

Ignatow's letters to Brooks revealed a proselytizing piety; he would write pages of rambling sentences on yellow legal paper extolling his newfound faith and belief in Jesus, regretting he'd taken so long to find him. In other letters he would explain in great detail the best place to buy tires for the Corvette, fine-tune its six-speaker stereo system, or repair an oil leak. The letters were precisely folded into four sections, fitted perfectly in an envelope.

In a February 1990 letter, he worried about a legal bill; he said it was running almost $1,000 a day. He asked about his former BYKOTA girlfriend whom he'd wanted to marry after dating a few months. He bragged in later letters that he had befriended an inmate who was a lawyer; he was learning how to file motions, work his way through the court system; there were many more motions to come; he and Ricketts were controlling the case.

He mentioned suffering a dislocated shoulder and a broken hand; no jail officials remembered them. He said his sister, Natalie Lisanby, had been working to sell their mother's old house, his boat, and finally, his Florian Road home and furnishings; everything he owned had to be sold to pay growing legal bills.

By March 1991, his letters had begun to darken, to take on a more desperate edge. His religious expressions became more fervent, more zealous. It was obvious that most of his former companions from Southeast Christian Church—caught in a tough position—were staying away from him. Ministers continued to come by, including Southeast Christian Church singles minister Ralph Dennison, new-member minister Ross Brodfuehrer, and on one occasion, Bob Russell, the man who had led the church's growth.

"I can assure you," Russell would say of the meetings, "that every time we talked to him our effort was: 'Mel, if you are genuinely repentant, if you want the right relationship with God, you should tell the truth.' "

The ministers and Ignatow would meet in private rooms in a fifth-floor conference area. The rooms were small, about six feet square, but well lighted and serviceable, with a small wooden table in the middle and room for two or three chairs around it.

Mel Ignatow had spent most of his life manipulating people, using them. No one could be sure when he was lying. Yet reports would persist—reports supported by Ignatow's statements in a taped interview he gave years later—that Ignatow had confessed to Bob Russell about two weeks after his arrest that he had murdered Brenda Schaefer.

Russell was not involved with that subsequent taped interview, nor did he ever hear it, although that tape was eventually heard by several attorneys, law-enforcement people,
and a representative of the news media. Russell was in an
impossible position; if a confession is made to a minister in
confidence, the minister would feel morally and ethically
bound not to reveal anything told to him.

"Every session we had with Mel before and after his arrest
was our attempt to motivate him to tell the truth," Russell
would say. "No one will be excluded from our fellowship
because of past sins. It's what a person does after he or she
commits their life to Christ when it becomes an issue for
us."

Russell also had legal support for that type of situation;
the Kentucky revised statute that applied at that time
(KRS421.210) said:

> No ordained minister, priest, rabbi or accredited practitioner
> of an established church or religious organization [shall] be
> required to testify in any civil or criminal case, proceedings
> preliminary thereto, or in an administrative proceeding, con-
> cerning any information confidentially communicated to him
> in his professional capacity under such circumstances that to
> disclose the information would violate a sacred or moral
> trust, unless the person making the confidential communi-
> cation waives such privilege herein provided.

When questioned, Southeast Christian Church officials
took the matter seriously enough to respond in writing. Michael Graham, minister of administration at the church,
would say of the Kentucky statute, "That means neither the
minister nor his penitent can be forced to testify in court
about the contents of a communication."

Graham also cited a U.S. Supreme Court ruling affirming
the Kentucky law:

"... in *Trammel* v. *United States* (1980) the United States
Supreme Court observed that 'the priest-penitent privilege
recognizes the human need to disclose to a spiritual coun-

selor, in total and absolute confidence, what are believed to be flawed acts or thoughts and to receive priestly consolation or guidance in return.' ''

Among lawyers and police who knew of the situation, a few questions would linger. Perhaps a minister could not be required or forced to talk in court, but *should* he testify in court, especially if he heard a confession to a murder? Where did "professional capacity" begin and end? Should the attitude, history, and mind-set of the confessor come into account? The Supreme Court ruling specified a "priest"; would other clergymen be more vulnerable on appeal?

Les Abramson, a professor of law at the University of Louisville, would say information passed on to a minister as merely a friend might not be privileged, but information passed on to a minister while in his clergy role probably would be privileged. If a minister was going to testify, a defendant could take legal action to stop it; Ignatow would have to give Russell permission to testify, a very unlikely possibility.

Russell did consult his attorney about his meeting with Ignatow. According to Assistant U.S. Attorney Scott Cox, Russell's office also contacted the U.S. Attorney's office and the Commonwealth's Attorney's office on the matter. Russell could never ethically divulge what happened during his meeting with Ignatow: "I had one session with him in jail. Because of the nature of that conversation I don't feel free to disclose that."

Eventually Ignatow would be asked to leave Southeast Christian Church.

"Over time we did not see evidence of true repentance," Brodfuehrer would say.

CHAPTER
22

No more than three minutes into his opening statement in the Mel Ignatow murder trial, Commonwealth's Attorney Ernie Jasmin was hitting his stride, his passion rising, a finger jabbing in the air toward the fourteen jurors—six women and eight men—seated before him in the olive-green chairs of Kenton County Circuit Court, Division 1.

It was midmorning on Monday, December 9, 1991, a gray, rainy, unusually warm morning in Covington, Kentucky, with patches of wispy fog clinging to the Ohio River outside the Kenton County Building just across the river from Cincinnati. The trial would finally begin more than thirty-eight months after Brenda Schaefer had disappeared.

Outside of Ignatow—and perhaps attorney Charlie Ricketts—no one in the case seemed especially happy about the change of venue. Nor was it a great time of year to begin a murder trial—so soon after Thanksgiving, only three weeks before Christmas.

Like everything else in the case, the decision to move the trial to Kenton County had not come easily. The legal maneuverings between Shore's July 23 testimony and the December 3 trial date were mindboggling, even in a case already barrister-deep in bickering and paperwork.

Ricketts had finally filed for a change of venue on September 12, asking that the trial be moved to Kenton County, or that a jury from Kenton County be brought to Louisville, because pretrial publicity made a fair trial impossible in Louisville. In truth, there were no other areas in Kentucky that had Jefferson County's demographics; it was by far the state's most populated, racially mixed area.

Jasmin had filed a motion asking that Johnstone temporarily step aside and let another judge decide the venue question because at an in-chambers meeting on July 25 Johnstone had already said he would "probably grant it." On October 7 Johnstone removed himself from the change-of-venue decision. At a November 1 hearing before Jefferson Circuit Judge William Knopf—who had been selected at random to fill in for Johnstone—a Western Kentucky University pollster testified nearly two thirds of the Jefferson County residents believed Ignatow was guilty. On November 15 Knopf ruled that because of possible "jury prejudice," a Kenton County jury would try the case. The decision to move the trial to Northern Kentucky, or bring Kenton County jurors to Louisville would be left to Johnstone.

On November 20 Johnstone ruled that the infamous thirteen-minute tape could be admitted into the trial. On November 21 Johnstone ruled the case would be tried in Kenton County, saying it would be easier to move the trial there rather than sequester Kenton County jurors in Louisville for the three weeks before Christmas. Although Charlie Ricketts and Ernie Jasmin had agreed on a December trial, Jasmin wasn't happy; the wife of a top assistant, Lloyd Vest, who had helped Jasmin prepare the case, was having a baby; Vest couldn't be at the trial. Charlie Ricketts was not sympathetic to Jasmin's problem.

Johnstone refused to again delay the trial. His patience was about gone. A good friend on the bench, Circuit Judge William McAnulty, had consistently advised him the only way to handle a death-penalty case was as quickly as possible.

"He told me time and time again to just get it over with," Johnstone would say. "To be quite honest I had gotten . . .

so fed up with the attorneys that at that point in time—except for hell or high water—I wasn't going to continue that case again.''

On December 2, a day before jury selection was to begin, Mary Ann Shore-Inlow pled guilty before Jefferson County District Judge Steve Ryan to tampering with physical evidence in connection with Schaefer's murder. Before her plea, Shore would have been a co-defendant with Ignatow. Her sentencing was set for February 3, 1992, well after the trial, raising the specter that the length of her sentence might depend on the success of her testimony against Ignatow.

Chief Region Circuit Judge Raymond Lape appointed Johnstone to preside at the trial, to be held in Lape's Kenton County courtroom. One reason his courtroom was open was that none of the area prosecutors wanted to have a jury trial in December; Kenton County juries had traditionally been less willing to find someone guilty near Christmas.

Kenton County, with a population of about 142,000, was a historic blend of sin and salvation. Covington, its county seat, was an exotic brew of old red-brick buildings, neighborhood taverns, huge churches, frame homes perched on hillsides, and gentrified grand homes. The town had an ancient reputation for easy sin it was still trying to live down. In the 1930s and '40s casino-supper clubs flourished near Covington's Dixie Highway; an area called the Gourmet Strip provided all the sin known to man.

Ringing the rolling hills around Covington were clusters of newer subdivisions, homes to the middle and upper-middle classes who wanted a little land but easy access to Cincinnati; many of them were people who had moved out of Covington. Caught between the two were shopping malls, industrial parks, river's-edge towns, and blue-collar neighborhoods; neat, tidy, churchgoing, heavily Catholic.

Kenton County was 97 percent white. Its minorities lived in tight pockets, attending all-black schools until 1965. Bill Martin, a black community leader who taught in Covington schools that were both all black and integrated, then became executive director of the Northern Kentucky Community

Center, estimated about 3,500 blacks lived in Kenton County, most in about a ten-block area in Covington.

"I go back to the days when you had black justice and you had white justice. Black-on-black crime was not considered crime, white-on-black crime was not crime, black-on-white crime was hate crime.

"I don't know that it's changed that much. The smaller percentage of blacks in Covington and all Northern Kentucky has always meant that they . . . they don't exist almost."

Martin said Covington had a black city manager, elected its only black city commissioner in 1971, and there was a black woman on the Covington School Board.

"The only time you might have a black attorney or a black at all in the criminal justice system would be from time to time when attorneys were hired from Cincinnati. Otherwise it is certainly a novelty for blacks to be anywhere.

"I'd say for jurors to see a black prosecutor here would be a novelty."

Jasmin was that prosecutor. As he rolled into his opening statement, he told the jurors, "I would sort of like for you to look at my opening statement as being a blueprint, or a road map, going on some long journey." Right arm pumping, his left hand thrust into his trousers pocket, he continued, "I would like you to use it in order to determine what the various twists and turns in the case may very well be."

Jasmin and Ricketts, along with their assistants, had spent most of the previous week picking the fourteen jurors from a prospective list of fifty-seven Kenton County residents, who would be paid $12.50 a day. Two of the final fourteen would become alternates, dismissed at the end of the testimony without being part of the final deliberation.

Prospective jurors were asked dozens of questions: Have you ever served on a jury, or been a crime victim? How do you feel about the death penalty? Have you heard anything of the case? Do you have trouble believing that one woman could kill another woman?

Jasmin expected to call about forty-five witnesses to the trial, Ricketts twenty-six. Once the jury was picked, Jasmin would lecture that it was not a jury's duty to play detective, but to judge the case on the evidence placed before it. Ricketts warned the jury that it was going to hear a case of love, hate, and emotions, that it must be careful finding the truth among those three treacherous characters.

The jury was an almost perfect blend of what Kenton County—if not Kentucky—had to offer; a clerk, a housewife, an assistant department-store buyer, a nurse, a city maintenance employee, a retired school principal, a food-systems general manager, a quality-control supervisor, a truck driver, a secretary, an IRS employee, a land appraiser, and several machinists. Only one of them—the city employee—was black.

Few of them had jury experience. This was not the law they saw on television. The very language of the court, the tedious questions, the theatrics, required they filter out much of what was placed before them. It sometimes seemed the lawyers were not always talking to them, but to some appeals court judge down the road. Despite Jasmin's warnings, a few jurors would find it easier to become their own detectives.

The courtroom was on the fifth floor of the ten-story Kenton County Building, a soaring, modernistic brick building lined with rectangular windows, fronted by what looked to be a huge white arch, none of it really compatible with Covington's mood or style. The dim courtroom was more staid, its back walls lined with wooden-framed pictures of former Kenton County judges dating back to 1850. They were somber, stern-looking men who appeared more than capable of hanging two horse thieves before lunch.

The spectators sat on long, dark, pewlike benches facing the judge and the witness stand. The jurors would be seated to the left of the judge's bench and witness chair; everyone who testified would have to swivel a little bit to the left to address the jury.

The jury room was only five feet away through a wooden door; court reporter Sharon Klosterman, the attorneys and judge, even the spectators, could easily hear through it when jurors' voices were raised. The judge's chambers were off a hallway right behind the courtroom, and adjacent to the jury room; the jurors' sounds would easily filter into the hallway, too.

The mood on the opening day of the trial was one of tension and expectation, an edge that would hold for the next eleven days. Ignatow was under constant surveillance. The courtroom was searched every day for weapons and explosives before the judge and jury went in.

Even before their opening statements, Ricketts complained to Johnstone that Jasmin was "wincing as though he were sitting upon a chair filled with tacks" when looking at Ignatow. Jasmin complained Ignatow was making "a concerted effort to stare me down. . . ."

Jasmin's opening statement had been short, to the point, lasting about twenty minutes. He moved quickly along his evidence trail, pausing to stress that the tire on Brenda Schaefer's car had gone flat while the car was sitting along Interstate 64, that the seat in Brenda's ransacked car had been found pushed way back.

"I expect the evidence to show that Brenda Sue Schaefer was roughly five foot three or five foot four and I anticipate the evidence showing that the defendant is roughly six foot four to six foot five," Jasmin said.

The bulk of Jasmin's opening statement covered the two strongest elements in his case: what Mary Ann Shore-Inlow had seen and heard on September 24, 1988, and the taped conversation between Shore-Inlow and Ignatow.

"I expect the evidence to show, through Mary Ann Shore, that some week or more prior to the twenty-fourth, that Melvin Henry Ignatow took a shovel over to her house, went to a wooded area in back of it to start digging a hole.

"I suggest the evidence will show to you that she got a bit concerned and he said, 'I'll just scare her.' And Mary Ann apparently didn't want to be involved in terms of any murder."

Jasmin quickly led the jurors through the rape, sodomy, photography, murder, and burial in the property behind Shore-Inlow's house, building up expectations of what she would tell the jury. Jasmin moved to the thirteen-minute tape, saying that Shore-Inlow had volunteered to wear a wire, then talk to Ignatow.

"I am not going to cover everything in the interview, ladies and gentlemen. But I am going to say to you that I expect the evidence to show that he did everything in his power to ensure that she didn't ever talk to the FBI or the authorities anymore.

"I expect the evidence to show that he made the statement: 'Don't get rattled. I don't give a shit if they're going to dig eight feet deep. . . . That's not shallow, that place. . . .' "

Jasmine touched briefly on Brenda's missing jewelry: Shore-Inlow had said Ignatow had stolen it; Ignatow told Tom Schaefer he was expecting insurance proceeds.

"I expect you to find Mel Ignatow guilty," Jasmin said, "and afterward . . . I would ask you to sentence the defendant to death."

One item missing from Jasmin's opening was a picture of Brenda Schaefer; the jurors would not see one until late in the trial, never get a sense of her ___ a person, a human being, a young and beautiful woman.

Ricketts's opening statement lasted seventy-seven minutes, setting his tone for the whole trial; grind it out, wear down the opposition with whatever it took, push the legal envelope so far that Jasmin might get tired of continually objecting for fear of offending the jurors.

Ricketts faced the jurors, *leaning* in to them, moving his eyes from chair to chair as he spoke, leaving ample early evidence of where he would try to take the trial, refuting many points Jasmin had not even raised.

"Don't be bowled over by the loud remarks of my opponent. Volume will not get it. Don't be bowled over by the stack of meaningless trivia that you will see placed on the evidence table. Examine it for what it is when it comes in. . . .

"You have to be on your toes in this case because the police were not . . . were not on their toes. Scientific proof, ladies and gentlemen, does not lie, has no reason to lie. A fingerprint is not given to jealousy or other emotions.''

Walking back and forth before the jury box, Rick̇etts began to hammer home his arguments: There was no physical
evidence linking Mel Ignatow to the murder of Brenda Sue
Schaefer; no fingerprints, pubic hair, blood, semen, fibers,
contusions, abrasions, or tears. He pointed out that both
Brenda Schaefer's car and the one found near it had been
vandalized; possibly the vandals had moved back Schaefer's
car seat.

Ricketts would document that Ignatow was having trouble
with the tires of his Corvette on September 24 when he asked
Brenda to drive. He charged the FBI's handling of reports in
the case was ''sloppy, negligent, purposeful.'' He went on
at length about witnesses—including Flaherty's waitress Sue
McKinney—who would corroborate Ignatow's story of being with Brenda Schaefer the Saturday night she disappeared.

He mentioned the public and media pressure put on the
police to find a suspect in the case. He spoke of Dr. William
Spalding, who ''permitted, insisted, expected'' that Brenda
Schaefer work from 7:00 A.M. until midnight. He alluded to
the jealousies within the doctor's office.

Ricketts rambled far afield, venturing into areas of press
leaks that made it impossible to get a fair trial in Jefferson
County, Ignatow's volunteered grand jury testimony, and the
''theft proclivities'' of Mary Ann Shore-Inlow. All brought
objections from Jasmin.

Ricketts brought Jim Rush's name into question as a suspect. With regard to Ignatow, Ricketts questioned how a man
who had just committed a murder could go out and eat chili
soon afterward. He challenged the validity of the thirteen-
minute tape. He saved his finest venom for Mary Ann Shore-
Inlow, referring to her as a deeply jealous woman, a
''Benedict Arnold Shore-Inlow'' because she had bargained
an agreement to testify against Ignatow while never spending
one night in jail. Ricketts would imply that Butch Inlow
might have been involved in the murder, that Shore-Inlow
would give the acting performance of her life.

''Passions have everything to do with this case,'' Ricketts

said, ". . . the most lurid and dark side of passions. The passions about which you will hear, ladies and gentlemen, are those of Mary Ann Shore.

". . . You'll hear the conflicting evidence from this woman's mouth as she gave one story, and then another, to the police. And then one story, and then another, to the federal grand jury; both under oath, one conflicting the other.

"Question that emotion. Question that passion. One, she saves her skin, she saves her life. And two, she fulfills that promise that she made to herself, and others: That if I can't have Mel Ignatow, then nobody can have Mel Ignatow."

Jasmin, wanting to first establish medical evidence, led the trial with George Nichols, who would testify to the condition of Brenda Schaefer's body. Nichols would show a videotape of the body being removed from the ground, the subsequent autopsy. About seventeen minutes of the original tape (the extraneous scenes and the cutting off of Brenda's hands) had been edited out. Ricketts had attempted to have the tape suppressed, calling it an "exquisitely grotesque, horrible depiction of what took place at that autopsy" that could inflame the passions of the jury. Johnstone overruled him.

Nichols carefully recited his findings, explaining the peculiar decomposition of Brenda's body that transformed soft tissues into a "great white mass"; the complex ropes around her body; the lack of external injury; no evidence of stabbing, shooting, or beating; the hysterectomy and the evidence of breast implants.

". . . And I might add," said Nichols, startling several members of the jury, "done in an excellent fashion by a very skillful plastic surgeon."

Jasmin followed with a basic question:

"Doctor," Jasmin asked, "do you have an opinion, based on reasonable medical probability, as to the manner of death?"

"As to the manner of death, a medical certainty: It is homicide."

"And, Doctor, do you have an opinion, based upon a reasonable medical probability, as to cause?"

"Asphyxia. Some form of suffocation."

Jasmin ticked off some possible causes of the suffocation: a pillow around the face, a rope around the neck, strangulation with hands. He did not mention the suffocating properties of chloroform; there was no way to prove it had been used. He asked Nichols if it would have done any good to attempt vaginal or anal swabs.

"No."

"Could you explain to us why, Doctor?"

"Under the best of circumstances the presence of semen and/or spermatozoa are there only for a relatively short amount of time . . . there will be no evidence of sperm or semen in a body that is decomposed."

Ricketts began his cross-examination of Nichols with a discussion of the aerial photos taken through the bare trees the day the body was discovered, the rakes and shovels used to unearth the body, the ability of Bingo, the cadaver dog. Finally Ricketts led him to the rope used to tie the body, the manner in which the rope ends were taped together, all leading to a specific question:

"Are you familiar with how firefighters tape the ends of their ropes to keep them from fraying?"

"I don't know how firefighters do," answered Nichols. "I know how a boater does."

"How?"

"Very similar to this."

Ricketts knew Butch Inlow was a fireman. Nichols knew Ignatow was a boater. Nichols's answer hung in the room for a second, but was not brought up again. Ricketts moved on to safer ground—the kind of knots used in the rope.

"If you are a boater, were these the kinds of knots that you would tie?" he asked Nichols.

"Not really. They were fouled miserably . . . it would have taken forever to get the knots apart."

Ricketts had another rope question:

"Did you see any marks on her neck which would indicate that a rope had been pulled tightly around that neck?"

"Clearly not."

Ricketts asked about beatings with a paddle:

"Doctor . . . being the erudite individual that you are, you are familiar with fraternity paddles?"

"Yes, sir."

"Since you don't know whether a fraternity paddle was used on that body, you can't tell from your examination of that body and its remains that, indeed, such a paddle was used on Brenda Sue Schaefer?"

"I can't tell whether it was, or was not."

Nichols was followed by St. Matthews police officer Thomas Gilsdorf, who had found Brenda Schaefer's car ransacked and abandoned along Interstate 64. The officer was shown aerial photographs of the area where the car was found.

"Can you point out for the jury where Flaherty's restaurant is in relationship with the little 'X' that you have depicted as being the location of Brenda Sue Schaefer's car?"

Gilsdorf estimated it to be 350 to 450 yards away.

"So we are talking about a short walk?"

"Yes, sir."

"And at night is the parking lot of Flaherty's well lighted?"

"Yes, sir, I would say it is."

CHAPTER 23

Having been provided with the testimony of Dr. George Nichols, the Mel Ignatow murder trial quickly settled into the drudgery of the prosecution presenting the broad outline of its investigation, sprinkled with a few of its clinical details.

The presentation was as necessary as it was tedious. The jury—any jury—had to be shown the nature of the crime, the course of the investigation, the physical evidence. Much of it would come from law-enforcement people or professional witnesses who had testified so often their presentation lacked any real drama. They knew what legal pitfalls to avoid, when to spar with an attorney, how to try to embellish a case, how to duck, bob, and weave.

Even then, under persistent questioning, witnesses sometimes had to deliver lines that hurt their case. Their only hope was that the attorney for their side was listening, could repair any damage during cross-examination or redirect.

The prosecution got off to a somewhat bumpy start the second morning when Keith Coffey, who towed Brenda's car to the family storage area after it was found, had to be reminded it was a Buick, not an Oldsmobile. Coffey was followed to the stand by Sergeant Malcom Deuser of the Jefferson County police K-9 unit, who briefly outlined how he and his bloodhound, A. J., unsuccessfully looked for evidence that Brenda Schaefer had walked away from her abandoned car, although such a trail might have been too old to discover.

The second day's main witness—his testimony would stretch into the third day of the trial—was Jim Wesley, now promoted to sergeant, a uniformed shift commander with the Jefferson County police. Even before Wesley took the stand, Ricketts approached the bench to be certain Wesley made no "inadvertent" mention of several subjects that would hurt Ignatow's case: abortions performed on Mary Ann Shore-Inlow; Ignatow's IRS conviction; the drug paraphernalia found in his home; Ignatow's drug overdose; or the insurance money for Brenda's jewelry.

"Can we have an admonition?" Ricketts asked Johnstone. "He's an 'anxious-to-please' with us, Judge. He has worked hand-in-glove with the commonwealth."

Johnstone refused.

"I am going to assume that Mr. Jasmin will not lead him in areas that he is not supposed to be in," Johnstone answered.

Wesley's testimony went on for hours, almost all of it regarding the course of the investigation and the people he had interviewed, although under the "hearsay" rules of the court, he could not testify as to what they had said. Jasmin needed Wesley's testimony. The prosecutor wanted to show the jury that police had worked very long and hard on the case, that it was not the sloppy effort Ricketts would portray. Jasmin would later bring in Jefferson County police detectives Dave Wood, William Hickerson, Jerry Bishop, and Lewis Sharber, each of whom went over case reports for the same reasons.

Wesley sat erect in his chair, speaking from notes he had culled from twenty-four separate reports. His testimony was interrupted to play the almost two-hour tape made with Ignatow in Ricketts's office a few days after Brenda Schaefer disappeared.

Jasmin zeroed in on the time sequence in Ignatow's initial

story, the many places he and Brenda had stopped the Saturday she disappeared. At first Ignatow had said he didn't get to Oxmoor shopping center until 8:00 to 9:00 P.M. He'd later recanted, saying he arrived at Oxmoor several hours earlier, putting his story more in line with those of people who said they saw him.

By early afternoon the jury already was getting restless, as were the attorneys. Ricketts approached the bench to note a spectator in a red coat was staring at him, distracting the jurors. Ricketts wanted Johnstone to order the jurors to pay more attention. Jasmin had also noticed the jury had grown restless; they were passing candy although Wesley had finished only four or five of his twenty-four reports.

". . . I hear some rumination over here from the jury," Jasmin said. "I wonder if we shouldn't give them a break."

Johnstone granted it. Ricketts returned after the break with another complaint. "Judge, as it happens, I walked out back with my water cup empty. I walked across the hallway putting water in my cup and I heard three of the ladies who had been sitting in the courtroom, all making remarks about me having stared at them.

"I did stare at them as you heard me say before we left the courtroom. That is to hopefully get them to cease what they are doing. . . . Again, I would ask for that admonition."

Johnstone promised to watch, adding, "Well, I suspect they are staring at you, Mr. Ricketts, because they don't like you."

Wesley continued, testifying to making hundreds of interviews and telephone calls. He was so thorough it would be midafternoon on Tuesday before Ricketts began his cross-examination of the officer, confessing he hardly knew where to begin:

"Was it Happy Chandler that used to say, 'I feel like a mosquito in a nudist colony'?"

Ricketts would always say he believed Ignatow to be innocent. He was determined to attack, question, and probe for any soft spots in Wesley's testimony; that was his job. Wesley still remembered Ricketts's implication that the county police might have been involved in the "death threat" letter mailed to Ignatow. Wesley could be professional and courteous, but Charlie Ricketts would not be the first name to come to his mind when Wesley put together a Saturday morning fishing trip.

Ricketts went over much the same turf covered by Jasmin, including the electronic surveillance of Ignatow by unmarked county police cars and an FBI airplane, the two veterans constantly jabbing at each other.

"You all were coordinating the efforts?" Ricketts asked Wesley.

"The Special Investigation Unit was coordinating with the FBI."

"And during that time what, if anything, did you learn about the habits of Mel Ignatow?"

"During that twenty-eight days, from the reports, I would say that he stayed home a lot."

"Well, it must have been terribly boring."

"Well, you would have to ask them. That is their job."

As the Tuesday afternoon testimony came to an end, Johnstone, as was his habit, kidded with one of the jurors, Debra McMillan:

"Ms. McMillan has her purse in her lap and is ready to go home. So I think we are going to take an evening recess."

The courtroom filled with laughter.

"I am bringing some cake in the morning and you are not getting a bite," McMillan fired back. "You are not getting anything."

Not only was the change of venue difficult on the Jefferson County contingent, it was expensive. The judge, his court reporter, the Jefferson County deputies, and the bailiffs needed to protect them and Ignatow were staying a few hundred yards north in the new Embassy Suites hotel, which hugged the Ohio River. Cincinnati's burgeoning skyline, with Riverfront Stadium in the foreground, was so close it seemed like an extension of Covington.

The prosecution team stayed a few blocks away at the older Quality Hotel, a fifteen-floor, mushroom-shaped tower with 236 rooms and a broad view of Covington and the Cincinnati riverfront. The government rates for the two varied from about $48 to $88, based on double occupancy.

Wednesday morning dawned cloudy and chilly, close to freezing, with fog on the river. Eager to hustle the trial along, Johnstone had Wesley back in the witness box a little after 8:30 A.M. Ricketts, with a night to think over his approach, spent about twenty minutes establishing that Wesley had been the lead investigator in the case for the Jefferson County police, that he helped coordinate with other police agencies, that he had access to all independent, county police and FBI laboratory reports.

Then he lowered the boom:

"In looking at all of those reports, Sergeant Wesley, and in being the chief investigative officer responsible for the prosecutive activity in this case, you have had an adequate opportunity to review all of your notes and materials that you and your department, and your allied departments who were feeding you information, all of those materials amassed, you have had a chance to review them, haven't you, sir?"

"Yes, sir."

"Do you know one piece of physical evidence which connects Melvin Henry Ignatow to the death of Brenda Sue Schaefer?"

"Physical evidence solely?"

"That's what I asked you."

"No, sir. I know of none. . . . Bearing in mind that most of the physical evidence was collected fifteen months after her death."

"Oh, we have to bear that in mind?" Ricketts asked.

"Yes, sir."

Ricketts repeatedly asked Wesley why he and the FBI agents had not returned to Oxmoor a second time to interview anyone who might have seen Mel Ignatow and Brenda Schaefer together the night of September 24, 1988. Specifically, Ricketts mentioned one possible witness, Brian Dilly, an employee of the Wild Pair shoe store, who told an FBI agent he'd seen a man resembling Ignatow in the store that Saturday night—without Brenda Schaefer.

Ricketts, eager to leave the impression of sloppy police work, went after Wesley as if Dilly were a vital witness, asking the officer why the Dilly lead wasn't pursued:

"... All I can say it was not done, probably because of ... what is considered a weak identification of a resemblance," Wesley answered.

"Does it say a weak identification in the 302?" Ricketts asked, referring to the FBI report involving Dilly.

"It says resemblance."

"It doesn't say anything about weak?"

"It says resemblance."

"It does not use the word 'weak'?"

"No, sir, I used the word 'weak.' "

Ricketts kept attacking:

"Sergeant, why wasn't that information that you were receiving from various sources being channeled back to Mel Ignatow so that he could assist you in remembering? ... Wouldn't that be normal operating procedure to want to verify those?"

Wesley had to pause, compose himself before answering.

"Mr. Ricketts ... in my twelve years of violent crimes I can never think of where I went to a possible suspect to ask for their assistance. ... We do not seek a suspect's assistance when we are investigating him in a case."

"Why not?" Ricketts asked.

Wesley looked at Ricketts, dumbfounded:

"Why not?"

"Yes, sir. Isn't that your best source ... ?"

Ricketts moved on to the photographs Mary Ann Shore-Inlow was supposed to have taken of the torture.

"Photos are keepsakes, aren't they generally, sir?" Ricketts asked.

"Yes."

"We take them of our children when they toddle. We take them of our daughters when they get married. And we take them of our sons when they graduate, and our daughters when they graduate. And sometimes we take them at other times that aren't so happy.

"Photographs help to reconstruct things. Photographs are things we use in advertising. There's lots of reasons for photographs. But typically, it's to freeze a moment in time."

Wesley was ready:

"I now understand the full meaning of photos. Yes, sir."

Ricketts moved on to more meaningful ground.

". . . With regard to these photographs, which were to have been taken of this despicable series of godless acts. If such a mind were to suggest that those photographs be taken, you would probably keep them, wouldn't you?"

"Yes, sir."

"And you found no such photographs at the home of Mr. Ignatow?"

"We found no such photographs after fifteen months, at the home of the defendant."

Near the end of his cross-examination, Ricketts asked the officer why Ignatow was arrested at 2:30 A.M., when there was nothing in the records to indicate he was going to run:

". . . After fifteen months you had to go and wake him up in the middle of the night to take him downtown? You couldn't wait until the body was found the next day, or sit someone in front of the house to make sure he didn't leave, if you were concerned, and let the poor man sleep."

Sandwiched in between Wesley's long testimony was that of Thomas Dodson, product-analysis manager for Smithers Scientific Service, the Ohio company that checked and tested the tire taken from Brenda Schaefer's car. Jasmin, Wesley, and the FBI had already seen the strangely contradictory test results; there were no road marks on the drywall nail—which had been pushed all the way to the bottom of a tire groove—yet the hole in the tire was elongated enough to indicate the nail had been stuck in a moving tire for some time. The outer, elongated hole was about $3/16$ of an inch long, the inner liner hole about $1/16$ of an inch.

"I can't make those pieces fit together," Dodson said. "If you wear the hole, you should wear the nail. . . . All we could do was address that from the perspective of the number of miles we would normally expect to see to give us a hole like we see here.''

"And that was," said Jasmin, finishing his thought, "several hundred to several thousand miles.''

"That's correct."

Dodson had one possible explanation; some other object besides the nail was shoved into the tire first, then the nail was placed in the hole. He said shoving a nail into a tire is easier than people believe; he was successful with a test-case tire just by pushing a nail with the back end of a screwdriver. He also verified that the tire had gone flat while Brenda Schaefer's car was sitting along Interstate 64, probably in less than forty minutes.

In cross-examination, Ricketts led Dodson into an elaborate discussion of hydroplaning, air molecules inside a hot tire, the weight of Brenda's car, and the ability to judge how much air is inside a radial tire by looking at it.

"Radial tires don't always readily admit from one standing outside of it, looking at it from a standing up person's view, give telltale clues as to what their pressure is, do they?"

"I'm sorry?" Dodson answered.

"What I'm saying is, you can't tell the pressure of a radial tire by looking at it?"

"Radial, or any other kind," Dodson answered.

One more question came from the jury box. Lowell Jarvis, juror number 6, wanted to know if a nail could be pushed to the bottom of a groove by driving the car.

"Yes, sir," Dodson answered. "For that to occur, however, you need to run the tire off some nonimproved surface such as grass . . . a piece of gravel is another way you could get the same result."

CHAPTER
24

Jurors quickly develop a sense of who should lead them, who seems the most qualified to help funnel a dozen shades of opinion into a single decision. With the jury in the Mel Ignatow case, it was David Whaley.

Whaley, sixty-two, had been principal of John W. Miles Elementary School for seventeen years, retiring in 1989. He was born and grew up on a small Northern Kentucky farm in Bath County, went to college because it was the right thing to do, served in the U.S. Army Medical Corps in Germany, married a Bath County girl, and became a teacher because a former principal had inspired him. Whaley welcomed jury duty. Two of his goals after retirement were to read the King James version of the Bible—which he did in about five months—and study the U.S. Constitution; the trial would be a living example.

Jury selection had begun alphabetically, then names were pulled at random. Whaley was there all day; he was the last person interviewed, but even then he felt good about his chances.

"I'd say I knew about one third of the people down there," he would say. "Kind of like any student does, you know where you stack up."

Whaley was a tall, lean man with the strong hands and worn face of a farmer; a little homely, but appealing. His years of being in charge of things, running meetings, dealing with parents gave him the unmistakable air of authority. He was everyone's pick to be foreman.

The Ignatow jury would require some authority. It was a varied collection of mostly good, decent, conscientious people—with a couple of potential problems.

One of them was Lonnie McMasters, twenty-five, a beefy, talkative, floppy-haired man who'd dropped out of school in ninth grade—eventually picking up a GED—and had worked a wide variety of jobs ever since: cook, laborer, long-distance truck driver, photo salesman, factory worker. Whatever McMasters lacked in formal education, he compensated for by being shrewd, observant, street smart. He was always able to dig up something to help support his family—a wife, who was a nurse, and three children.

"I had eight jobs in one year one time," McMasters would say. "I'm the type of person that if I don't like a job I won't work it. I don't believe a man should have to work a job that he doesn't like."

McMasters should never have been on the jury. Earlier that year he had filed suit against the city of Covington asking for more than $64,000 in damages after an automobile in which he and his wife were riding was rear-ended by a Covington police car on an emergency run—a suit to be settled out of court in McMasters's favor.

The standard form all jurors were asked to fill out asked very specific questions, including: Have you or any member of your family ever made claim for a personal injury lawsuit? Although the form came with a warning—No person shall willfully misrepresent a material fact on a juror qualification form—McMasters would say he forgot to check that blank. The form also asked if he or his family had ever been party to a lawsuit. The family had been through several involving unpaid bills.

McMasters would admit that in the years before the Ignatow trial he had been arrested several times for public intoxication and disorderly conduct, owed the IRS $4,000 to $5,000, and was very familiar with local police, on a first-name basis. He did mention a disorderly-conduct charge on his jury form, but those forms were very rarely checked for inaccuracies; McMasters's other charges were lost in the swirl of juror questioning.

A second potential problem was Debra McMillan, who sat on the front row next to McMasters. A half dozen other jurors would say McMillan was emotional, high-strung, constantly complaining she did not want to be on the jury; she wanted to be home helping her daughter prepare for a school Christmas play. During many of the jury breaks she would get on the telephone to call her employer, Cincinnati Bell, to talk with fellow employees.

Jurors would say that despite admonishments from the judge, McMillan repeatedly stated in the jury room she believed Ignatow to be guilty; she would bet on Jasmin as the winning attorney. If true, those comments could be grounds for a mistrial.

McMillan's closest companion during the trial would be Sheryl Cook, a pretty, brown-haired woman with a soft voice and sweet disposition. Cook, twenty-three, worked in the deli department in a chain grocery. Her first child, Nicholas, was born just six weeks before the trial; Cook was very surprised to be picked for the jury, and not especially happy to be there. Not one to argue, she just accepted it, and made very complex family arrangements to have someone watch her baby.

"I explained to them that I didn't have a baby-sitter," she would say. "The only thing they were really concerned about is they asked me if I was breast-feeding."

Cook and her husband shared a rented house with her mother. They were very close; Cook would discuss the trial with her mother almost every day. Cook and McMillan also discussed the trial during lunch breaks. Cook hadn't liked McMillan at first, regarding her as too loud and opinionated. Once they began to discuss families, their children, all barriers melted. Cook said they talked often about the case, grounds for dismissal from the jury, if not mistrial.

"I know we weren't supposed to talk about the trial," Cook would say. "We would go to a restaurant or for a walk. . . . I'd ask her, 'Debbie, what were they talking about? What did they say? Clear it up for me.'

"I would get most of it but there were a few things I didn't get. Debbie was pretty sharp."

Another force in the jury room would be Charles Cox, fifty-nine, who worked for the state of Kentucky twenty years, most of it negotiating property right-of-way. Cox didn't really want to be involved with a jury; he at first tried to get out by saying he had a conflict of interest, he worked for the state.

"Once I was on," he would say, "I did my duty. . . . We did our duty."

Cox was a stocky man with enough belly, wispy patches of white hair, and large-frame glasses to give him an owlish look. He would say that McMasters was not a leader in the jury, but he was a disruptive factor, especially early in the trial before things settled down, when he talked often of his brushes with the law. McMasters and McMillan would also exchange barbs—and hard candy—during court proceedings.

"Lonnie was the youngest in the group," Cox would say. "He spoke out a lot . . . in fact he irritated a lot of jurors because of his yapping."

Juror Pam Davis, thirty-five, was an assistant buyer for the Lazarus department-store chain. She worked in downtown Cincinnati, commuting from Kenton County. She was a small woman, five feet tall and 110 pounds, who quickly commanded respect because of her thoughtfulness and her ability to express herself. She would say that overall the jury got along fairly well.

"You just can't stack a jury with fourteen similar personalities," she would say. ". . . People who totally agree what's right or wrong."

Greg Laukhuff, thirty-nine, direct, straight-ahead, politically conservative, was a University of Cincinnati graduate with an M.A. in public administration from the University of Dayton. He was of medium height, with bright blue eyes that seemed almost centered in the middle of a round face. He was general manager of a very successful Hardee's restaurant. He had never before served on a jury, welcomed the opportunity.

Laukhuff remembered well the phrase he'd used during jury questioning that got him selected.

"I told them I could make a decision without emotion. When I said that, bing, I was selected."

Andrew Wilder, fifty-three, was a machinist, a short, curly-haired, pugnacious-looking man who had strong opinions; he needed his information to be precise, to the point.

"There were five Masons on that jury," he would say. "When we go into Masonry we're taught the four cardinal virtues: temperance, fortitude, prudence, and justice. And we went by those. If the evidence isn't there, then you've got to give the man justice."

Jerry Sebastian, forty-five, was a senior quality-control supervisor for Reliable Casting in Cincinnati. He'd lived in the same brick house twenty years, worked for the same company twenty-three years, had been married twenty-four years. A compact, good-looking man with neatly trimmed brown hair and modish aviator glasses, Sebastian would drive across the river and work three or four hours after jury duty to catch up.

"I feel that as an American citizen you have certain obligations, and one of them is jury duty," he would say. "That's part of citizenship."

Lowell Jarvis, the juror who asked questions from the jury box, also worked in the milling-machinery business. He was short, of medium build, and drove a red Ford Ranger pickup. Patricia Bruin, a Kenton County nurse, preferred to remain in the shadows, as did Sherry Grieme, a card-shop clerk who did stained-glass windows for her home and friends.

Two more jurors who were mostly quiet, but would find themselves placed in a more stressful situation than they ever could have imagined, or wanted, were Lois Reber and William Miller.

Reber, an IRS employee who was married to a Baptist minister, was often silent during the trial—and very reluctant to talk about it afterward. Miller, forty-three, the only black on the jury, was employed by the city of Covington as a heavy equipment operator in the Department of Public Works. He'd worked for the city twenty-one years, beginning in garbage collection.

He was a tall, slim, thoughtful man with a mustache and goatee and a tendency to wear a baseball cap turned backward. He'd never before been on a jury. Of all the jurors, Miller was the only one ever to mention love:

"I've had some bad times in my life, too. A lot of times you do things out of spite. Especially when you're getting ready to break up and you're in love with somebody. . . . Love is the thing."

Collectively the jurors would have little bad to say about Judge Martin Johnstone's handling of the trial, although several felt he might have done a little more to stem the sniping between Jasmin and Ricketts; perhaps the judge allowed a little too much as a way of preventing serious fireworks.

Jasmin's oratorical delivery did not bother them as much as the occasional little things he did to upstage Ricketts: tossing a pencil on the table in disgust, looking askance when disagreeing with the defense attorney. The jurors would all say race was never a factor, but such things are often unconscious, something Jasmin had lived with all his life.

Some jurors found Ricketts patronizing, insincere, much too wordy, but they did not seem to take it personally; they wrote it off to his courtroom style. The jurors tried to filter out the mannerisms of both attorneys; they might believe one did a better job than the other, but few found serious faults. They innately understood the combative nature of adversarial law.

All during the trial, the better jurors would watch the attorneys and Ignatow, trying to gauge him by the way he dressed, his body language, the expressions on his face. All the jurors were hoping Ignatow would eventually testify, the better to judge the full nature of the man.

At the same time, the Schaefer family, the judge, his court reporter, Sharon Klosterman, and the attorneys watched the jurors. The Schaefers, always six to ten strong in the spectators' area, thought the jurors much too inattentive, bored if not sleepy. Johnstone, who had seen hundreds of juries, saw little to distinguish this one from others.

Ricketts and Jasmin—and their assistants—would constantly analyze the jurors, try to read body language, their actions and interest. The lawyers and staff would gather at night over their respective dinners, or at breakfast, to discuss strategy, picking out jurors on whom to concentrate their arguments. They paid a lot of attention to certain people: Whaley, Cox, Laukhuff, Jarvis, Reber, Miller, and especially McMasters and McMillan.

Just before the jury filed in Thursday morning to hear the fourth day of testimony, Ricketts approached the bench to ask about having it sequestered—kept in motel rooms for the duration of the trial.

"Judge . . . It appears that each and every paper of the *Courier*, and some radio spots in the area that are delivered in the area, are mentioning this case, and these people are not walking around with Bell jars over their heads."

Johnstone, with Jasmin in his corner, ruled against it.

"Quite frankly I'm a little surprised that there hasn't been more media coverage," the judge said. "I haven't heard anything on any local coverage."

Thursday's testimony included Roger Coffey, the owner of the Coffey towing service, who testified he'd found the front bench seat in Brenda's Buick pushed all the way back to the number 5 position. Coffey testified he had two of his employees—a short woman and a tall man—verify that a short woman couldn't drive the car with the seat pushed back that far.

A somewhat conflicting FBI report filed by special agent Steve Shiner was also introduced Thursday in which Shiner said "the seat position was noted in number four of six positions. The car mirrors appeared to be adjusted to the number four position of the seat."

Shiner had gone to Coffey's garage on November 3, 1988, causing Ricketts to argue strongly that anyone could have moved the seat in the more than two months it had been at Coffey's, despite the owner's claims it was safely locked away.

Most of Thursday was taken with the testimony of Robert Stine, who had been on the Jefferson County police Evidence Technician Unit while the Brenda Schaefer case was being investigated, but had retired in June. Stine, away from the case for almost two years, retired for almost six months, was a very heavyset man, halting in his delivery, unable to supply information immediately. His give-and-take was slow, laborious; most of the jurors found his clinical review of the evidence poorly prepared, boring.

Stine began his long day by explaining to the jury the condition of Schaefer's car when found, the blood droppings found on the rear shelf and the broken rear window—which didn't match Schaefer's blood type—the several methods used to take fingerprints from the car. The car was fingerprinted right after it was found, and again on February 1, 1989, with no matches. No relevant fingerprints were found in the black Dodge that had been found near the Schaefer car, either.

Stine led the jury through the January 9, 1990, scene where Brenda Schaefer's body was found in the woods, and the autopsy afterward. None of the information was of much use to the jury until Stine said he did find some "ridge lines . . . fragments of a fingerprint" on the sticky side of the tape used to bind the black plastic bags that went around her body.

"And when you say fragments," Jasmin asked, "what are we talking about? Just little pieces, big pieces?"

"Little pieces. Very little pieces."

Stine said he tried to photograph the fragments, but was unable to, so he sent them to the FBI.

"They had only slightly better luck than you, is that correct, sir?" Ricketts asked Stine in cross.

"Yes."

"They did find a print on there that you didn't find?"

"I believe that is right."

"A print that was not the print of Melvin Henry Ignatow, is that correct, sir?"

"Well, you are saying a print. I am taking it for granted that you are saying a fragment of a print."

"Fragment, part, whole. Whatever you want to call it. They found no indicia that that was Melvin Henry Ignatow?"

"No, sir, they did not."

Ricketts asked Stine if the blood samples, the heel print found in the car, or the fragmented print found on the tape were ever compared to those of Butch Inlow.

"No, sir."

Ricketts noted that numerous animal hairs and fibers were recovered from Brenda Schaefer's car, logical since Brenda had three pets, a poodle named Jockey and two cats, Yoda and Boo.

"Did you know that Mary Ann Shore-Inlow had a dog?" he asked. "Two dogs . . ."

"No, sir, I didn't know she had any dogs."

Ricketts asked if any of the nails found in Ignatow's garage were sent to the Smithers lab.

"No, sir."

He asked Stine about the big Oster vibrator-massager taken from Ignatow's house.

"In your thirty years of police work, Detective Stine, you no doubt have come in contact with crimes of every description. Would that be a fair assessment?"

"Yes, sir."

"Some of which had to do with sexual activity?"

"Yes, sir."

"Some of which had to do with deviate sexual activity?"

"Yes, sir."

"Do you know what a sexual or dildo vibrator is?"

"Yes, sir."

"Is the vibrator that we have shown you as exhibit twenty-two . . . a dildo vibrator?"

"No, sir."

Ricketts noted both he and Stine were present when Ignatow provided head hair and pubic hair for a "sexual assault kit" by sitting on a large napkin and combing himself, and that due to a series of police problems, Ignatow had to be fingerprinted three separate times to get a workable set.

He asked if Stine had checked the fraternity paddle for any K-Y jelly or chloroform—even if it wasn't seized until almost sixteen months after Brenda Schaefer disappeared.

"No."

He asked about hair samples found in a brush in Brenda's car, Caucasian hair samples that had been dyed. Brenda dyed her hair; so did Mary Ann Shore. Ricketts was building to his big finish, another moment that would stick to the jurors' minds after sitting through hours of testimony.

". . . Indeed, there is no physical evidence in all of the evidence in all of the pages that you have, and all of the files, and all of the photos . . ."

Jasmin, knowing what was coming, objected to the question even before Ricketts finished it. The judge quickly overruled him, telling Ricketts to continue.

"In all of the files, in all of the photos, all of the materials, you have nothing to physically connect Mel Ignatow with the crime. Isn't that correct, Detective Stine?"

"I believe so, yes, sir."

Jasmin tried to turn the question around.

"*Sir*," he said to Stine. "In looking at all of the evidence in the case file does it exclude . . . the defendant Melvin Henry Ignatow?"

"No, sir, it does not."

Ricketts came right back:

"But it certainly does not implicate him, does it?"

"No, sir. It did not implicate him. I did not say that."

CHAPTER
25

Mike Schaefer sat nervously in the spectator area of the Covington courtroom on Friday morning, December 13, waiting for his brother Tom to testify. Mike sat in the same place every day, near the end of the second bench, looking directly at the witness stand, with Charlie Ricketts, Mel Ignatow, and Ricketts's associate seated well to his left.

Schaefer hoped Ignatow noticed him, at least sensed his presence. Schaefer wanted Ignatow to feel uncomfortable. Schaefer often caught Ignatow staring at the jury, or at him, playing mind games. Schaefer planned to stare down Ignatow if and when he testified. There were brief moments when Schaefer—as if in a daydream—thought about leaping across the wooden railing that separated them, confronting Ignatow, finding some physical release for the family's mental torment.

Mike Schaefer had also been through a lot in the years before the trial. He, too, was upset by the release of the Tinsley brothers, and worried about the condition of Tom's daughter, injured in the Florida accident. To add to that, on August 6, 1988, just six weeks before Brenda's disappearance, Mike and his wife of almost twenty years had angrily separated, beginning prolonged, sometimes bitter divorce proceedings. Mike had two young sons, John Nels, six, and Jesse, three. John—who was continuing the family name—had had his birthday on August 6.

Mike was a civilian editor of army training manuals and circulars at Fort Knox, about thirty miles southwest of Louisville, where he had worked for sixteen years. He was a good writer and editor, with a master's degree in communications and one in library science. In his early years he'd been program director of WFPL-FM, a public radio station in Louisville. He'd had seven or eight pieces on National Public Radio's *All Things Considered.*

"That was a great job," he would say. "I had a lot of fun. It just didn't pay anything. I couldn't survive on it."

Mike was a handsome, neat, smooth-faced man, his hair turning to silver. Where Tom preferred a beard and mustache, Mike was clean-shaven. Mike also could be more direct than Tom, who most often dealt with the media. Mike's sense of humor was dry, biting; he found it less difficult to be rude than Tom.

Mike had no early sense that Ignatow might have harmed his sister; indeed, the early police investigation left him with the impression her abduction might have been one of those terrible, random incidents. Mike never liked Ignatow and Ignatow knew it. Mike tolerated him because of Brenda, but Mike had not been as close to the situation as Tom, who lived with Brenda in the family home.

The brothers were often together during the trial. Tom couldn't sit with Mike until closing arguments, but the brothers would walk around in the park near the Quality Hotel where they were staying, even as late-December temperatures dropped into the mid-teens and the cold winds blew off the river. The Schaefers would lunch together at a cozy restaurant called Otch's, with its blue awnings, "soup and sandwich" specials written in grease pencil on a wallboard, and lights that dangled like white flowerpots over their tables. One night they went to the nearby Oldenburg Brewery, another to a sports bar across the interstate highway. There, they briefly bumped into Judge Johnstone, who wished them well.

No matter where they went, the brothers talked mostly of the trial, where it was headed. Outside of the bare bones of the case, the Schaefers had been given only a few investigative details; the trial was a continual learning experience for them, too.

Mike had been a married graduate student at the University of Kentucky when his brother Jack was murdered. A Lexington police officer came to his door and told him to call home; when he did, Pete Van Pelt had told him about Jack. It was Mike who combed Jack's hair while he lay in the casket; it needed shaping because the bullet wounds had distorted the shape of Jack's skull. Now, twenty years later, he was at the trial of the man accused of murdering his sister.

Family members and friends huddled together on the benches near Mike: a cousin, aunts, uncles, sisters, and many in-laws. Some stayed in Covington; others commuted every day from Louisville. For the most part they were confident the trial was going well, but felt the need to support each other.

The Schaefers—at least Tom and Mike—basically under-. stood the role of the defense attorney; he had a job to do, too. The public defenders in the trial of Jack's murderers had made it a point to buy the brothers a beer while the jury deliberated. But there was just something about the way Charlie Ricketts went about defending Ignatow that irritated them, embittered them. On Friday morning, as he began to watch Tom testify, Mike felt almost if he were trying to protect one of his children from Ricketts:

"You're sitting there and you want to jump up and say, 'Charlie, you son of a bitch, get away from him.' "

Tom Schaefer had left Jeffboat and was now a corrections officer at the Kentucky Correctional Psychiatric Center in LaGrange. Prohibited from watching the trial, he would hang out in the halls or in the grand jury room, sometimes peeking through the small window of the courtroom door. Tom was very nervous, eager to help Brenda. His testimony would help close out the first week of the trial. He wanted to give the jurors something to think about over the weekend.

He took his rosary with him to the witness stand; he had it every day of the trial. He began his testimony by listing what had happened the day Brenda disappeared; Ignatow's whimpering and programmed reaction, Ignatow's presence irritating his mother.

". . . He was just real skittery, real nervous, kind of babbling back and forth to members of the family," Schaefer said of Ignatow. "And I was trying to stay away from him, basically."

Schaefer took the jury through his recorded conversations with Ignatow at the KingFish restaurant; the night he walked out onto the Interstate 64 overpass; a night Ignatow came to the Schaefer home to sit in Brenda's bedroom and meditate—the FBI had secretly videotaped that episode, but the quality was poor.

"I could hear him running around the bedroom," Schaefer testified. "You could hear drawers slamming. . . . I wondered to myself . . . what is he doing? How come there is so much commotion up there?"

Jasmin and Schaefer worked to show Ignatow's interest in the insurance money from Brenda's jewelry. Jasmin showed the jury the list Ignatow had made of Brenda's assets, the one he'd given Tom at the KingFish restaurant. -

"Did your sister specifically tell you, sir," Jasmin asked, "that she had communicated that desire to break up or not marry the defendant?"

"Yes, sir."

Jasmin spent an hour questioning Schaefer; Ricketts's cross-examination would take four and a half hours. Knowing he had a real public-relations problem with the family, Ricketts tried to get off on the right foot:

"I hope that nothing that I say to you will be taken by you in any way other than completely respectful. And if, sir, you feel that I am not being respectful, please raise your hand or signal in some other way, and I will change my demeanor so that there won't be any miscalculation on my part in terms of how I convey, not only in what I say verbally, but in what I say nonverbally. Do we understand each other?''

"Yes, sir.''

A few minutes later Ricketts asked about Schaefer's referring to Ignatow as "the defendant'' rather than "Mel.''

"I know you have spoken with Mr. Jasmin but please feel free to call him Mel. You have for many years, haven't you, sir?''

"Yes, sir. I used to.''

"In fact you all were pretty good buddies, weren't you?''

"No, sir.''

Schaefer made it plain he thought Ignatow a strange person, hard to be around. Ricketts quickly sawed off the corners of the criticism:

"Are you trained in psychology to the degree level?''

"No, sir.''

"You probably have heard the old phrase, 'We are all a little crazy to a limited extent,' haven't you?''

The men argued about the accuracy of the appraised value of the missing jewelry. Brenda told Tom that Ignatow had it appraised too high even if the pro-rated settlement eventually went into his parents' estate. Ricketts would say the long list of Brenda's belongings that Ignatow had given Schaefer was only to help the family determine Brenda's worth. Most irritating, Ricketts continually referred to Brenda as Ignatow's "sweetheart.''

". . . My question to you, sir,'' Ricketts asked Tom at one point, "do you know whether Mel had ever lost a sweetheart before?''

"No. I do not know.''

"You therefore have never seen him under this kind of condition before, ever in your life before this occasion, had you, where a sweetheart had been lost?''

"No.''

It was on redirect—Jasmin's second chance to talk to Schaefer—that the prosecutor asked Schaefer if he ever drove his sister's car, and if he did, what seat position would he use?

"I would have to move the seat back," Schaefer answered. "I told her one day, 'I don't see how you can drive with that seat sitting all the way against the steering wheel.' And she said, 'That's the only way I can drive it.' "

Tom Schaefer felt relief when he was off the witness stand. He quickly found Linda Love, who would testify after him. He gave her a kiss, opened her hands, pressed his rosary into them. The rosary helped Love hold her composure. She, too, was nervous, afraid of saying the wrong thing when Ricketts cross-examined her. Assistant Commonwealth's Attorney Rob Hickey—taking over briefly for Jasmin—questioned her about a breakup with Ignatow.

"I called her on Friday . . . and asked her if she was going to go through with it," Love told the jury. "She said yes. . . ."

Love testified Brenda had been very unhappy for many months; she hated Ignatow.

"I would ask her, 'Why don't you just leave him and forget it?' She looked at me and said she was afraid. She said, 'You just don't understand. I am afraid.' "

Ricketts asked Love how long Brenda had used the word "hate" in connection with Mel. She answered ever since Ignatow had returned from his ill-fated Florida venture in early spring, 1988.

"What did she say she was afraid of?" Ricketts asked.

"Things that he was doing to her."

"And she stayed around for eight months?"

"Yes, sir."

"If someone was doing something to you for eight months that made you hate them . . . would you call the Abuse Hot Line? Would you get out of the relationship? Would you tell that person to pound pineapples?"

"I can't answer that. If I am afraid for my life I don't know what I would do."

By Monday, December 16, it had become obvious the trial was moving more slowly than everyone had hoped, so slowly that nine witnesses were sent home without testifying Friday. Christmas Eve was only eight days away, and Commonwealth's Attorney Ernie Jasmin still had a dozen more witnesses, including his major weapon, Mary Ann Shore-Inlow, and the thirteen-minute tape. Then Ricketts had to put on his defense. Time was beginning to worry the attorneys, the judge—and the jurors.

"We would ask," Ricketts told Johnstone, "for some kind of admonition to the jury so that if the commonwealth's portion of the proof lasts so long as to thereby give us just but a few days left thereafter to present our proof before Christmas break, or we would be into Christmas break by virtue of it, that they would not hold it against Mr. Ignatow."

"I will consider that," Johnstone answered.

Jasmin's list of Monday witnesses included all three of Brenda's co-workers at Dr. William Spalding's office: Marlene Ash, Joyce Smallwood, and Laverne Burnside. Ash testified that Brenda had told her the Monday before her disappearance that she was going to break up with Ignatow. Smallwood, who had since married a man named Basham, testified Brenda had told her on Wednesday she'd already broken up with Ignatow, and was returning his ring and fur coat that weekend.

"She told me she would meet him in a public place because she felt safer there."

Ricketts asked Smallwood why Brenda had continued to date Mel if she was so unhappy, even afraid.

"Did she ever or did you ever call any police authority or any spouse abuse center . . . ?"

"No, sir."

"Neither of you did; neither of you reported that fear?"

"I didn't. I'm not aware that she did."

"And yet she continued to date him?"

"She continued to date him."

Ricketts then put into evidence a card Brenda had mailed to Mel in Florida in March 1988:

I am sorry we have to go through all of this mental anguish. I don't think Mom is going to make it with me leaving and I really don't know how much more I can take. It almost seems that my world is falling apart instead of getting better. I am sorry if this is depressing but day-by-day this is not getting any better or easier. Well I better go because I am at work. Love you, Brenda.

Burnside testified about the office phone call from Ignatow when Brenda had slammed down the phone. Brenda had confided in Smallwood—and to a much lesser extent Ash and Burnside—many of the sexual details of her relationship with Ignatow: the chloroform, the pills, the bondage, the items found in Ignatow's house. Smallwood could not testify to any of that. What Brenda had told them could not be admitted in court because Brenda was not around to be cross-examined by Ricketts; the women's testimony would have been considered hearsay.

There are certain cases where, through a "dead man's rule," such testimony could be allowed, but Johnstone did not believe it applied in this case. Nor, of course, did Ricketts. Smallwood, who considered herself Brenda's best friend, didn't understand the rules of law; she was terribly frustrated because she couldn't say more.

"It just never seemed fair," she would say.

The most enthusiastic, effusive witness Monday afternoon was Tom Tilford, Brenda's hair stylist. She had been going to him since May 1988, and had an appointment with him at 9:00 A.M. on the day she disappeared. Tilford considered Brenda a friend and confidante; he vividly remembered Brenda's feelings toward Ignatow that morning:

"She said to me: 'If I never see that asshole again it will be too soon.' "

Tilford had also told investigators from Ricketts's office that Brenda felt overworked, hated her job, and was probably influenced by money. Ricketts sent Tilford a confirming letter after that interview; Tilford, having second thoughts about some of his statements, refused to sign and return it.

"There were some things that I said in his letter that needed to be like readdressed and reissued and redone and everything," he told the jury.

Monday's final witness was Robert Longshore, Jr., the man who had served Mel Ignatow at Skyline Chili in the early hours of September 25. Longshore said Ignatow ordered two or three Coney dogs and a soft drink. He remembered Ignatow as being talkative; there seemed to be some mixup on the order.

"I think there was twenty cents or a bunch of pennies laying on the counter," Longshore said, "and he commented on how good a tip that was I received."

By Monday afternoon the jury was getting bored, eager to see Mary Ann Shore-Inlow, who was to testify Tuesday morning. The jurors had a good sense of the commonwealth's case, but much of it seemed circumstantial; Shore-Inlow was the key. Meanwhile, Johnstone had something to tell them before they went home:

"Ladies and gentlemen of the jury, the good news is that we are going to be leaving early today because we got through all the witnesses. And now it appears . . . that the commonwealth's case will be finished tomorrow.

"The bad news is I don't know how long the defense will take. But just to put you on notice early, I don't want to be here Christmas Eve, or Christmas, any more than you all want to be here. And I may be talking to you all about a Saturday session depending on how tomorrow goes."

The judge told the jurors he wanted to get the case finished that week, perhaps by having lunch ordered in and by sticking in extra time where possible. Before the jury left, juror Debra McMillan asked, "How long are you talking about on Saturday? Just roughly what time frames?"

"I haven't thought about it. . . . I am willing to let you all get together tomorrow and talk about what would be the most convenient. . . . We will bend our schedules because we are going to have to be here anyway."

Lowell Jarvis also had a question.

"If it gets into next week we wouldn't be here on Christmas Day or Christmas Eve?"

"No," Johnstone answered. "I haven't even told the lawyers this, but my anticipated schedule if this case is not fin-

ished by Monday is to adjourn this trial and start back
January second. Or if the jury decides they would rather
come in after Christmas and finish it up at that time.''

Jarvis said it was his understanding that once a jury begins
to deliberate, it can't stop until a verdict is reached.

''That's right,'' said the judge.

''Well, we don't want to go in there before Christmas.''

CHAPTER
26

The long-awaited appearance of Mary Ann Shore-Inlow on Tuesday, December 17, added a layer of tension to the courtroom, a sense the trial was moving to some sort of needed climax. The jury was ready; early in the week David Whaley, Andrew Wilder, and Greg Laukhuff had decided during a noon walk that there were too many ad-lib comments coming from the jury box, a little too much talk from some of the jurors.

"Nobody was boss," Whaley would say. "We just brought it up and everybody said that's right, we probably are talking too much."

The situation with Debra McMillan had grown more serious; jurors said she had continued to declare Ignatow guilty. It became so bad that during the second week of the trial Lonnie McMasters went to Judge Martin Johnstone and told him something had to be done because McMillan was driving him crazy; McMasters wanted off the jury, or he wanted McMillan off.

"She really made me mad," McMasters would say. "She was sitting in there saying, 'I have to be home for Christmas. I have to fix my little girl's hair for the Christmas play for church and I'm not going to be here.'

"This woman really got to me. She was betting Jasmin would win. She had the guy convicted. You might as well hang him. You might as well just go out and lynch him."

Johnstone had been watching McMillan—had heard how emotional she could be—but he delayed any decision. He had two things to deal with before he could even begin the Tuesday session. One, Charlie Ricketts was frantically trying to have Sue McKinney, the Flaherty's waitress, brought to court; McKinney had told his investigators she would not come although Johnstone had ordered her to appear.

The second was Barbara McGee, Mel Ignatow's old girl-friend, the woman to whom he had taken a dildo, K-Y jelly, and condoms after Brenda Schaefer had disappeared. It was only in the second week of the trial that Jefferson County police learned of McGee's relationship with Ignatow, partly through a call to Crime Stoppers. McGee may have been a vital prosecution witness, a more direct link to the evidence against Ignatow.

At Jasmin's request, McGee would go to Cincinnati late in the trial's second week and wait to testify, but Johnstone considered it too late to let her on the stand. Ricketts had a right to know who the witnesses against him would be; Johnstone didn't believe he could allow this caliber of a surprise witness at this late stage of an already contentious, much-delayed trial. When McGee was discussed at the bench early Tuesday morning, Ricketts said he had heard that McGee wouldn't be called until the following Monday or Tuesday, Christmas Eve.

Johnstone strongly disagreed:

"Let me just say that if anybody gave that type of information it is pretty erroneous," he told Ricketts. "And people that don't have their witnesses here when this case gets to the shank, they are not going to have witnesses."

Ironically, McGee believed that at one point Ricketts considered having her testify as a character witness for Ignatow, which might have given Jasmin an opportunity to question her.

Two other prosecution witnesses were to testify Tuesday

morning before Shore-Inlow. The first was Louise Petrie, who had lived next door to Shore-Inlow on Poplar Level Road. Her daughter, Jeanetta Spoelker, owned the house Shore-Inlow rented.

Petrie, elderly, opinionated, with a country edge, rambled at times. She'd lived in her rectangular brick Poplar Level house more than forty years. She had a big window in the back of her kitchen that offered a broad view of Shore-Inlow's yard and the woods behind. Petrie told the jury that Ignatow and Shore-Inlow walked her dog in the woods, and that Mary Ann would use her phone because she didn't have one. Ignatow would call Shore-Inlow at Petrie's home several times a day; the one Petrie remembered most was the call Mary Ann received after Ignatow returned from Florida in the spring of 1988, reestablishing contact.

"The first time he called her she cried and went on. I thought she was going to die. I thought someone was going to die in the family. . . . She was so happy she was just screaming."

Ricketts asked Petrie several questions about her neighbor, providing another moment that stuck in the jurors' minds.

"Now you describe Mary Ann as being very physically strong. Do you recall that?"

"She is very strong."

"Do you recall saying that Mary Ann could have, quote, 'killed Mel in a lick,' close quote?"

"I imagine she could. I tell you. . . . We had concrete put down in the ground. . . . My father had it put down for a grape arbor and we were going to get somebody to come and take it all up. And she pulled that thing right out of the ground and you wouldn't believe it. It had been there for thirty-five years."

"And Mary Ann did this all by herself?"

"She sure did. She was like a bull."

Ricketts got in several more damaging blows after that, quick hits to which Jasmin instantly objected, but damage was done.

"Ms. Petrie, did you state to our law clerks that you were afraid of Mary Ann?" Ricketts asked.

"Yes, I was."

Ricketts then moved Petrie into the area of Shore-Inlow's character, integrity.

". . . Now among those who know her in the community, is she known to be truthful?"

"No."

"Your Honor, I was getting ready to object . . ." Jasmin began.

"I said, 'No,' " Petrie finished.

"Thank you . . ." said Ricketts, "And is this a generally held opinion?"

"Your *Honor*?" pleaded Jasmin.

"Sustained. Sustained," Johnstone said. "Ms. Petrie, please don't answer any more questions. Mr. Ricketts, don't ask any more."

Petrie was briefly followed on the witness stand by hairdresser Lauren Lechleiter, Shore-Inlow's old friend, who testified that Shore-Inlow would watch Ignatow's house, spying on him when he dated other women.

"She would follow him?" Ricketts asked.

"Right."

So when Mary Ann Shore-Inlow—the key to the entire trial—took the stand near midmorning she was following two prosecution witnesses who had helped characterize her as a liar and a jealous woman strong enough to cause bodily harm. Her effectiveness was further damaged by her appearance, which surprised several jurors.

". . . We kept hearing from the attorneys about this mystery witness and I think we expected some beautiful foreign woman," Charles Cox would say, "but this is a big, strong woman. . . . Her next-door neighbor had already said she was so strong that she pulled up a concrete pillar out of the front yard."

Shore-Inlow had gained a lot of weight. Her dyed-blond hair was severely pulled back into a short ponytail; her bangs were puffed up over her forehead. Her plump face was accentuated with too much rouge, her blue eyes blinking owl-like behind large-framed tinted glasses. She was wearing a gray jacket, a white blouse with a modest V neck, and a short black skirt. She sat back in her elevated witness chair, right leg often crossed over the left, exposing much of her thighs to the jury.

Greg Laukhuff, conservative by nature, was appalled: "She wasn't dressed properly. Maybe her posture, the way she presented herself on the stand in terms of length of skirt . . ."

Streetwise Lonnie McMasters would say it more brutally: "She was dressed like some of the girls you would see in downtown Covington on Friday or Saturday night. She came across like she really didn't give a shit."

The murder trial—especially Shore-Inlow's testimony—was covered heavily by the Louisville television stations and the *Courier-Journal*; photographers for all of them were at the back of the room directly facing Shore-Inlow's crossed legs. Their pictures and videotape would cause a sensation in Louisville, where it had mostly been a foregone conclusion Ignatow would be found guilty.

Jack Vittitow, Shore-Inlow's lawyer, believed that Shore-Inlow thought she was nicely dressed. Jasmin, whose office was ultimately held responsible for the appearance and preparation of his key witness, would say there was very little he could have done about Shore-Inlow's looks, actions, or demeanor; witnesses who are coached often speak as if they were, raising jury suspicion.

"Mary Ann was Mary Ann," he said, "though sometimes I wished that Mary Ann could have been equivalent to Ms. Percival Pureheart."

Even before questioning began, Jasmin approached Johnstone to tell him something that might have affected Shore-Inlow's demeanor:

"Your Honor, I have been asked to bring to the court's attention as delicately as I can that this is Ms. Shore-Inlow's time of the month and she's having some difficulty. And there might be some frequency with which she may have to request to be allowed to go to the ladies' room.''

Shore-Inlow testified about her early relationship with Ignatow. She said she occasionally saw him after they broke up about 1984, even while he was dating Brenda Schaefer. She was overjoyed when he called her after returning from Florida in the spring of 1988; he seemed to need her again. Her testimony was halting; Jasmin almost had to badger his own witness. It took several minutes for Shore-Inlow to explain how Ignatow had come to her house on a Saturday in mid-August to dig a hole in the woods behind her home, a hole to be used as part of a sex therapy class for Brenda Schaefer. Shore-Inlow went with him.

''. . . He started digging the hole and I think there was some mention he was going to bury her in there,'' Shore-Inlow told the jurors. ''I told him I didn't want any part of that. . . . He said don't worry about it. We were just going to scare her.''

''Did you ask him what he meant by scaring her?'' Jasmin asked.

''He said that she was a very timid person and if you raised your voice you could scare her; like a timid little mouse.''

Shore-Inlow said Ignatow broke his shovel while digging the hole, threw the two pieces back into the woods, then went and bought a new one to finish the job, a shorter shovel with a red handle and a flat blade. She quickly added more detail:

Ignatow had wanted to have his sex-therapy class the weekend of September 15, but she couldn't; she had promised to take the Spoelker children to Mammoth Cave.

Early on Friday evening, September 23, Ignatow returned to Shore-Inlow's house with a brown paper sack containing black plastic garbage bags, duct tape, and clothesline rope cut to exact lengths with its ends meticulously taped and an Olympus 35mm camera and several rolls of color film.

He also brought a white, battery-powdered dildo, K-Y jelly, work gloves, a wooden fraternity paddle, and a wide-mouth, dark-brown bottle of chloroform. He placed the bag behind the bedroom door of her home. Ignatow had taken the items to Shore-Inlow's in his mother's car; he didn't want his Corvette recognized.

"He seemed to be in a hurry," Shore-Inlow said. "I had to get back to the baby-sitting. I had someone else watching the kids and I couldn't be gone very long."

The morning of September 24, Shore-Inlow went to Jeanetta Spoelker's home. The women had become friends; Shore-Inlow did odd jobs around Spoelker's house, cut their huge lawn with a hand-pushed mower for $15, ingratiated herself with Spoelker, who was a devoutly religious woman.

"Mary Ann was very sweet to me," Spoelker would say. "She never did curse in front of me."

Shore-Inlow liked to drive Spoelker's car, a dark blue 1986 Thunderbird. Spoelker hated to drive expressways, so Shore-Inlow would chauffeur. The two women went to B&B Lamps in eastern Jefferson County early Saturday afternoon. They bought two lamps but skipped their usual lunch, which Spoelker would always buy.

"Mary Ann said she was sick," Spoelker would explain. "She did seem nervous, edgy, very fidgety."

Spoelker would often play Christian tapes on her deluxe Thunderbird stereo system as the women traveled together.

"I like to listen to them," Spoelker would say. "I thought that would go to help Mary Ann as a Christian. She said she would become a Christian as she became nearer to death. . . ."

Shore-Inlow got home to Poplar Level Road about 5:00 P.M. As ordered by Ignatow, she parked her 1974 Vega on the grass behind her house, leaving room in her garage for another car.

Over the course of the trial, the jurors would hear all the terrible details of what happened that night in 1988. At the same time Mary Ann Shore-Inlow waited at home, Brenda Schaefer prepared for what was to be her last evening out. As was her custom, she had gotten her hair done that Saturday morning. Early that afternoon, before going to Ignatow's house, she had stopped by her condominium, which her brothers and father had been painting for her.

"Can I help?" she asked them.

Mike Schaefer noticed Brenda seemed preoccupied. She wasn't dressed to paint.

"No, thanks," he said. "We'll have it wrapped up pretty soon."

Brenda picked up Ignatow at his home between 3:30 and 4:00 P.M. She was wearing white, woven-leather shoes, nylon stockings, and Oscar de la Renta blue jeans, size 8. Her white knit sweater, an R. G. Arnold, size medium, was covered by a yellow Avon windbreaker with drawstrings at the hip. Her undergarments were white, lacy panties, size 6, and a white bra with lace top, size 32-C.

They went to the Gold Star Chili at Hike's Point; then Ignatow told her he had a friend who would like to see her jewelry. It was almost 6:00 P.M., the sky a drizzly gray, when she pulled her Buick into a ramshackle garage behind the small white house on Poplar Level Road. Investigators would later be told that Shore-Inlow and Ignatow had "scream-tested" the house, Shore-Inlow screaming inside while Ignatow stood near the busy road in front to determine if she could be heard.

Shore-Inlow's testimony continued. Her voice very low key, matter-of-fact, she began describing in detail the rest of the events of the night Brenda Schaefer died.

When Brenda and Ignatow came through the front door, Shore-Inlow locked the door behind them; the back door already was locked. As Ignatow had ordered, Brenda Schaefer was trapped; she had no way to run. She stepped into a living room painted off-white on three walls, its fourth covered in cheap gray wallpaper. The hardwood floor was bare, the drapes pulled across the front picture window, the room dim. Two couches covered in floral print faced each other across the narrow room, the space between them narrowed by a brown, worn-looking coffee table, its top divided into rectangular glass sections. Brenda sat in the middle of the largest couch, Ignatow on one side, Shore-Inlow on the other.

Brenda had never met Shore-Inlow; she was surprised when she was introduced to her.

"After all the stuff you said about Mary Ann?" she said to Ignatow. "Why did you bring me here?"

"You're here for a sex-therapy class," he told her. "This will get you into better sex."

Startled, Brenda quickly got up.

"No, I want to go home."

Ignatow grabbed Brenda's arm.

"You are *not* leaving!"

A piece of Brenda's bracelet fell off. She sat on the couch, frightened. She argued with Ignatow, pleaded with him.

"As soon as you do this, you can go home," Ignatow told her.

Ignatow's first concern was Brenda's jewelry; he didn't want it damaged. He had her remove it, putting each piece aside; watch, necklace, bracelet, engagement ring. He ordered Brenda to stand against a wall near the front door, then slowly remove her clothing: sweater, bra, jeans, panties. Ignatow had a piece of yellow paper in his hand, a checklist of exactly what he wanted to do in the order he wanted to do it. Ignatow began taking pictures with a 35mm camera Brenda had given him as a Christmas present. He had her pause at each step, posing her, checking her position against his list.

"What are you going to do?" Brenda asked.

"Show these to your high, influential attorneys and people you know."

Ignatow's camera was focused on a frightened woman, her face contorted in fear and disgust, her eyes filled with dread and hopelessness. When she had stripped to her panties, Ignatow had her pull them up high on her waist, as if wearing a thong bathing suit. Ignatow insisted Brenda clasp her hands behind her head, elbows out; the classic image of a prisoner of war, total submission.

"Get this over with," Brenda told Ignatow. "I want to go home."

Shore-Inlow testified that Ignatow forced Brenda to lie

facedown across the top of the coffee table, her knees on the floor. Using the precisely cut and taped pieces of rope, Ignatow tied Brenda's hands to the legs of the table, the glass top protected with a white towel. He removed all his clothing except his dark socks. His body was thin, with distinctive hair on his back, a scattering of moles on his body, especially his legs. He wore his Ebel "Discovery" watch: expensive, Swiss-made, with a stainless-steel band and 18-karat-gold bezel, a watch worn by boaters and underwater divers.

He got down on his knees behind Brenda—all his weight on the floor—and licked at her anus. He spread K-Y jelly on her, penetrated her with his penis, then the vibrator. Shore-Inlow watched from the hallway, saying nothing. As Ignatow knelt on the floor behind Brenda, he ordered Shore-Inlow to take pictures, to focus on Brenda's face.

"Just be sure my face isn't in any of the pictures," Ignatow told her.

Brenda was tied to the coffee table almost forty-five minutes while Ignatow raped her anally, used a vibrator on her, took close-up pictures of genitals. Ignatow untied her, let her use the tiny bathroom just off the bedroom. Following orders, Shore-Inlow followed her into the bathroom, wiped tears from Brenda's eyes with Kleenex while she sat. The woman did not speak.

Brenda was led into the bedroom at the right front corner of the house. The room, ten feet square, was barely big enough for a queen-size bed, two dressers, and two end tables. Brenda sat on the edge of the bed, which had side rails and a headboard. As Shore-Inlow watched, Ignatow licked at Brenda's vagina, then ordered her to perform fellatio on him.

"I didn't take pictures of that," Shore-Inlow told the jurors.

The jurors were as interested in Shore-Inlow as they were in her story. She was telling a terrible tale, but her words were rote, matter-of-fact, her body language indifferent; she continually slouched back a little in her chair, legs crossed; her head was slightly cocked, resting against her right fist.

She looked tough, hardened, mostly unaffected by what she was saying; she'd told her story many times in recent years; she seemed weary of it, numb to its horror. She talked as if she, too, were a victim of Ignatow, but displayed little vulnerability. She evoked some sympathy, but what she needed to sell was credibility.

"He kept making remarks to Brenda," Shore-Inlow testified. "He said Brenda was taking this better than she ever had before."

Shore-Inlow had told police in one confession that once Ignatow got Schaefer into the bedroom he forced her to lie on her back. He tied her arms to bed rails, one on each side. Ignatow spread her legs, pulled them back over her head, then tied them tightly to the bed rails, her thighs angled up in the air, the rope cutting into her skin. Ignatow raped her, then took more close-up photographs.

Shore-Inlow said Ignatow was focused, methodical, continually checking his list, which lay on the bed next to Brenda. His sexual excitement seemed heightened by being in total control. Ignatow turned Brenda onto her stomach, again tying her, then pushed a pillow under her stomach. He spread K-Y jelly across her anus, shoved a finger inside, then put it under his nose.

"It smells good," Shore-Inlow would remember Ignatow saying, ordering her to do the same thing.

"Go on. You'll enjoy it."

Shore-Inlow complied. "He told me to do it and I was afraid of him."

". . . Then what happened?" Jasmin asked.

"Then he put his finger in her. He just put it in there and kept it in there and said it smelled good, and stuff like that."

Shore-Inlow continued:

Ignatow asked her to slap Brenda on the buttocks with the fraternity paddle. Then Ignatow took the paddle, began striking Brenda. She screamed, her cries unanswered.

Shore-Inlow fled to the kitchen, not wanting to see more, but afraid to run to get help; she could easily have unlocked the back door. Ignatow shouted at her to get a washcloth, bring it back, wipe Brenda's face. When Shore-Inlow returned, Brenda was on her back, stretched out, still tied to the bed. Shore-Inlow leaned over, wiping away her tears.

Brenda was sobbing, defeated. Her pale-white skin was bruised, jagged-red rope burns along her wrists, ankles, and feet. Her life was almost over; she may have sensed that, perhaps welcomed it.

Shore-Inlow left the room, returning to the kitchen for a glass of water. She could hear voices in the bedroom, voices growing lower, more distant. She could not see what happened next. Ignatow did not want Brenda Schaefer to leave the house alive; that was part of his plan. He opened the wide-mouth jar of chloroform, a chemical once used as an anesthetic, and poured some into a handkerchief. He pressed it against Brenda's mouth and nose, the chloroform depriving her of oxygen, sending her brain into narcosis, until he couldn't feel a pulse. Uncertain if she was dead, he placed a rope around her neck, prepared to choke her.

He walked into the kitchen, looking at Shore-Inlow.

"Are you okay?"

"No."

He went back into the bedroom. Shore-Inlow followed him. Brenda was stretched out on her back on the bed, hands tied. Brenda's brown eyes were pale, still open.

"She didn't suffer," Ignatow said. "She went to sleep just like you'd be going to sleep."

Throughout the trial Ignatow had constantly fidgeted with his tie, adjusting the knot. Now he sat almost motionless at his table, head slightly bowed, listening intently to Shore-Inlow.

"What happened next?" Jasmin asked Shore-Inlow.

"I went back in the bedroom. . . ." Shore-Inlow said.

"And what, if anything, did you see?" Jasmin asked.

"There was a rope around her neck . . . and the rope . . . was like hanging over the bedpost. You understand? A piece of it. But . . . I could see marks on her neck."

Shore-Inlow ran back to the kitchen, shaking and upset.

"Then what happened?" Jasmin asked.

"He came back out and he started shaking me and he said, 'Pull yourself together.' And he maybe cried just a little bit and then that was it."

"What do you mean, 'That was it'?"

"He didn't seem like he was too upset about it."

Shore-Inlow said that Ignatow bent Brenda's body into a tight fetal position, her head nearly pressed between her knees, her feet drawn up to her buttocks. He carefully tied the body into a tight package, wrapping the rope several times around ankles, wrists, and neck. He pushed the body into garbage bags. Shore-Inlow held the body, preventing it from rolling.

"I don't know how many bags he put on her," Shore-Inlow testified. "Then he proceeded to take tape and started wrapping it around the body, tearing it with his teeth."

Shore-Inlow and Ignatow carried the body to the kitchen, placing it on the counter, the body fitting neatly in the space beneath the blue cupboards. Shore-Inlow unlocked the back door, which led to an unheated back room with a rough-plaster ceiling and dirty blue rug. They lifted the body off the counter, carried it into the back room, made a tight left turn, and went down three steps into a fenced-in backyard.

"Why did you help pick her up?" Jasmin asked.

"Because he told me to and I was afraid. I didn't want to be in there, too."

Ignatow carried a flashlight and the red-handled shovel, along with trying to hold the body. A light rain was falling. They they had to hurry because of the yard light in Louise Petrie's side yard.

"I was carrying one side and he was carrying the other," Shore-Inlow testified. "He kept getting mad because I had to keep setting it down."

They carried the body into the woods, lifted up the metal that had been protecting the hole, and placed Brenda Schaefer at the bottom, with her clothing in another bag beside the body. Shore-Inlow sat on a nearby fallen log in the rain and watched Ignatow.

". . . He covered her all up," she said. "He covered her up completely."

They went back into her house, where Ignatow changed clothes. He ordered her to dump the dirty clothes in the garbage can near Louise Petrie's house. Ignatow placed the dildo, brown bottle, camera, tape, rope, and whatever items he had left into a bag, went outside, and put them into the trunk of Shore-Inlow's Vega, along with the shovel. Although Ignatow had previously led her to believe she would get some of it, Shore-Inlow said she did not know what happened to the jewelry—or Brenda's purse.

"He had that stuff. I don't know where he took it," she testified.

Shore-Inlow continued:

Before leaving her yard, Ignatow, working in the dim glow of the yard light, stooped behind the right rear passenger tire of Brenda Schaefer's car, sliced a small hole with a paring knife, then pushed in a nail. He put on brown gloves, got into the car, and told Shore-Inlow, "Follow me and I will tell you what to do."

"So he pulled out on Poplar Level," she said. "I was having trouble starting my car. He was sitting right there waiting for me to pull out."

She followed Ignatow about two miles to the Watterson Expressway, a belt road around Louisville. She drove about eight miles east toward Interstate 64, then turned west on I-64 for about a mile, pulling off on the north side of the road just past Breckenridge Lane. Shore-Inlow said she pulled behind Schaefer's parked car, killed her car lights, and watched Ignatow get out of Brenda's car.

"He still had his gloves on," Shore-Inlow said. "He went back to the rear tire that he had put the nail in and let the air out of the tire. . . . He got into my car after he did that."

Shore-Inlow was so turned around that Ignatow had to give her directions to his house. They arrived there about 11:30 P.M.

"He told me to back up into the driveway. He got out of the car; took all the stuff out of the trunk. He told me he would contact me later; not to contact him."

CHAPTER
27

Mel Ignatow did not testify in his own defense. It was a disappointment to the jurors—and to Ernie Jasmin, Rob Hickey, and Jim Wesley—but made legal sense to the defendant and his attorney, Charlie Ricketts.

Ignatow was cocksure of his persuasive abilities, but his testimony could have created problems. It could have resulted in some mention of Ignatow's IRS felony conviction. Ignatow's tax problem would eventually come up obliquely, but never to the point where Jasmin could make a federal case of it.

Ignatow may also have feared the prosecutorial wrath of Jasmin, who could have sliced him up with questions about why Ignatow's story of what happened on September 24, 1988, did not fully agree with any of the stories of his own defense eyewitnesses. Ignatow also knew that the jury would be instructed to disregard the fact he did not testify; the entire burden of proof rested with the prosecution.

Ricketts told a Louisville television station Ignatow did not have to testify because his grand jury interview and lengthy interview with police were put into the trial record.

"There is no need to put him on the stand," Ricketts said.

Certainly after Mary Ann Shore-Inlow's dismal performance, the jury wanted to have a shot at hearing Ignatow. Sherry Grieme thought Shore-Inlow looked angry, like a jilted lover. Jerry Sebastian couldn't believe she would ever be afraid of anyone. William Miller had believed her story. Miller came from the streets; he was less concerned with her appearance than with what she was saying. Juror Sheryl Cook also believed Shore-Inlow's story, with a twist of her own:

"Mel buried her alive," Cook thought as she listened to the testimony. "He knocked her out and tied her up and put her in that plastic bag. I think he buried her alive and she suffocated in her grave."

Jim Wesley, who had worked five murder trials with Jasmin before this one, had a bad feeling about the jury; it just wouldn't have the same interest in a Louisville murder as in a Kenton County murder, might have difficulty convicting a man so close to Christmas. Wesley could see that Ricketts had been working hard on jurors David Whaley and Charles Cox. Wesley didn't trust Lonnie McMasters. He didn't want him on the jury, but Jasmin had liked him; McMasters seemed to have a gung-ho attitude: Get the truth and burn somebody.

The person who best understood Shore-Inlow's matter-of-fact testimony was Yulee Schafer, the victim's advocate for the Jefferson County Commonwealth Attorney's office. Schafer had long worked with the Schaefer family, but in previous cases had worked with spouse-abuse victims; she understood their fear of authority. During one break in her long testimony, Shore-Inlow told Schafer she was very emotional, nervous but feared to show it.

"I'm afraid I'm going to start crying," she told Schafer.

"Mary Ann, it's okay to cry. Just try not to break down."

"I can't cry. The judge will get mad at me if I cry."

Schafer was in a strange position. She knew tears would show a side of Shore-Inlow the jury needed to see; emotion, remorse, guilt. But Schafer couldn't ask her to cry, and Shore-Inlow couldn't let herself go; she'd been afraid of authority too long.

"Mary Ann, the judge won't get mad," Schafer told her.
"Yes, he will."

In his cross-examination of Shore-Inlow, Charlie Ricketts
worked hard to establish Shore-Inlow's long relationship
with Butch Inlow. Late in the day, as the jury again began
to wear down, Ricketts suddenly began bombarding Shore-
Inlow with questions about Ignatow's safe—a safe that had
never before been mentioned in direct connection with
Shore-Inlow. Jasmin didn't challenge it.

"Do you recall, Ms. Shore-Inlow," Ricketts said, "that
you called Mel and asked to borrow that safe?"

"No."

"That call was sometime in advance of, or before, August
of 1988?"

"No. I have never called to use that safe."

Ricketts kept pushing; he couldn't use the word "safe"
enough.

"Do you also remember, Ms. Inlow, that when you called,
Mel brought that safe to you and the two of you off-loaded
it at 4921 Poplar Level Road?"

Shore seemed genuinely perplexed by the questions. She
became as animated as she had been all afternoon.

"I have never seen that safe in my house; only in his
house or his father's house."

Ricketts suddenly brought Butch Inlow into the equation.

"Do you recall, Ms. Shore-Inlow, calling upon Mr. Ignatow and saying to him, 'Butch and I have taken care of it.
We don't need it anymore. Come get it'?"

"No. I never said no such thing."

"Do you recall telling Mr. Ignatow, Ms. Shore-Inlow, that
you wanted to bury something in the backyard and needed
a safe?"

"No."

Ricketts made sure the jury knew that Shore-Inlow had
earlier lied to a grand jury, that she had worked a deal with
Jasmin's office to testify in exchange for a tampering-with-
evidence charge—and a one-to-five year prison term.

"You jumped at the chance to take that, didn't you?" Ricketts told her.

Becoming emotional, hoping he could further soften the impact of Shore-Inlow's testimony, Ricketts went after a strong finish.

"You haven't told Mel Ignatow that you had killed his sweetheart and buried her remains?"

"I did not kill her."

"Your life is on the line now, isn't it?"

"I did not kill her."

"Just answer my question. Your life is on the line? Just answer my question."

"Yes."

It was dramatic theater that inevitably made its way onto Louisville television stations. It had some impact on the jury. But Mary Ann Shore-Inlow's life was no more on the line than was Charlie Ricketts's; she had already pleaded guilty to tampering with evidence; she faced a maximum sentence of five years.

"No further questions," said Ricketts.

Jasmin had closed the prosecution's case by calling Maury Berthon and Mike Griffin, the two FBI special agents who taped the conversation between Ignatow and Shore-Inlow. Maury Berthon had been transferred to Miami in the two years it took to get the Ignatow case to trial; he showed up wearing the beard of a narcotics officer. In anticipation of Ricketts's charges of shoddy FBI work, Berthon explained that interviews with FBI witnesses were not officially made into FD302 reports until almost a year later through an "oversight," but the information was given to the Jefferson County Police.

Berthon led the jurors through the eventful day of January 9, 1990, describing how Shore-Inlow's apartment was wired, how she blew her assignment, that the sudden change prevented FBI agents from putting the normal preamble on what was also an old tape. Berthon explained the gaps in the tape: FBI transmissions to county police cut into the recording. He solved the problem by using a hand-held radio outside the car. There were about fifteen gaps in the tape, the longest about 3½ seconds, most others in milliseconds.

Ricketts, in cross-examination, jumped on the chance to prove his former employer had done a poor job of investigation. He dropped a half dozen references to his FBI experience into the questioning, using FBI code, lingo and references, at one point saying to Berthon, "Mr. Hoover always wanted us to be as accurate as possible, didn't he?"

Near the end of the very lengthy questioning, Johnstone told the jury: "Ladies and gentlemen . . . I am sure Mr. Hoover would want us all to go to lunch. . . ."

After lunch, Ricketts used the same line of questioning on Griffin he'd used on Berthon. After Griffin explained that the taping was made in an FBI car using a cassette tape recorder with the induction coil stuck in the bureau radio, Ricketts asked if the batteries had been checked beforehand, eventually arguing weak batteries made Ignatow sound more "rushed" than the conversation had been.

Griffin understood adversarial legal relationships, believed Ricketts had done an outstanding job of defending Ignatow, but thought Ricketts was being too personally disparaging of the county police and the FBI in the process.

"That was infuriating," Griffin would say.

The jury listened closely when the tape was finally played, straining to hear every word. To solve the long dispute near the end of the tape over the word "got" or "dug," the jury was given a transcript that left both words out. It said, "That place we . . . is not shallow." The phrase "that area right by where the safe is" was left in the transcript.

Jasmin had one more piece of unfinished business before resting his case. He wanted to place a statement from Barbara McGee, Ignatow's old girlfriend, into the court record:

"That on or about March of 1989, Melvin Ignatow, who at that time she was dating, brought to her house a pack of condoms, a tube of K-Y jelly, and a dildo and asked her to keep this paraphernalia for him. . . . She kept this for several weeks and at this time stated that she did not want it in her house and she threw it in the Dumpster.

"She also stated that this was about the time that Mel had received a letter . . . regarding Dr. Spalding making threats toward Ignatow. Ms. McGee stated that Ignatow wanted her to keep the paraphernalia because he said it would not look good if the police obtained a search warrant and found this in his home.

"Ms. McGee further stated that if she had known that the paraphernalia had been used in the course of committing a crime at the time, she would not have destroyed it but would have turned it over to police."

Although he did not testify, Ignatow, as usual, had been very busy behind the scenes working on his defense. He'd been moved to the Kenton County jail on December 1, even before jury selection began. Sergeant April McGuire, a corrections officer, noticed Ignatow brought seven videotapes from his hearings in Louisville; he had access to a VCR and television where he could watch them. The officer was amazed by the volume of court papers Ignatow had with him, fascinated at how clean he kept the ninth-floor area he shared with three other inmates.

"He had tons of papers," she would say, "but they were always neat and tidy. He must have kept every document he ever had, and he would take his yellow pad to court with him every day."

Ignatow was also a model Kenton County prisoner, always polite and punctual. He was taking ten pills a day for a heart condition and high blood pressure. He would change from his jail clothes to his three-piece suit, then wait to be taken to court in the jail's property room. McGuire could watch him there through a security mirror:

"It was scary. He would stand there every day in his three-piece suit combing his hair . . . comb it . . . fix it . . . comb it . . . fix it. . . . He'd be at it constantly, a half hour, forty-five minutes at a time. He was very particular."

Ricketts opened his defense Thursday afternoon, after Berthon and Griffin had testified. Only three of the defense witnesses were the clerks and salespeople who believed they saw Ignatow—or Brenda Schaefer—the afternoon and evening of September 24. The other nineteen were all family, friends, former co-workers or members of Southeast Christian Church—Bob Russell's church—who would willingly testify to Ignatow's honesty, thoughtfulness, and good character.

This was another part of the Ignatow puzzle the jury had to snap into place. It was given that the immediate Ignatow family would support him. Yet the Mel Ignatow these other defense witnesses described would be nothing like the sexually sadistic monster portrayed by Mary Ann Shore-Inlow. This Ignatow was portrayed as a good, honest, often personable man, a solid contributor to society. Ignatow had convinced them of that.

Ricketts's first defense witness, Danita Dilly, set the tone for much of the defense testimony. Dilly had been Ignatow's assistant at Rosalco for seven years, handling his letters of credit. She testified he had a loving relationship with Brenda Schaefer, had cried when she disappeared; Ignatow had a good reputation at Rosalco: honest, reliable, compassionate.

"Did you ever talk to anybody in the community in which he lived about his truthfulness?" he asked Dilly.

"Only the people at work."

"Do you know who really knows him best?"

"Other than family, no, I don't really know. . . . I have spoken with his mother, his sister, his daughters."

"You ask my mother . . . she would say I'm a nice guy," Jasmin said.

"Maybe," said Ricketts, jumping into the fray.

Nancy Heid, Ignatow's secretary at Rosalco from 1981 to 1984, told the jurors Mary Ann Shore-Inlow had been extremely jealous of Ignatow, kept his old love letters, pestered him with telephone calls. Julie Swinghammer Simpson, a former Rosalco receptionist-secretary, had begun dating Ignatow after leaving an abusive relationship, had lived with him for almost a year in the early 1980s.

"Did you leave that relationship for any reason at all associated with how Mr. Ignatow treated you?" Ricketts asked.

"No. It had nothing to do with it."

Joyce Harper, the woman Ignatow began seeing just six weeks after Brenda Schaefer had disappeared, said she had first met him at Parents Without Partners in the early 1980s.

"I would say that he would be a very peaceful type," Harper said.

Three more Southeast Christian Church members—Ken Verone, Linda Brooks, who had bought his Corvette, and Jim Westerman, a boyhood friend—praised him. Verone was effusive; he had seen Ignatow and Brenda Schaefer together only once, perhaps for thirty minutes, but thought "they were obviously in love with each other. At least from what I could sense."

Most helpful to the defense were Norma Leslie, a supervisor with the Louisville Alcohol Beverage Unit, and Jean Frank, an old friend of Ignatow and Mary Ann Shore-Inlow

The Louisville Alcohol Beverage Unit was responsible for licensing taverns, taxi drivers, and adult entertainment centers. Leslie told the jurors that Shore-Inlow worked in her department as a temporary Kelly Girl employee in the early 1980s. Leslie intimated Shore-Inlow was so jealous of Ignatow that she wanted to use the office's National Crime Information Computer to check the license numbers of women Ignatow had been dating.

Frank portrayed an even more sinister Shore-Inlow, a woman totally obsessed with Ignatow. It was Shore-Inlow, Frank intimated, who turned Ignatow in to the IRS because he wouldn't marry her—even if he did see her again after he got out. Frank said Shore-Inlow had become pregnant by Ignatow. Ignatow worried she might file a palimony suit if they lived together.

Frank quoted Shore-Inlow as saying of Ignatow: " 'If he don't marry me, he will never marry anybody. I will see to that. . . . ' She has repeated that to me at least a hundred times."

The next defense witness, James L. Hampton, said he got to know Ignatow and Brenda Schaefer during the summer of 1987 when Ignatow's boat was tied up near his Tartan's Landing marina.

Hampton described an excited Brenda Schaefer showing her engagement ring to his wife, Connie. Hampton said Ignatow made careful plans the Monday before she disappeared to bring Brenda to their home Saturday night, September 24, to "share a bottle of wine and enjoy our hot tub." Those plans were canceled that Wednesday because Hampton's mother-in-law had a severe stroke.

"Mel called me on Thursday, as best I can recall, to confirm our plans for Saturday evening," Hampton said. "I said, 'Mel, I hope you can forgive me and understand, but my mother-in-law is in the hospital seriously ill . . . could we postpone our plans?'

"Mel said certainly. Absolutely no problem. He and Brenda had other plans to go to a boat show or craft fair that they could do. . . ."

Ricketts asked Hampton whether, if his mother-in-law had not become ill, the hot tub party would have been held.

"We would have shared a bottle of wine and enjoyed the hot tub, I assume."

"On the Saturday night?" Ricketts asked.

"On the Saturday night."

The Ignatow trial, like the years of problems and delays leading up to it, was a magnet for odd happenings and unusual testimony. Hampton was followed by Sharon Stratton, a waitress at Pitts Smokehouse and Grill on Upper River Road near Prospect, Kentucky. She testified that between 6:00 P.M. and 9:00 P.M.—the times Ignatow had told police he and Brenda were at Oxmoor shopping center about eight miles away—she was certain the couple was in Pitts. Stratton said most of her attention was focused on Brenda.

". . . There was just something about her. She was very happy; smiling a lot. I noticed her lipstick right away."

Kentuckiana Yacht Sales general manager John Scott Pullem was an incredibly talkative witness, his language embroidered with fractured syntax and repetition. Pullem insisted—and would still insist years later—that Mel Ignatow and Brenda Schaefer came onto one of his boats during a show at Harrods Creek on September 24, 1988.

Pullem estimated the couple was on the boat about fifteen minutes sometime between 11:00 A.M. and 3:00 P.M. Ignatow had told police several times he and Brenda never left her car to get on a boat; it was too rainy.

Under Ricketts's questioning, Pullem acknowledged, "It was raining. A slight drizzle of sorts, as I remember, because it was kind of all day long. But they had an umbrella with them. We had the umbrella put on the deck. . . ."

Pullem's mention of a drizzle was followed by a verbal deluge.

"At that particular time Mel wanted to go through the front of the boat. . . . Brenda was more in the direction of either being tired or not as interested as much as Mel was. Of course, you know, Mel is enthusiastic in the boating sport. . . .

"So Mel went scouting to the front of the boat and I kind of went with Mel in the front of the boat and he was looking up there in the galley area, a little bit toward the front section. And Brenda kind of went to the aft portion of the boat and it had a large, large salon area in the aft portion of the boat like a big living room."

Rickets stopped Pullem for just a second, reminding jurors that the aft portion is the rear of the boat.

Pullem raced on:

"The back portion of the boat. Thank you very much. The back portion of the boat. And Brenda went to the back and sat down in the back of the boat for a while. And Ivan Ryan, one of my salesmen, went in the aft portion of the boat and was talking to Brenda at that particular time. While Ivan had known that I was always in communication with Mel, whenever Mel was talking in terms of boats in our business, he just kind of stayed back, because communicating with Mel was being handled by me."

Jasmin, in cross-examination, reminded Pullem that Ignatow told police he had not been on the boat, adding:

"Sir, would it change your opinion as to what time and what day . . . if you knew Brenda Schaefer did not leave her hairdresser until around twelve o'clock. Would that change your opinion of the twenty-fourth?''

"No, sir," Pullem answered.

"Would it change your opinion, sir, if you knew or had heard that she was at a condominium which she owned, where her brother was painting, at around three P.M.?''

"No, sir."

Hearing this, Mike Schaefer was livid, barely able to keep from shouting into the courtroom, ''What the hell's the matter with you? She was with us!'' He would never be certain if Pullem was sincerely wrong or too deep into a mistake to get out.

Jasmin continued the questioning:

"So regardless of what else is shown, you are going to stick firm that you are correct?''

"Yes, sir."

As Pullem left the stand, Johnstone told the jurors a story:

''. . . Ladies and gentlemen, we have a circuit judge in Louisville that they say if you ask him what time it is, he will tell you how to build a watch. This is what you ought to reflect on. Let's take a recess.''

As his list of witnesses wore out, Ricketts was still desperately seeking Sue McKinney, the Flaherty's waitress he believed essential to his defense. The attorney had already told a Louisville television station that because McKinney knew many of the police officers who went to Flaherty's on off-hours, it was possible they had persuaded her not to testify for the defense. At that point Johnstone had signed an order for her arrest; he wanted McKinney brought to Covington.

Two of Ricketts's assistants, Linda Keesey and Kevin Mathews, had filed affidavits in court saying they had spoken with McKinney in December. Keesey said in her affidavit that McKinney made it clear she did not want to testify, that Mel Ignatow could take the subpoena and ''shove it up his ass.'' Mathews said in his affidavit that McKinney did not want to testify, adding, "I'm tired of you sons of bitches bothering me."

Mathews said when he talked to McKinney on December 16, she had told him, "You have no idea how mad I am. I'm mad enough to grab you by the throat and strangle you."

Before dismissing the jury on Thursday, Johnstone told them that it appeared that Ricketts could finish his case on Friday, leaving Saturday, December 21, for closing arguments and jury deliberation.

"I would like you to plan your schedules that way," he said.

The judge also dismissed Sheryl Cook from the jury, paring their number to thirteen.

Cook was the logical choice. She had talked to Johnstone earlier in the week. She had already been struggling with baby-sitters, but her sister-in-law's father had died, and twelve hours later her sister-in-law's uncle had died. There were no baby-sitters left in the family. Cook had considered having one of the court attendants watch her baby, perhaps even take the baby into the jury room for deliberations.

"All I really needed was somebody for that one day," she would say. "I really wanted to stay."

When dismissed, Cook was leaning heavily toward convicting Ignatow. Debra McMillan had somewhat convinced her, but Cook had also carefully kept notes in a small spiral notebook. She didn't agree with many of Ricketts's arguments, and even had difficulty understanding some of his sentence construction.

"He was real arrogant, real pompous," she would say. "It was like he was trying to teach a class."

Johnstone still had one more juror to dismiss. He told the jury that person would be dismissed on Friday or Saturday, right after closing arguments. That juror would be selected by drawing a number at random. Although her name was not mentioned at the time, the juror everyone had in mind was Debra McMillan.

On Friday morning, defense witness Helen Stainback came into the courtroom through a method Johnstone had never before tried; Stainback was in bed in Louisville with the flu; she testified over the telephone that on September 24, 1988, while she was working as a clerk at Embry's clothing in Oxmoor between 5:00 and 9:00 P.M., Brenda Schaefer had been in the store, accompanied by a man similar to Ignatow. Stainback had seen a picture of Brenda Schaefer in the *Courier-Journal* about the same time the woman had come into Embry's.

"Are you convinced that this was Brenda Sue Schaefer?" Ricketts asked over the telephone.

"Yes, sir," Stainback answered.

Jasmin reminded Stainback that she had told FBI agent Maury Berthon that the woman in the store was "similar" to Schaefer.

"Do you remember making that statement, ma'am?"

"No. I do not."

Stainback was followed by Natalie Lisanby, Ignatow's sister, and two of his children, Donna Ignatow Evans and Mike Ignatow. Lisanby showed jurors a picture of Mel and Brenda taken on her boat at a family gathering on September 18, 1988, the weekend before Brenda disappeared.

"It was just a very enjoyable time," Lisanby told the jurors. "She seemed extremely relaxed. She smiled a lot and enjoyed that day. . . . There was no evidence there was any problem of any kind."

Donna Evans—as with her brother, Mike—repeatedly tried to volunteer information about having Mary Ann Shore as a baby-sitter. She gave the appearance the children left home as soon as possible to get away from Shore.

"My sister left the house before I did," Evans said. . . . "My brother left after I did, when he joined the army. I left because of the strange things that were happening around the house. . . ."

"Your Honor," Jasmin said, "commonwealth objects."

"Sustained," said Johnstone.

Ricketts looked at Evans. "Did you all routinely lock your doors at the house?"

"Your Honor," said Jasmin, "commonwealth *objects*."

"Yes," Evans answered before the judge could sustain the objection.

Patricia Ignatow Wood, Ignatow's other daughter, testified that there had always been a good family relationship in their house, that her parents got along well even after their divorce. Wood also volunteered the information—Ricketts hadn't even asked—that her father's old fraternity paddle hung on a basement bar where everyone, including Mary Ann Shore, would have seen it.

There was relief—and anticipation—in the courtroom when the final witness was gone. Final deliberations would begin the next day. Juror David Whaley summed up what was on the jurors' minds with one question.

"Should we bring our own provisions for lunch," he asked, "or should we bring our own provisions for overnight?"

Everybody laughed. Johnstone told the jury lunch would be provided, adding, "The jury should be prepared, if a verdict is not returned tomorrow, to be here overnight. But not in this building, in a hotel somewhere."

Huddled at the bench, Jasmin, Ricketts, and Johnstone turned to the matter of juror Debra McMillan.

"It is my opinion that everyone involved in this case, including the court, would be better off if we excused Ms. McMillan one way or the other," Judge Johnstone said. "If she has to be the lucky winner of the drawing or if we say she has got too many hardships. But she's gotten to the point where she's not listening to evidence."

The judge said McMillan had been in tears in the back, concerned about her job, and did not want to participate.

"I would sure hate to end up here with a jury that is doomed from the beginning [not] to have any meaningful deliberations, possibly causing the thing to be hung up just because we've got somebody that everybody is not going to stay in the jury room with."

Jasmin asked if McMillan might not be questioned before something was done. All the men were aware of Lonnie

McMasters's comments to the judge; he had said she had long ago declared Ignatow guilty. Johnstone suggested they just all agree that McMillan would go; she might become very embarrassed, emotional, and resentful if openly questioned by them about her behavior. The judge knew if he, Jasmin, and Ricketts couldn't reach unanimous agreement, it could present appeal problems.

Ricketts, for the first time in a long while, sided with Jasmin.

"I kind of think we ought to have on the record what it is this lady is going to do," Ricketts said.

Jasmin was caught between a legal rock and a hard place; he suspected McMillan was in his corner, but even if Ignatow was found guilty, McMillan's presence on the jury could lead to his losing an appeal; they might have to endure the whole trial all over again.

Ricketts would see a juror dismissed who seemed to be leaning toward a guilty plea, but he still balked at making an agreement.

"I don't think I can do it, Judge," he said. "I don't know what I'm dealing with."

Jasmin finally suggested they think about it overnight and decide after closing arguments in the morning.

Johnstone agreed.

"See you in the morning," he said.

CHAPTER
28

Charlie Ricketts's closing argument lasted almost four hours.

Likening jury duty to paying taxes, military service, and voting, he went on to praise the Bill of Rights, the brave men and women at Pearl Harbor, the 4-H, Boy Scouts, Girl Scouts, Thomas Jefferson, James Monroe, John Jay, John Hancock, ministers, the great American mix of Irish, German, Lithuanian, Catholic, Jew, Baptist, the FBI, J. Edgar Hoover, Christmas, and the Prince of Peace.

The Kenton County courtroom was packed for this final day, filled with nervousness, apprehension, a sense of drama. All Louisville media were expectantly in place. Mel Ignatow's family, including his sister, brother, two daughters, and son, were in the courtroom. Court reporter Sharon Klosterman, who sat near the door leading to the jury room, didn't sense the same somber mood from the jurors.

"They hadn't brought the jury out yet, but you could hear them, they were so loud," she would say. "I made eye contact with a deputy, who went in and told them to be quiet."

The Schaefer family, a dozen strong, sat as close together as possible; Tom, who had testified, was allowed to join them for the closing arguments. The Schaefers were anxious but optimistic; Mel Ignatow would finally get his due.

Ernie Jasmin, Rob Hickey, and Jim Wesley had been up until 1:00 A.M. going over all their notes, laying out arguments. Jim Wesley felt good, mostly confident.

"I wasn't *that* positive but I didn't feel any negatives," he would say. "It was a sleepless night."

Ricketts, Valerie Herbert, and his associates had been up until 3:00 A.M. preparing his closing argument. Its focus was a list of fifty-one reasonable doubts—virtually a point-by-point review of his entire case—which would be shown to the jurors with the help of an overhead projector and screen. Attorneys are given more leeway in closing arguments; where many attorneys will release a red herring or two into their arguments, this had been a trial with entire schools of blinking red fish.

In closing, Ricketts continued to attack the credibility of Mary Ann Shore-Inlow, defending the integrity of Mel Ignatow.

"Ask yourselves what the terms of that deal with Mary Ann Shore were with the prosecutor. Why did we throw thousands upon thousands of your dollars and mine at prosecuting a man who has no involvement in this case?

"Don't speculate. I don't run for my job. The commonwealth's attorney runs for his job. He must please people. Oftentimes when prosecutors prosecute they get confused about win/loss records."

Ricketts did have one very strong argument in his favor, and he used it like a club:

"There is not one piece of evidence, and they have admitted it over and over and over again . . . except the testimony of Mary Ann Shore. She had to go a step further after she went down and purged herself of her guilt; the guilt of killing sweet, sweet and precious Brenda Sue Schaefer."

In the absence of Flaherty's waitress Sue McKinney, who never was found, Ricketts was able to use McKinney's statement to police in his closing argument:

". . . There was only one night when Sue McKinney could have seen Brenda Schaefer. . . . That was Sunday morning at one o'clock . . . after she experienced automobile problems."

Ricketts's voice was strong, clear; his television experience helped him. He argued that the position of Brenda's car
seat was no indication of who had been driving; someone
from the Coffey Wrecker Service, or Robert Stine, the very
heavyset county police evidence technician, or vandals could
have moved the seat. Ricketts rolled on for almost two hours
before even beginning to list his fifty-one points of reasonable doubt.

"Reasonable doubt," he reminded the jurors. ". . . The
commonwealth's attorney must prove its case beyond a reasonable doubt. Any reasonable doubt, you've got no conviction."

For reasonable doubt number 4, Ricketts pointed out that
Dr. George Nichols said Brenda Schaefer's body was tied in
"complex knots," not nautical knots; Mel Ignatow would
have used nautical knots.

"Mary Ann Shore is not a boater," Ricketts said. "Mary
Ann Shore is a murderer and a liar, a jealous liar."

In full cry, continuing his long, numerical march, Ricketts
reminded the jurors Jim Wesley had not shown a photograph
of Brenda to his 170 cab drivers; that Brenda's jewelry was
still missing and no photographs were ever found; that police
and FBI procedures were weak; that Ignatow and Schaefer
had boarded a boat at the Harrods Creek boat show, and had
been at Pitts Smokehouse and Grill to eat, even if Mel said
they had not.

As Ricketts hit reasonable doubt number 40, after almost
three hours of argument, Johnstone called him to the bench.

"Excuse me," Johnstone told Ricketts. "I hate to interrupt
your closing argument, but your client has to go to the bathroom."

After a forty-five-minute lunch break, Ricketts picked up
where he had left off; the one fingerprint found on the tape
around Brenda's body did not match Ignatow's—or anyone
else's. He intimated Shore-Inlow and Butch Inlow might
have buried a safe in the woods behind her house. He said
if Mel had dug the hole, it would have been more than nineteen inches deep. He showed the jury a picture of the bed

on which Brenda was supposedly murdered, the bed from which Shore-Inlow had seen a rope looped around a bedpost. The bed had a headboard, but no posts.

Finally—his fifty-first reasonable doubt—he asked the one question many people had always asked: If Brenda Schaefer was so afraid of Ignatow, why didn't she just stay away from him?

In closing, Ricketts proposed a scenario to the jurors to pull many of his fifty-one reasonable doubts together, give them life:

A jealous Shore-Inlow was spying on Ignatow the night of September 24, 1988. After Brenda Schaefer dropped him off at his home about 11:30 P.M., Shore-Inlow followed her down Interstate 64 in the rain where she motioned to Schaefer that she was having car problems.

Schaefer pulled off the interstate just past Breckenridge Lane near Dupont Circle. Shore-Inlow suggested to Schaefer that she walk across Interstate 64 and up the wet, grassy embankment to Flaherty's to make a telephone call while Shore-Inlow watched Brenda's car.

When Brenda was out of sight, Shore-Inlow let the air out of the right rear tire of Brenda's car—not knowing that a nail was already lodged in it. Shore-Inlow then drove to Flaherty's, abducted Schaefer, murdered her, meticulously wrapped her body in rope, placed her in plastic garbage bags, and buried her 130 yards behind her house in the thick woods.

Jasmin leaned over toward Wesley.

"If the jury buys that piece of shit," Jasmin said, "I've got some land in Florida for them."

Ricketts finished with a preacher's flourish, Jasmin's technique. Jaw set, his voice powerful, he told jurors Shore-Inlow had invented "all this sex-therapy stuff . . . to sicken us." Staring at the jurors, rage in his eyes, Ricketts dramatically shouted his final message:

". . . She was strong enough to do it. And she was mean enough to do it. And she lied well enough to cover it up. 'And if I can't have Mel Ignatow,' says Mary Ann Shore, 'nobody is going to have Mel Ignatow! He will go to hell first.' Hell hath no fury like a woman scorned.

"Remember, we are in 1991 Christmastime, celebrating the birth of the Savior, a man who was to grow up, and in his thirties be accused falsely.

". . . Please don't be sitting in church on midnight on Christmas Eve wondering if you have done the wrong thing, failed to be responsible.

"Godspeed in your deliberation . . . Thank you."

Ricketts had begun his closing arguments about 9:30 A.M. It was almost 2:00 P.M. when he was finished. He had already exhausted many people, including Wesley.

"It threw a curve at us," Wesley would say. "The first thing Ernie said to the jury was he wasn't going to respond to all that."

Jasmin didn't. He would speak for about an hour; he believed responding to many of the "reasonable doubts" would give them a credence they didn't deserve. He wanted to play from his strength, attack some of the fifty-one that made the least sense, get on with what he had to say. Jasmin had always felt confident of winning the case; he still felt confident.

"I am not going to try to answer, point by point, all that nonsense he has come up with," Jasmin said. ". . . The only evidence presented in this courtroom, with reference to the events which occurred on September the twenty-fourth, 1988, were presented by the commonwealth. And it has not been refuted."

Jasmin was transformed into his preacher mode, voice rising, tapering off, swelling again. His hands sliced through the air like a choir conductor's, forming blocks, semicircles, and rectangles in space. He would pound on the jury-box railing to make a point, bristle with indignation.

"What I am suggesting to you, ladies and gentlemen, is that this is what we as prosecutors call 'The Great Octopus Defense.' When we were in law school we all learned this: If the facts are against you, you argue the law. If the law is against you, you argue the facts. If the facts *and* the law are against you, you put everybody on trial in hopes your client can walk away.

"I have been put on trial. The police department has been put on trial. The FBI has been put on trial. We aren't defendants in this case.

". . . I am not going to apologize to Mr. Ricketts, or anyone else, because Mary Ann Shore got a break. What I am going to say to you is this: In every police officer and prosecutor's life, there comes a time when crimes are committed where, as we say, you sometimes give a little devil a break in order to get to a big or truer devil."

Jasmin asked jurors to consider several points: Ignatow knew Shore-Inlow well, knew her supposed jealousies; why did he never once mention her to police as a likely murder suspect? The prosecutor questioned the testimony of Sharon Stratton, John Scott Pullem, and Helen Stainback, and the police report on Sue McKinney.

"I was trying to figure out . . . how a person is going to be in all of those places at one time. Back where I come from, when people come up with stuff like that, they just say, 'That dog don't hunt.' "

The lack of physical evidence to connect Ignatow to the crime—such as K-Y jelly on the paddle—was understandable:

"Ladies and gentlemen," thundered Jasmin, "it is always difficult to find any physical evidence if you cannot get to the crime scene until fifteen months later. What are you going to have left on a paddle?"

Jasmin's task was daunting; Ricketts had dragged everything imaginable into this case. Near the end of the closing, the prosecutor made brief mention of the safe.

"And there is another red herring in here that sort of bothers me," he said, "I just don't understand this safe. How can the safe be back in the woods near a hole, and be at his house at the same time? Because that's where the safe came from."

Jasmin finished with an oratorical rush, mixing an odd

blend of poetry, blues, and a plea, quoting from Omar Khay-yám's "Rubáiyát":

" 'The moving finger writes, and having writ, moves on. For all your piety, nor wit, shall lure it back to cancel half a line, nor all your tears wash away a word.'

"Look at how smart the defense attorney is: He can't wipe away the fact that the only evidence presented here in this courtroom about murder, robbery, sodomy, kidnapping, sex abuse, has been presented by the commonwealth.

"All I can ask you to do, ladies and gentlemen, is sort of, in the words of a blues song by a fellow named Z. Z. Hill, say: " 'I ain't buying what you're saying. I can't believe in what you're telling.'

"You have a guilty man, ladies and gentleman. I am just asking you, please, don't let him go."

Had the Mel Ignatow murder trial been a bench trial—with no jury involved—Judge Martin Johnstone would have ended it immediately after Charlie Ricketts finished his closing argument; the veteran judge had no problem making that decision:

"I wouldn't have even had to take a recess. I would have just declared Ignatow guilty . . . and we could have gone directly into the sentencing hearing."

Johnstone liked this jury. With the jurors passing by his door every day he'd gotten to know them, felt good about them; David Whaley seemed like a solid, thoughtful man. Johnstone was confident the jury would find Ignatow guilty, but now he, along with Jasmin and Ricketts, had to make a decision on eliminating one more juror.

"What about Ms. McMillan?" Johnstone asked.

"We agree, Your Honor," said Ricketts.

Johnstone asked one of the sheriff's deputies to come to the bench and pull a number at random from the thirteen numbered balls.

"Juror number nine," the judge said. "Ms. McMillan is the alternate. . . . At this time, I would ask you all to accompany the sheriff."

Jasmin had spoken a little less than an hour. The jury was

led out about 3:30 P.M. on Saturday, December 21, for a final gathering. One of the sheriff's deputies told Johnstone he heard Lonnie McMasters say something about a lack of evidence against Ignatow; McMasters hoped the others had brought a suitcase. All the jurors had brought clothes with them, prepared to stay the night. David Whaley had his clothes in the car.

"I went in the jury room with an open mind," the foreman would say.

The jury room was rectangular, perhaps ten feet by fifteen feet, a brown wooden table down the center flanked by an ugly mix of cushioned straight-back chairs. A built-in kitchen lined one wall: electric stove, sink, overhead cabinets. A coffeemaker sat on the porcelain counter, a telephone on top of the stove near the wall. An almost lifeless potted plant stood in one corner, an old, dirty terrarium on a shelf.

Jurors had just enough room to get up, walk around their chairs, look out the windows at the brown Cincinnati hills, an arched bridge over the Ohio River. An old picture on the wall was labeled *The Jury*: twelve old men, most looking bored, uninterested, passing gossip and yawning.

Whaley sat at one end of the table, William Miller near the other; the jurors scattered evenly along the sides. Most of them—in their hearts—believed Ignatow was somehow involved, perhaps even guilty of murder. They had been looking for reasons to convict him, but had two major problems: Shore-Inlow hadn't been believable, had come across as jealous and vindictive, and the thirteen-minute tape was a major disappointment.

Ironically, the tape—whose admittance Ricketts had relentlessly challenged for almost two years in a dozen different ways—would be a major factor in the jurors' final decision. The jurors were continually surprised and disappointed that the tape made no mention of Brenda Schaefer, a body, a crime, or a grave. Their interest centered on the tape's last minutes. The FBI transcript provided them read:

"It's isn't going to stir up anything. Believe me. That's not shallow . . . that place we [ ] is not shallow, so don't let it get you rattled. Besides, that one area right by where the safe is, does not have any trees by it. The trees are down. . . ."

The jury had heard the tape twice during the trial, then played it over and over in the jury room, straining to understand the words. They had to determine on their own if the missing word was "got" or "dug," although either one fit the general context. The word "safe"—described as "site" in early news reports because "site" made more contextual sense—was conveniently printed out for them. Listening to the tape, it sometimes sounded like "site." But the FBI printout was clear. It said "*safe.*"

Ricketts had covered his bets. He fought the tape tooth-and-nail; when he lost, he found a way to use the tape; Ignatow had taken his safe to Shore-Inlow's house.

Not one of the jurors gave credence to Ricketts's final scenario: that Mary Ann Shore-Inlow had followed Brenda Schaefer in the rain to Interstate 64, picked her up, murdered her. It wasn't taken seriously, never discussed. Nor did the jury see any help in almost two weeks' worth of common-wealth testimony; there was no clinical evidence linking Ignatow to the crime. The jurors would be guided, in large part, by Ricketts's continual drumbeat about shoddy investigative work. Much of that was unfair; the various agencies had interviewed at least two hundred people, compiling thousands of pages of reports, interviews, and documents over three years. Their mistakes—made mostly in the heat of the January 9, 1990, chase—were greatly magnified by defense counsel.

The jury was in a quandary. It didn't believe Ricketts's scenario, the commonwealth's case, or Mary Ann Shore-Inlow. It was convinced the investigators had been sloppy. The jury turned detective; it went off on its own to find meaningful evidence. Whaley began searching right after Jasmin's closing argument, which had disappointed him.

"The first thing we thought was that the tape was probably going to spell this thing out in detail without question," Whaley would say. "We were waiting for the shoe to drop.

Well, the shoe just didn't drop. So we kind of expected maybe Jasmin to come back in the final argument. . . .''

Whaley actually believed a safe might have been buried in the woods, that Shore-Inlow and Ignatow had been speaking in some ''code''; perhaps the two had buried some jewelry in it, or something.

''They had been together and done so many things together that the safe could very well have been hiding something else.''

Whaley was leaning toward acquitting Ignatow, but not wanting to influence other jurors, he voted guilty on the jury's initial straw vote. Charles Cox was ready to acquit Ignatow. Cox didn't trust Shore-Inlow. He found it very suspicious that she hadn't insisted Ignatow come to her apartment to be taped, but met him at Ehrler's; it bothered Cox that Shore-Inlow just wasn't very good at following instructions.

Cox and Whaley had emerged as two jury leaders, men who set the tone, helped guide decisions. Cox also began to believe Ignatow and Shore-Inlow had buried a safe eight feet deep behind her house.

''We didn't know,'' he would say. ''It was just speculation. We knew there was jewelry missing.''

Sherry Grieme wanted to find Ignatow guilty, but couldn't see enough evidence to convict him. She had been impressed by Ignatow's appearance; he was also so nicely dressed, looked so innocent. Echoing Ricketts, she would be critical of the FBI's investigative work.

''The police were doing a super job when it first came about,'' she would say. ''Then as soon as the FBI came in, it seemed like it got screwed up.''

Pam Davis was wrestling with her decision. She wasn't comfortable, but was reluctantly leaning toward acquittal—the commonwealth had rushed the case; Jasmin should have gathered more convincing evidence. Davis was convinced that Mary Ann Shore-Inlow was strongly involved.

''I didn't expect her to be Mary Poppins,'' Davis would say, ''but she painted a bad picture.''

Lowell Jarvis was ready to acquit. He was critical of the FBI taping, the poor police work, the lack of evidence. Greg Laukhuff was leaning toward conviction, but was a long way from making a final decision; it bothered him that Ignatow had not taken the stand in his own defense.

Lonnie McMasters wanted to acquit Ignatow and go home; the whole trial had been a total waste of time and money. McMasters—who had a lawsuit against the Covington Police Department—believed police had done a poor job; as for Shore-Inlow, she was a "snitch"; she'd turned herself in for self-gain, which violated his personal code.

William Miller was certain Ignatow was guilty; Miller didn't buy into the now-popular buried-safe theory. If Shore-Inlow had murdered Schaefer, why would she tell the police anything? Why even get involved in taping Ignatow when she could just walk away from it? Was she that insanely vindictive?

"Why would she confess?" he would ask.

Lois Reber, a minister's wife, also was certain of Igna-tow's guilt. She was unhappy with some of her fellow jurors; they were not taking their job seriously, goofing around when a man's life was at stake.

"I think Mary Ann was telling the truth," she told her fellow jurors. Jerry Sebastian, thoughtful, cautious, also was leaning toward acquittal: "I really believed the evidence placed against Mr. Ignatow was circumstantial."

Andrew Wilder, hard-nosed, decisive, blunt, had come to admire Ricketts's court style, his speaking abilities, his defense of Ignatow:

"The evidence the state put forth was almost laughable. They had forensic experts sit there and tell us not one hair of Ignatow's was found on that body. And hair follicles live for years.

"If he had intercourse with her, or whatever, something would have rubbed off."

After an hour Whaley took a count; some people were still on the fence but it was roughly 8 to 4 to acquit Ignatow. A momentum was building. Whaley had the sense they would reach a decision that night, perhaps in a few hours. He believed the jury was taking its job seriously; one detail that had continually bothered him began coming up in its general discussion:

"The sex act on the glass table," he would say. "I guess most glass tables that most of us know about probably couldn't withstand upwards of three hundred pounds. That seemed incredible.

"And in evidence we didn't expect to find any sperm, of course . . . but no pubic hair?"

Whaley, who grew up on a farm, also had trouble believing Ignatow would use such a short-handled shovel to dig Brenda Schaefer's grave; it wouldn't be practical.

"That's a factor," Whaley would say. ". . . Ignatow being his height and the short-end-handle shovel that they showed us. You could dig a hole with it . . . but it would seem anybody would have chosen a longer-handled shovel to dig a hole like this."

Nor did the foreman believe Shore-Inlow had any fear of Ignatow; she didn't look as if she feared anything. He could never understand one person controlling another to the point where she would just stand there and witness rape and murder, even take pictures of it.

"She could have run and got help," he would say.

The jurors picked over the evidence; Brenda's clothing, the car tire, the fraternity paddle. Sherry Grieme went through the pockets of Brenda Schaefer's yellow raincoat, now faded, filled with rust holes. Grieme reached in a pocket and pulled out an old Kleenex.

"Look at this," she said, holding it up.

The Kleenex, almost meaningless by itself, caused an almost righteous stir among the jurors, more proof of what Ricketts had been saying—poor investigation. The jurors voted again. This time Greg Laukhuff voted for acquittal:

"I was wanting to convict Mel Ignatow. . . . The other shoe never dropped. . . . There just wasn't anything conclusive beyond a reasonable doubt."

This time Whaley voted to acquit Ignatow, adding his momentum. At the same time he would worry that the legal system didn't tell jurors enough, they were left to their own devices. Whaley knew of the standard of double jeopardy—which prevents a person from being tried twice for the same crime—but had never been in a situation where he had to understand its application and limits.

"I was thinking," Whaley would say, "that if more evidence came up Mel could probably be taken back and tried again."

The vote was now 10 to 2 to free Ignatow. The last holdouts were William Miller and Lois Reber.

Reber felt the pressure. She had been shocked to see the way the vote was going; they all needed to step back a second and look at the big picture: Was that whole thirteen-minute tape, the excitement and rage in Ignatow's voice, only about a *safe*? Surely there was more to it than that.

So what if a Kleenex had been found in Brenda Schaefer's jacket? What did that prove? So what if Mel Ignatow had used a short shovel? He'd broken the old one and rushed out to buy what he could to finish digging the hole. Nor did Reber think Whaley was an especially good leader; he wasn't always clear in his thinking, or his arguments. Reber felt these things, but wasn't capable of forcefully arguing them. She'd begun to feel in the way; it was her fault all these other people had to stay.

Miller also was feeling the pressure. Outside of some subtle confrontations with McMasters, he didn't believe his race had ever been a factor with the jury, nor had it seemed to be a factor in the jury's opinion of Jasmin. But some jurors did whisper he was holding out because both he and Jasmin were black. Whaley had heard some of that. The foreman would say:

"Miller was the last one and it seemed to me it was maybe . . . being colored. This was the only factor that ever came in about color. That maybe Mr. Miller was leaning toward Jasmin."

Miller simply believed Ignatow to be guilty, would *always* believe Ignatow guilty. Miller knew passion was involved;

something happened inside men who felt jilted by women. He believed Ignatow to be obsessed with passion, dangerous.

The jurors began to focus on the two holdouts: "We gave our opinion," Jerry Sebastian would tell Reber. "You gave your opinion. You're more than welcome to that. . . . But convince me that I'm wrong."

Reber could only say she just believed Ignatow guilty. It was something beyond evidence; it was a gut feeling that went beyond reasonable doubt. Reber sat there, feeling trapped; no one could go home until she changed her mind.

"I feel as though almost everybody in this room is against me," she said.

"We're not against you," Laukhuff answered. "We're just trying to show you what our point of view is."

Reber grew tired. This wasn't fair; she had taken the job very seriously while other jurors hadn't; now the pressure was on her. She would feel a terrible guilt about changing her vote—guilt she would have for a long time—but there seemed no other way out.

"I just got to the place where I didn't care," she would say. "One of us had to go home."

William Miller was the last holdout. If Sheryl Cook had found a baby-sitter, or if Debra McMillan hadn't become such a legal liability, there might have been other jurors to support him—and Reber. Three—perhaps four—guilty votes might have been enough for all of them to hang together, perhaps force a hung jury.

Miller had talked to Reber, telling her that the other jurors obviously didn't believe Ignatow was guilty; maybe the best thing to do was to go along with the crowd. Miller never did change his mind; he just changed his vote.

"That's the way I felt," Miller would say. "These people wanted to go home during Christmas and everything. We all sat around arguing and we're not getting anywhere. So that's the reason I said, 'Let's get it over with. If you find him not guilty it's going to be on your all consciences.'

"All night long the whole thought that was in my mind after we left the courthouse was the man was guilty. The thing was in my mind all night and all day, all week, all month; the man was *guilty*."

The jury had deliberated a little more than two hours. Once that decision was made, jurors believed they had to absolve Ignatow of all other charges; if he hadn't committed the murder, he couldn't have been there to commit sodomy, kidnapping, assault, robbery, and tampering with physical evidence.

The jury had gone out late on a Saturday afternoon. As promised, a meal had been ordered for them—and all court officials—Chinese food from Sechuan Gardens in nearby Park Hills, Kentucky. The jurors were beginning to unwind, pass around phone numbers, make plans to meet again. In their euphoria their loud voices—and occasional laughter—easily passed through the closed door to the adjacent courtroom where, among other people, the Schaefer family waited.

Mike Schaefer was astounded, dismayed:

"What in the hell is going on in there?"

If Schaefer had known, he might have been even more dismayed: They were waiting to eat.

"We had already decided the verdict at that point," Greg Laukhuff would say. "We had already ordered food. We were very professional in our deliberations, but we simply didn't want to leave because somebody, I don't know if it's Kenton County or Jefferson County, is paying about one hundred plus dollars. . . .

"We wanted to leave, but didn't want to waste the food. We didn't want to waste the taxpayers' money."

The word of the verdict spread long before the jury officially returned. One of the deputies guarding the jury room thought he overheard the verdict. He went into Johnstone's chambers.

"They're going to acquit this guy."

Johnstone was stunned.

"No."

"Yes. I can hear what's going on. They're going to acquit this guy."

It was several hours before the Chinese food arrived. Johnstone couldn't eat, nor could the few members of the staff who heard about the verdict. The jury finished its meal, then announced about 8:30 P.M. it was ready to return with its verdict. Ricketts and his staff had gone back to their motel; they had to be brought back, another long delay. Television crews had set up all along the hallway, eager to make the 11:00 P.M. news, reporters shooting video in anticipation of the verdict: "Melvin Henry Ignatow was found guilty Saturday night of the murder of Brenda Sue Schaefer. . . ." All the media would announce the jury had deliberated about six hours and fifteen minutes.

The Schaefer family had been moving around, waiting in the witness room, sitting in the crowded hallways. Just before they were to hear the verdict, a deputy took them aside and warned them: No matter what, strictly as a precautionary measure they would be ushered from the courtroom. It was almost 10:00 P.M. before the jury, the attorneys, the judge, and the families were all back in place. The courtroom was packed, incredibly tense. Among the spectators were Dr. William Spalding and his wife.

Mike Schaefer believed Johnstone already knew the verdict; there was something about the look on the judge's face, his somber air. Rob Hickey turned to look at the Schaefers, a lost look on his face. Jasmin stood perfectly still facing the bench, never looking at the family.

"Ladies and gentlemen," Johnstone said, "at this time the court will review your verdict. And Mr. Ricketts, I will ask you and your client to stand as the verdict is read."

Aside from Johnstone's voice, the courtroom was silent, tense; eyes flickering and back and forth from the bench to the jury. Ignatow, wearing the light gray suit he wore often during the trial, stood with his head bowed, trembling. Ricketts stared at Johnstone, jaw set.

"Ladies and gentlemen of the spectator section, again, let me ask you that there be no outbursts during the reading of these jury verdicts. If someone feels like they can't contain themselves, I would ask you to exit the courtroom at this time."

No one left the room. Sharon Klosterman looked out into a mass of anxious faces, counting at least ten police officers and sheriff's deputies, a few standing near the Schaefer brothers, an eye on them, an eye on Ignatow. Whaley handed the jury's verdict to a court bailiff, who passed it to Johnstone. Ignatow lowered his head a little more, eyes fixed on the floor, lips shuddering, as if in violent prayer.

"The jury's verdict is as follows: 'Under instruction number one, we, the jury, find the defendant, Melvin Henry Ignatow, not guilty.' "

For a moment there was dead silence, then a widening gasp of surprise, disbelief, anger, joy. Mike Schaefer felt his legs go numb, his shoulders and head slump forward. A black glue oozed through his body; he couldn't move, didn't want to move. Tom Schaefer sat next to him, staring at the floor, struck dumb by what he had heard.

Carolyn Kopp burst into tears. Mary Ann Hilbert, the Schaefers' foster child, and her husband, Bernie Hilbert, were crushed, angry, confused. All around them, the Schaefer aunts and uncles asked the same question: "Why?" What had gone wrong?

One by one, Johnstone read off the charges: kidnapping, sodomy, assault, robbery, tampering with physical evidence—all not guilty. He asked Ricketts and Jasmin if they wanted the jury polled; they declined. It was over. Mel Ignatow was forever acquitted of the murder of Brenda Schaefer. He gave Ricketts a huge hug, exultant in victory.

"Thank God," he told Ricketts. "Thank God."

Ricketts had more legal business to worry about.

"Judge," he asked Johnstone, "when can we get Mr. Ignatow out?"

Ricketts didn't get the answer he wanted; Ignatow's legal problems were far from over.

"You may wish to check. I understand the United States marshal has placed a hold against him."

Sharon Klosterman fled the courtroom, found her husband, and cried in his arms. The Schaefer family was quickly led from the courtroom to the empty one behind it. Jim Wesley had sensed trouble early; the jury had finished too soon, and the deputies were avoiding eye contact. Jasmin, Hickey, and Wesley had sat in the courtroom while waiting for Ricketts, hearing laughter from the jury room. As Wesley left the room, Charlie Ricketts came up to him and stuck out his hand. Wesley instinctively shook it—then hated himself for doing it.

Jasmin refused to shake Ricketts's hand.

"Charlie, I just can't do anything like that right now."

Ricketts walked triumphantly out to meet the television cameras, where one of Ignatow's daughters had been exultantly shouting, "Justice is done! Justice is done!" Jasmin, Wesley, and Hickey joined the Schaefer family in the back room. Almost everyone was crying, in shock, as if suddenly learning of a terrible accident.

A deputy came over to Mike Schaefer.

"Do you want to make a statement to the media?"

"No. Shut the damn door."

Jasmin sat on a bench facing the door, looking numb. Wesley took a seat near him. Tom and Mike Schaefer paced the floor, as angry and hurt as they had ever been. Somehow they had again let Brenda down. Tom walked over to Wesley. The officer looked up, bewildered.

"We screwed up," he said.

"No, you didn't," said Tom.

Tom went over to Carolyn Kopp, put his arm around her.

"Tommy, it's okay if you cry."

Tom gave her another hug.

"Carolyn, I don't know what I want to do."

Jasmin sat stunned. He would later say the two most surprised people he saw in the courtroom that night were Charlie Ricketts and Mel Ignatow.

"Is there something that can be done?" somebody asked Jasmin.

"No, he's home free."

The jurors were hustled out of the county building, given protection to their cars in the parking lot. The temperature was hovering around freezing, the air wet, chilly to the bone.

There were no media there. The reporters were too busy talking to Ricketts Jasmin, the Ignatow and Schaefer families; their 11:30 P.M. deadlines were an hour away.

Juror Greg Laukhuff had never in his life felt the emotion that filled the courtroom when the verdict was announced. He watched Ricketts and Ignatow hug, saw tears in their eyes.

"I also kept my eye on the judge. Maybe I was reading something into this, but I thought I saw disgust."

Juror Pam Davis glanced into the eyes of a sheriff's deputy as she left the jury box, saw the hurt and tears in them. Davis felt a sudden pang of remorse, an emotional chill that would last a long time; something was wrong, dreadfully wrong.

The Schaefer family, trying to regroup, met in Dr. Spalding's room that night to talk about the verdict. They were numb, disoriented. Being among family and friends didn't help; being alone was worse. Tom Schaefer didn't sleep. He lay in bed for hours, staring at the ceiling, trying to understand; it would be the worst night of his life. Mike Schaefer got up, went out onto the balcony, stared out into the night. Carolyn Kopp cried until she couldn't cry anymore.

The next morning, after the family returned to Louisville, Tom Schaefer went to Cave Hill Cemetery and walked up the hill where Jack, Brenda, and his parents were buried. He felt hollow, depressed, barely able to function. Jack had been murdered, Brenda had been murdered, his parents had been hurried to their deaths in their grief. Now all the people who had put them there—the Tinsley brothers, Mary Ann Shore-Inlow, Mel Ignatow—were free, walking around, enjoying life. It wasn't right. It wasn't fair. Schaefer stood there for a long time, head down, alone with his thoughts.

For Johnstone, the trip back to Louisville Sunday morning was the longest, most silent of his life. He was in a van full of people—it was three days from Christmas—and nobody said a word. Sharon Klosterman cried all the way back to Louisville.

CHAPTER
29

Roy Hazelwood was seated in his small office in the Behavioral Sciences Unit at the FBI Academy in Quantico when the telephone call came from Assistant U.S. Attorney Alan Sears in Louisville.

Sears had known Hazelwood—and of the FBI's Behavioral Sciences Unit—for years. Sears had a special interest in pornography and adult sexual crimes, having served as executive director of the U.S. Attorney General's Commission on Pornography in 1985–1986. One of the eleven members of the pornography commission was Dr. Park Elliot Dietz, who worked with Hazelwood.

Sears believed that if the federal government was to convict Mel Ignatow on perjury charges lingering from Ignatow's voluntary appearance before the federal grand jury on October 16, 1989, it needed the expertise of Hazelwood and Dietz.

At the time, Ignatow's carefully arranged grand jury appearance had seemed a public-relations triumph. It gave Ignatow—and Ricketts—a chance to sell Ignatow's good intentions to the media. It was also a minor embarrassment to the U.S. Attorney's office, which had provided the platform. If Ignatow hadn't volunteered to testify before the federal grand jury, his legal troubles would have been over; there were no more state charges against him. But Ignatow couldn't resist. When asked by U.S. Attorney Scott Cox if he had killed Brenda Schaefer, his answer had been short, forceful:

"No, absolutely not. I did not kill her."

In essence, the only way the government could prove a perjury charge was to have a federal jury find Ignatow guilty of the murder. After what had happened in Covington, Sears knew they could profit from the mistakes made in the state trial: put together a new plan of attack, better prepare Mary Ann Shore-Inlow, perhaps even find some new evidence.

"We talked to Dietz and Hazelwood for a long time," Sears would say. "We knew we had to develop a stronger case."

Sears was the picture-perfect federal prosecutor, lean, handsome, highly organized, a Ronald Reagan conservative filled with near-patriotic fervor in his pursuit of men like Ignatow:

"It may sound hokey but . . . we almost felt like we knew Brenda. She was an important person in our lives and protecting her dignity was a very big concern."

Justice and dignity for Brenda Schaefer had become very important in Louisville. Although several letters to the editor in the *Courier-Journal* reminded readers that the "reasonable doubt" doctrine must always apply, Ignatow's acquittal infuriated and confounded many Louisvillians. They had heard or seen portions of the thirteen-minute tape on radio and television a dozen times. They had seen the pictures of Ignatow and Mary Ann Shore-Inlow linked to the tape. They had long since judged Ignatow guilty.

Louisvillians did not understand—never would understand—that the case against Ignatow had weaknesses: the lack of damaging physical evidence; a confusing, ambiguous tape; the "safe"; a poorly presented star witness. The change of venue had done what it was supposed to do: It moved the case to an area where reasonable doubt was in greater supply. The phrase "the Ignatow Jury" became a pejorative, a brief description of indifference, stupidity, and injustice that became permanently etched in the Louisville lexicon.

Courier-Journal columnist Jim Adams would rip the jury to the point where the Kenton County jurors—through an attorney—would hold a meeting to discuss it, through the attorney writing an angry letter in reply. Doug McElvein's Sunday-morning talk show on WHAS radio—a popular outlet for Louisville outrage—crackled with callers unable to understand the verdict; Ricketts took phone calls to defend the verdict, and appeared on WHAS-TV that night. Ricketts was quoted in the *Courier-Journal*—with a circulation of 320,000 reaching into every corner of Kentucky—as saying, "Justice has been done. We are elated." Ricketts said the verdict sent a message to prosecutors that "you must study your case before you take it on. You must be sure you have probable cause" before indicting people.

Jasmin was criticized for being overconfident, for not being better prepared, for not having Mary Ann Shore-Inlow better prepared. He would answer there was nothing he would change; he had never been involved in a case where a jury had been so hell-bent on playing detective instead of examining the evidence.

"I make *no* apologies for *anything* I've done in this case," he would say.

Reluctantly—never making a public issue of it—Jasmin believed his race could have been a factor in Kenton County:

"I cannot count that out. I make the basic assumption that the defense counsel specifically wanted to go to that area for a reason. I understand what the profile is in terms of black folk in that particular area. I am aware of the fact that those folk are not accustomed to seeing a black professional do anything.

"I can't say altogether unequivocally, but after reflecting upon it I have a tendency to believe that it could have had an effect."

Ignatow, smiling broadly, surrounded by family, walked out of the federal courthouse in Louisville on Monday, December 23, free for the first time in two years. He thanked God for his release, said he was looking forward to sleeping in a soft bed. Ricketts complained that any pursuit of the federal charges against him amounted to persecution; the federal authorities had no case.

U.S. Magistrate William Clark had ordered Ignatow's release on the condition that he have no contact with any of the trial witnesses, that he call his probation officer daily, that he stay in the home of his son, Michael, with whom he would live at LaFontenay Apartments, a five-hundred-unit complex in Middletown. Ignatow was not required to post a bond, but would forfeit $25,000 if he failed to show up for a January 13 hearing. He could not leave town.

At the urging of federal prosecutor Scott Cox, Ignatow's request to be allowed to go to church was refused.

"I was worried about public reaction to that," Cox would say, "but the next day a minister from Southeast Christian Church called to thank me."

Cox had gone to Covington for the final day of the trial to hear closing arguments, and had left believing Ignatow would be convicted. The minute he heard the verdict, he began leafing through his Uniform Federal Code lawbooks at home, looking for other federal charges. At first he thought Ignatow could be charged under Section 242 with violating Schaefer's civil rights, a charge used in several highly publicized national cases. Cox later learned that law applied only if a state "actor" was involved in the case—an employee such as a police officer or prison guard.

Ignatow's future lay in the hands of Cox's boss, U.S. Attorney Joe Whittle. The federal perjury charge served as a detainer, but to continue prosecution Whittle had to obtain an indictment within thirty days of Ignatow's acquittal. Whittle's decision was more difficult than it seemed.

There was enormous public pressure for him to go after Ignatow, coupled with the urgings of the Schaefer family, Whittle's own staff, Jefferson County police, Ernie Jasmin, and FBI special agent Deirdre Fike, who lobbied very hard for federal indictments. Many of those pleas were professional, but there were personal reasons, too. Mel Ignatow had been arrogant, aloof, infuriating. In many minds Charlie Ricketts's criticism of the prosecutor's office, the police, and the FBI had been stronger than his professional responsibility required. Pride was at stake; it was time for a little payback.

That pressure had to be balanced by the high cost of another trial—financial and otherwise. A federal trial was certain to require another expensive change of venue. The new jurors would know—or find out—that Ignatow already had been acquitted in a state court. Federal perjury and obstruction charges carried only five-year penalties; would a full-scale murder trial be worth a five-year sentence?

Whittle was all too aware that the evidence used against Ignatow in Covington didn't do the job. What would the public reaction be if Ignatow was again acquitted? Whittle didn't take long to decide. He'd been home the Saturday night the verdict was announced:

"I absolutely could not believe it. The first thing I did Monday morning was to call a meeting to see what we could do about it."

Another man convinced justice had not been done was Judge Martin Johnstone. He wrote Tom Schaefer a letter shortly after the trial, the type of letter Johnstone had never before mailed as a judge—and would never mail again.

DEAR TOM,

I WANT TO EXPRESS TO YOU, AND YOUR FAMILY, MY SHOCK AND DISMAY OVER THE IGNATOW VERDICT. I AM STILL UNABLE TO FATHOM HOW A JURY COULD COME TO SUCH A DECISION. I FEAR THAT IT HAD LITTLE, IF ANY, TO DO WITH THE EVIDENCE. YOU CAN IMAGINE HOW MANY TIMES THAT I HAVE BEEN ASKED—WHAT HAPPENED?—AND I STILL DON'T HAVE A RATIONAL EXPLANATION. I DON'T BELIEVE IT WAS THE FAULT OF THE COMMONWEALTH.

YOU AND YOUR FAMILY HAVE MY UTMOST RESPECT FOR THE MANNER IN WHICH YOU HAVE SUFFERED

THROUGH THIS TRAGEDY. I CAN ONLY HOPE THAT
YOUR FAMILY WILL SOME DAY BE ABLE TO PUT THIS
BEHIND YOU. WHETHER IN THIS WORLD OR AN-
OTHER—ONE DAY JUSTICE WILL BE DONE.

WITH WARM REGARDS, I AM,
SINCERELY YOURS,
MARTIN JOHNSTONE

From the moment of the verdict, the Schaefer family had
been numb, angry, bitter, anesthetized to almost everything
around them. Driving home to Louisville Sunday morning,
Carolyn Kopp's daughter, Cindy, heard the WHAS radio talk
show. She flagged down Tom and Carolyn as they traveled
southwest along Interstate 71, told them to listen. The Schaefers were heartened by the public reaction—a direct extension of what they were feeling—but remained depressed
there was little they could do beyond listen.

Tom, Mike, and Carolyn went to a press conference on
Tuesday, December 24. The Schaefers were reluctant—they
mostly went to show support for Jasmin—but under questioning their anger and frustrations poured out. The family
had prepared a statement, trying to explain that Brenda was
not Ignatow's "sweetheart"; she feared him, was murdered
because she wanted to escape him. Mike Schaefer, his face
frozen in anger, was blunt, barely able to control himself as
he faced the cameras.

"What do you think was Ignatow's motive?" someone
asked.

". . . I think he did it for the fun of it. . . . That's the kind
of person he is."

What about the jury?

"Brenda was just somebody from down the road; she was
not from their community."

What would the family do now?

"Try very hard not to go crazy," Mike answered, speaking more truth than most people realized; several family

members would require psychiatric counseling to deal with the shock, grief, and depression.

For months afterward, the family could not escape the questions. What happened, what had gone wrong? Book authors and tabloid television producers hounded them, wanting to do stories; the family wanted only to be left alone, to do what it could to help any federal prosecution. Their worst fear was accidentally running into Ignatow in public. It was a nagging, uncomfortable feeling; neither Mike nor Tom really knew what he would do if suddenly confronted with him.

On January 8—only eighteen days after Ignatow's acquittal—the federal grand jury met in its room at the top of the stairs to consider a three-count indictment against Ignatow. Whittle, who rarely made grand jury appearances, was there, as was Deirdre Fike, the FBI case agent, who briefly outlined the case. The jurors were also given an edited copy of Ignatow's October 16, 1989, testimony.

Federal grand juries rarely fail to act as directed. Within fifteen minutes, Ignatow was indicted for perjury—lying to the grand jury, including telling its members that Shore-Inlow had never met Brenda Schaefer, that he didn't know what happened to her engagement ring, and that he had nothing to do with her death. The second indictment—subornation of perjury—charged that Ignatow had induced Shore-Inlow to lie before the grand jury. The third was that he had lied to FBI agents by telling them Brenda had dropped him off at his house the night she disappeared.

None of the three charges carried the emotional weight of the state murder charge; the maximum cumulative federal sentence would be fifteen years in prison and a total of $750,000 in fines. No one ever got the full sentence, and a destitute Ignatow couldn't pay fines anyway. Ricketts complained the federal government was bowing to public pressure by trying to "get a second bite out of the apple." Joe Whittle had quit talking; he imposed a gag order on his whole office; no one was to say a word about the case.

On January 20—less than two weeks later—Charlie Ricketts quit as Mel Ignatow's attorney, taking Valerie Herbert with him. In a four-page, single-spaced letter to U.S. District Court Judge Edward H. Johnstone—who was no relation to Circuit Judge Martin Johnstone—Ricketts said he and Herbert had worked on the case for more than three years. Ricketts again complained that much of the time, money, and effort that should have gone into trial preparation were diverted to repeatedly file motions against Jasmin's office. Ricketts's bottom line was that his law firm had accumulated about $30,000 in pro bono services and that Ignatow owed the firm well in excess of $65,000 for work approaching $100,000 in value. Ricketts said he knew long before the trial Ignatow could not pay his bill, but his firm continued to defend him as responsible attorneys. He told Johnstone that he was very disappointed in the federal indictment; he'd been led to believe by the U.S. Attorney's office there would be no federal prosecution.

Ricketts closed his letter by saying that if the United States was going to prosecute Ignatow at the expense of the taxpayers, then taxpayers should pay for his defense. Ricketts would later say he also dropped Ignatow because he believed he probably would be called to testify in the federal trial about Ignatow's unwillingness, given his angina problems, to take an FBI lie-detector test. Whittle, ignoring his own gag order, called the move "vintage Charlie Ricketts."

On paper, Ignatow was broke; the man who always had need to prove himself through material things had none left. His children had received the Florian Road house after his mother's death. His Corvette had been sold to Linda Brooks for $10,000, money that presumably went to legal fees. His $67,000 boat, the *Motion Lotion*, had suffered badly in dry dock and needed a lot of work. It would be sold early in 1992 for about $31,500 to Wayne Teether, a Jeffersonville salesman. Teether said the boat had been deeded to Natalie Lisanby, an old friend, with whom he negotiated. Teether said the law firm of Ricketts & Travis had a lien on the boat.

Ownership of Virginia Ignatow's former home at 3741 Avon Court, valued at $70,000, had been deeded over to

Ridgeway Properties on August 23, 1991, about three months before the trial. Ridgeway Properties was listed as a Kentucky general partnership that included Charlie Ricketts, Janice Ricketts, William Clifton Travis, and Paula Travis. Virginia Ignatow had willed the house to Natalie Lisanby and Jim Ignatow, but Charlie Ricketts would say the transaction was made to help pay some of Mel's legal expenses. Lisanby, the executrix of her mother's estate, signed the deed.

When Ignatow appeared in federal court on January 21 to plead not guilty to the three-count federal indictment, he stood alone, wearing his gray three-piece suit, holding a folder of legal papers. After two years of standing—or sitting—in the shadow of Charlie Ricketts, the image of Ignatow standing alone seemed odd, a little unnatural.

Meeting with reporters afterward, Ignatow, his head characteristically bobbing like a tin can on a stick, said, "I have faith in the justice system. It will prevail."

His new, court-appointed counsel would be Thomas Clay, forty-six, a veteran Louisville defense attorney who had worked often in federal courts.

"I knew he was going to be prosecuted vigorously," Clay would say. "I felt he ought to be defended vigorously."

Clay was always called "T"—the first letter of his name. His great-grandfather, grandfather, father, and two of his brothers had been attorneys in and around Danville, Kentucky, a family tradition he couldn't resist.

"I really had no burning ambition to become a lawyer. It just seemed like the logical thing to do. I didn't have any idea how much fun it was."

Clay was a 1974 University of Louisville Law School graduate who was first drafted into the army, then spent twenty years in the Army Reserve, rising to the rank of lieutenant colonel. He was a lean, articulate man with short-cropped hair, who carried his military bearing into court; aggressive, straight-ahead, look-you-in-the-eye; anticipating trouble before it came up. His pay—by lawyers' standards—

was low: $60 an hour for courtroom work, $40 outside the
courtroom.

Whittle decided he would prosecute with Sears and Jim
Lesousky, with Lesousky sitting in the lead chair. Using Lesousky made good sense. Not only was he respected, he had
a long history with the case; he had worked for Commonwealth's Attorney Ernie Jasmin when Brenda Schaefer disappeared. Lesousky had been eating lunch with John Stewart
when Scott Cox had called on January 9, 1990, looking for
Jasmin. For a very brief time, Lesousky had been Jasmin's
lead prosecutor. He had been with Stewart during much of
the day of Ignatow's arrest. Lesousky—who moved to the
U.S. Attorney General's office in 1991—had prosecuted
many murder cases.

Given Ignatow's incredible luck, his history of being able
to dodge judicial bullets, Lesousky knew a conviction
wouldn't come easy.

"We used to say Mel had a pact with the devil," Lesousky
would say.

Lesousky could say that with some authority. The Louisville native had attended Mt. St. Francis Seminary in Indiana,
where he studied six years to become a priest. He left there
to attend Bellarmine College in Louisville, receiving a master's in counseling psychology; he worked ten years for the
Kentucky Cabinet for Human Resources. In the early 1980s
he began going to the University of Louisville Law School
at night, taking a job with Jasmin's office in 1985.

Sears and Lesousky made an interesting—if not odd—
couple. Both men worked hard, often eating lunch at their
desks while reviewing court documents. Sears—either playing devil's advocate or leery of the odds of winning the
case—had initially argued within the office that Ignatow
should not be indicted. But once on board, Sears was relentlessly organized; he did much of the early sexual-sadist
research while Lesousky was finishing another case.

Lesousky had more of a social worker's air about him—
he often relied on instinct, gut feeling—but he was a bulldog,
meticulous, well prepared, a tough and respected opponent.

There would be some tense moments between the men. Both were experienced prosecutors accustomed to being in charge. They found ways to defer to one another, to bend a little for the common good. They combed all the evidence looking for clues, made it a point to debrief Jim Wesley, use his experience. Both prosecutors became convinced a key to the federal case was better preparation for Mary Ann Shore-Inlow, who would again be the star prosecution witness.

Shore-Inlow continued to make news. WLKY-TV's Steve Burgin featured her and the Kenton County jury in a series of follow-up stories that included taped interviews with jurors Pam Davis, Lowell Jarvis, Sherry Grieme, William Miller, and Lonnie McMasters. In one brief, bizarre scene, Shore-Inlow was shown partially bent over the glass-topped coffee table in her living room. In other moments she was seated on a couch wearing a red sweatshirt, her face framed in long blond hair, red Christmas candles spread out on the coffee table. Her voice as flat and unemotional as it had been on the witness stand, Shore-Inlow stayed with her story: Ignatow was guilty.

"I still believe he has the photos," she told Burgin.

On February 3, Shore-Inlow appeared before Judge Martin Johnstone for her sentencing on the tampering-with-evidence charge. Conservatively dressed, wearing a long flower-print dress, dark blue blazer, and a pearl necklace, with her blond hair cut and softly shaped, she presented a much more appealing figure than she had in her Kenton County fiasco. With Jack Vittitow standing at her side, Shore-Inlow made her first public apology, reading slowly from a card she held in her hands.

"I realize my involvement in this whole situation was wrong. I'm very sorry."

Even had Ignatow been found guilty—and Shore-Inlow's testimony against him had done more harm than good—it's doubtful Johnstone would have been sympathetic. He described Shore-Inlow's actions as "shocking, reprehensible," her remorse evident only now that she was being sentenced. The judge again deviated from standard judicial script, still obviously troubled by the Kenton County verdict. "To be quite frank about it," he said, "I believe that Ms. Shore's testimony under oath was truthful. Ms. Shore is the only person who had knowledge of this crime before the crime, during the crime, and after."

Yet he was compelled to sentence Shore-Inlow to only five years in prison, the maximum. The sentence provided another incongruous turn in the bizarre case; Mel Ignatow was free, his chief accuser in prison.

It was a turn not lost on Commonwealth's Attorney Ernie Jasmin, who said nothing about probation for Shore-Inlow, leaving the sentencing up to the judge.

"That's one of those anomalies, I guess you would call it," Jasmin told the media. "The clear inference to be drawn by the evidence presented was that Melvin Henry Ignatow was as guilty as homemade sin."

The words "guilty as homemade sin" had barely cleared Jasmin's mouth before T. Clay, Ignatow's new attorney, added them to his growing pile of reasons to request a change of venue in Ignatow's federal trial. On February 4 Clay and Ignatow both said the trial should be moved, perhaps to Paducah in far Western Kentucky. Clay also said Martin Johnstone's comments about Shore-Inlow's telling the truth could also affect potential jurors. In fact, U.S. District Court Judge Edward Johnstone had already hinted to Clay that he should prepare for a change of venue.

On March 4 Clay filed a motion that the trial be moved to Nashville, Tennessee, about 160 miles south of Louisville. The arguments in the federal trial quickly began to echo those in the state case, although with a lot less personal rancor. Lesousky and Sears replied that if Mike Tyson, William Kennedy Smith, and Oliver North could receive fair trials in their local jurisdictions, so could Mel Ignatow.

Johnstone quickly sided with Clay; for the second time Mel Ignatow was given a change of venue; the case would be moved south to Nashville or one hundred miles north to Indianapolis. The only thing both sides agreed on was that the case could be ready for trial by July. Meanwhile, Sears had persuaded the FBI's Roy Hazelwood, and his assistant Steve Mardigian, to come to Louisville early in March to help them work on a profile of Ignatow. Sears was eager to demonstrate what had never really been made public, that this was not just a crime of greed and passion; Mel Ignatow was a criminal sexual sadist, a dangerous, evil man who preyed on vulnerable women, seduced them, manipulated them, used them.

Ignatow had done it without remorse, cloaked in upper-middle-class respectability, hiding behind his job, the members of Southeast Christian Church, his family and friends. Sears was convinced that if he remained free, Ignatow would eventually murder again.

Sears believed Hazelwood could give federal jurors a very specific profile of the sexual sadist, the twenty-two telltale characteristics of the criminals and their crimes. Lesousky and Sears could then try to match them to Ignatow. There was no guarantee Hazelwood would be allowed to testify. The special agent had testified in about fifteen federal cases—had never been refused—but Clay would surely challenge his appearance, make him jump through all the legal hoops, make Johnstone decide the issue.

Edward Johnstone, sixty-nine, was the son of a University of Kentucky agronomist, was decorated for heroism at the Battle of the Bulge in World War II, then graduated from the University of Kentucky Law School in 1949. He was six feet four, with broad shoulders, a farmer's hands, and large, ungainly feet he would prop up on his desk, spreading them out like fan blades. Age, a craggy face, and a knack for storytelling gave him the presence of a Lyndon Baines Johnson. Johnstone enjoyed the label of country lawyer, but was too perceptive, too knowledgeable in the law to draw the legal line there. He tended to be very strict in protecting the constitutional rights of defendants; he cultivated an image as a judicial pragmatist, but liked to be unpredictable; he liked to settle cases without going to trial.

Not surprisingly, federal prosecutors believed that Johnstone was just too liberal, he had too much sympathy for individual defendants.

"He was always a big thorn in our side," Whittle would say, "always on the side of the defendant. We were worried at one time that the judge would toss out the whole case."

Lesousky saw problems getting Hazelwood on the stand as a witness.

"We knew we had a tough row to hoe but we were prepared for it. We anticipated having the judge defer a ruling until some point in the trial."

Sears remained encouraged. Hazelwood and Mardigian promised to spend four days with them and Deirdre Fike, who was case agent for the FBI.

"Roy Hazelwood could produce a number of things for us, a lot of places to look, a lot of things to look at," Sears would say. "He was vital to our case."

CHAPTER
30

Roy Hazelwood was a teacher, a storyteller with a knack for distilling complex medical jargon into psychiatric vignettes. He had one custom-made for Mel Ignatow, who—from a clinical point of view—Hazelwood found very interesting.

"... The thing about a psychopath is that they have the ability to manipulate people.... They could say to you it's raining in this room right now, and you would say, 'No, it's not.'

"And they would say, 'Well, it just finished.' "

Hazelwood and Steve Mardigian held court at the FBI headquarters in Louisville from March 2 to March 4, with Deirdre Fike, Alan Sears, and Jim Lesousky their prime students in the ten-to fourteen-hour days. Fike and the attorneys were amazed at how much Hazelwood seemed to know about Ignatow just by fitting his character traits—and the details of Brenda Schaefer's brutal murder—into the FBI's criminal sexual sadist profile.

The pieces fit everything Mary Ann Shore-Inlow had said happened: A partner assisted in the murder; the victim was taken to a preselected area and tightly bound; there was anal rape, dildo penetration, torture, murder; the body was concealed, the sexual torture recorded on tape or film for future gratification.

Often seated around a big conference-room table in the FBI's fifth-floor headquarters, Hazelwood led his group as it developed a list of "stressors" from Ignatow's immediate past: losing his job, moving to Florida, Brenda's refusal to leave her mother, Brenda's growing detachment, their final breakup. Together the team developed a time line of events in Ignatow's life, beginning in 1974 when he first dated Mary Ann Shore-Inlow, continuing until the day Brenda Schaefer's body was found.

They worked late into the night, ordering pizza for dinner; the cardboard pizza boxes shared the table with charts, outlines, and notes. A telephone line was put in the room, an FBI computer-link made available for sessions that began at 7:30 A.M. and lasted until 11:00 P.M.

"It was like a think tank," Fike would say.

Hazelwood gave them almost forty specific leads to check, all of them indicators of Ignatow's true personality.

"Capture the relationship," Hazelwood told them. "Everything about this guy. What's his favorite type of movie? What did he like to read? What kind of music did he like? What were his pastimes and hobbies? What kind of collections did he keep? How did he treat animals?"

Mary Ann Shore-Inlow also was approached from a more clinical perspective; she easily fit the profile of compliant victims of the sexual sadist.

"Interview Mary Ann," Hazelwood said. "Don't go in there judgmentally and attack her, because she was the victim of this guy up to the point where he got her to assist him.

"Guys like Mel have ways to transform these women into ways that are sexually gratifying to them."

From the day they had held hands in the U.S. Attorney's office, Fike was the prime link to Shore-Inlow. The women had grown close, built trust between each other. Shore-Inlow, who was being held in the Kentucky Correctional Institution for Women in Pewee Valley, Kentucky, about twenty miles from downtown Louisville, didn't want to cooperate with the

FBI. She'd already testified against Ignatow, done everything asked of her; Ignatow was free and she was in jail.

She was angry and bitter, believing she was the scapegoat because Ignatow had walked. There had been nothing in writing, but she had always expected much less than the full five-year sentence, some type of parole or home incarceration. It might look good with the Kentucky Parole Board if she willingly testified in the federal trial, but there were no guarantees; why the hell should she get involved again?

Fike never condoned what Shore-Inlow had done, but Mary Ann had always been truthful with her. Fike had met Shore-Inlow's family, knew they were strong Catholics who were very hurt and embarrassed by what had happened. Fike was sympathetic; she could see Shore-Inlow as another Ignatow victim.

"I think people can be controlled by different things," Fike would say, "some by guilt and fear, others by their emotions and attachments, their love for somebody.

"Mel controlled Brenda Schaefer by guilt and fear, Mary Ann by her emotions and attachment. I think Mary Ann was controlled by Mel but she was also more of a willing partner to him in his life. . . . I don't think Mel always had to force Mary Ann like he did Brenda."

Fike was now the FBI's lead investigator; she took notes of everything Hazelwood had to say. Like Jim Wesley, Lewis Sharber, Maury Berthon, and every other law enforcement officer who got near the case, she became personally involved. Her growing hatred of Ignatow, her sympathy for the Schaefer family, had pushed her to pursue the indictment, was now pushing her to finish the job.

FBI special agent Mike Griffin, Fike's immediate supervisor, relieved her of all other duties to work on the case. Griffin believed Fike was too involved; it was affecting her health. She worked with Wesley, now a shift commander in the county police David District, meeting him weekly. She made regular trips to Pewee Valley to talk to Shore-Inlow; the agent knew an unhappy witness would not help the FBI's case, especially this witness.

"Mary Ann," Fike would tell her, "I can't promise you anything. All I can ask is that you do the right thing."

Griffin admired Fike, respected her work, worried about her. They talked several times about the case.

"A lot of times when you have sources of information, you force yourself to have a relationship for the benefit of the case," Griffin would say. "Deirdre's [relationship] went beyond that. Deirdre did become attached to Mary Ann, did become friendly to her, went to bat for her a number of times trying to make things better for her.

"This was when Mary Ann was still saying, 'No, I'm not getting involved anymore. He got away with it.'

"Deirdre would say, 'That's fine, that's fine,' and kept working with her. Finally Mary Ann said, 'OK, I'll do it.' As far as Mary Ann goes, without Deirdre it never would have happened."

Collectively, with a budget and resources that Commonwealth's Attorney Jasmin couldn't have duplicated, Fike and the others mapped out a new strategy. Sears carefully choreographed his opening statement to include jury-friendly graphics: a large color photograph of Brenda Schaefer, a street map of key locations, a diagram of Shore-Inlow's house, and photographs of the grave site and autopsy.

Sears had a witness who would testify that Ignatow and Schaefer's relationship splintered during a trip to Gatlinburg, Tennessee: Ingatow had again forced himself on Schaefer, using chloroform as his weapon. Brenda left their room, was locked out, started to walk home.

That was the weekend—Labor Day, 1988—when Ignatow first fully understood Brenda would leave him. Ignatow and Shore-Inlow had already dug their hole in the woods. Ignatow's plans to murder Brenda accelerated quickly after that, as did the phone calls to Shore-Inlow.

The prosecution team made certain that Barbara McGee, the woman Ignatow had given the dildo and condoms to, would be subpoenaed to testify. Sears was going to put Ignatow's voice into the trail even if Mel never testified. He would play segments of Ignatow's testimony at the October

16, 1989, grand jury hearing, Ignatow's first call to the police, and the interview in Ricketts's office. More important, Sears would open with a segment of the thirteen-minute tape, which would be stopped while he read his interpretation of the key sentence that had so confused the Kenton County jury.

Judge Johnstone would rule the jury had to decide on its own what the tape said; all words in question would be left blank in the transcript. Sears would launch a preemptive strike in the opening statement by eliminating the words "got" and "safe," replacing them with "dug" and "site": "that place we *dug* is not shallow so don't let it get you rattled. Besides, that one area right by where the *site* is, does not have any trees by it."

The prosecutors discussed bringing Mel Ignatow's ex-wife to the trial; let her testify about Ignatow's form of punishment. Brenda Schaefer's car would be taken to the trial; let the jury see the position of the car seat. Mary Ann Shore-Inlow would be better dressed, better prepared; Fike had spent hours with her to help ensure that.

FBI visual information specialist Cyrus Glover III met with Sears and Fike a half dozen times either in Louisville or at his office in FBI headquarters in Washington to develop detailed diagrams, maps, and blowups of the crime scenes, including Shore-Inlow's house.

More important, Glover introduced "Susie"—a life-size Brenda Schaefer look-alike mannequin. Glover had found Susie at the Johns Hopkins School of Medicine. He carefully reworked the mannequin's arm and leg joints, making her more pliable. The Kenton County jury had never understood that Brenda Schaefer had been on her knees when anally raped, her assailant on his knees behind her; there was very little weight on the coffee table.

The coffee table would be brought into the courtroom. Shore-Inlow would get up from the witness box, use Susie to demonstrate the assault on Brenda Schaefer, the position of her knees. Susie would be dressed in a leotard, but the mannequin's wig would be dark brown—the color of Brenda's hair.

Susie had been used well before the trial. Shore-Inlow, Glover, Fike, Sears, and Lesousky spent much of one day re-creating the torture and murder. With Shore-Inlow directing, Susie was shaped into all the sexual poses that had been forced on Brenda Schaefer. The mannequin was bent over the coffee table, placed on the bed where Brenda was raped and sodomized, a rope tied around her neck as Brenda had been tied when Ignatow felt the chloroform might not be enough. Photographs were taken at each stage, just as they had been taken during Brenda's murder.

Hazelwood talked continually about those photographs. It had been almost four years since the murder. Jefferson County police had twice searched Ignatow's house. He'd lived there almost sixteen months between September 24, 1988, and his arrest on January 10, 1990, plenty of time to destroy them. It seemed inconceivable they could still exist, but Hazelwood was persistent:

"He's not going to throw away the pictures. They're his trophy, a sign of conquest, a sign of victory."

Ignatow had not been able to get back into the Florian Road house after his acquittal. On December 6, 1990, while he was still awaiting his first trial, it had been sold for $175,000 to Ronald B. and Judith Watkins, who had moved to Louisville from Indiana.

Hazelwood took pleasure in thinking Ignatow might have outsmarted himself. Ignatow had deeded his half of the house to his mother, apparently to avoid having it involved in any legal costs or suits. Virginia Ignatow died while he was in jail, willing the house to his three children, who sold it. Natalie Lisanby was the executrix. Mel was out of the loop, with no way into the house.

Hazelwood had urged the FBI to search the house one more time, but the Watkinses politely refused them admittance; they were tired of the intrusions, the drive-by gawkers. They knew county police had twice searched the home already; what was the point of another search?

As March rolled into April, Louisvillians put aside the Mel Ignatow controversy to focus on more important matters: the blossoming of the flowering crab and dogwood trees, the arrival of Derby Week with its grand parade, Great Steamboat Race, and street festivals, all of it building toward the race on the first Saturday in May.

Derby Week was a long community binge inevitably followed by a communal hangover. The Ignatow case maintained a low profile until May 22 when Mary Ann Shore-Inlow once again appeared before Judge Martin Johnstone; she had served about 110 days in prison and was seeking immediate release on shock probation.

By then Shore-Inlow had developed a classic defendant's case of selective amnesia; her new life had begun on January 9, 1990, the day she began cooperating with the FBI. The events before that were in the dim legal past; her subsequent cooperation was all that should matter. Shore-Inlow had fired Jack Vittitow, his reward for engineering her a five-year deal in a capital-murder case. He was paid very little—less than $1,000—but he did have some bad checks as souvenirs.

"We met when she wrote some bad checks," Vittitow would say, "and we parted with some bad checks."

She tersely notified Vittitow of their parting:

JACK VITTITOW,

I WANT ALL RECORDS ON THE CASE TURNED OVER TO MY HUSBAND, CHARLES INLOW.

MARY ANN SHORE-INLOW

She replaced Vittitow with Maury Kommor, an aggressive Louisville attorney who said the Inlow family—believing Vittitow had done a very poor job—had sought him out. Kommor didn't believe Shore-Inlow should have served *any* time.

"Mary Ann should have been given complete immunity," he would later argue. "Without her they never would have found the body, there would be no case.

"There's no doubt in my mind that if Mel gets convicted, she gets probation."

Shore-Inlow's shock-probation hearing was contentious, confrontational, emotional. She wept as she testified she'd twice become pregnant early in her relationship with Ignatow, who forced her to have abortions. On one occasion, when she was eight weeks pregnant, Ignatow knocked her off a chair.

"He said it embarrassed him publicly when I became pregnant," Shore-Inlow testified. "He didn't want to be forced into marriage."

"Mary Ann," Kommor asked, "when he first started beating you, why did you go back?"

"I was afraid of him . . . I was always afraid of him."

"What did he do to keep you in line?"

"He tied me to the bed and performed anal sex on me."

Butch Inlow, a man who looked uncomfortable in a suit, made his first court appearance, ready to defend his wife's honor. Angry, with tears in his eyes, Inlow testified how much he missed her, that she had been misled into believing she would receive a lighter sentence if she cooperated.

Jasmin had only contempt for that argument:

"It is not true that Mary Ann did not come forward until sixteen months after Brenda Schaefer disappeared?"

Kommor complained Jasmin met with Shore only twice, each time for about sixty to ninety minutes, in "the biggest murder case of all time." He said Shore-Inlow had been an abused victim with no family support, no place to turn; she deserved shock probation, to be home with Butch.

Judge Martin Johnstone did not agree. He had always believed Shore-Inlow's story but could never personally or legally excuse it; he denied Kommor's request. During the same week—in what was a little bit of a surprise—U.S. District Court Judge Edward Johnstone ordered the perjury trial to Chattanooga, Tennessee, about three hundred miles from Louisville. The trial was set for July 13.

CHAPTER
31

The final piece of prosecution evidence—a dramatic, almost mystic finding that would have sold Shore-Inlow's story to the Kenton County jury if it had surfaced earlier—came almost by accident.

Jim Lesousky had known a Louisville document examiner named Steve Slyter for several years; Lesousky had used him a half dozen times in the prosecution of credit-card or bad-check charges when he was in Jasmin's office.

Slyter, forty-six, was an interesting man. His office was on the third floor of a hundred-year-old Victorian mansion in Old Louisville, a gentrified area of stone and brick mansions that had been divided into apartments, the once and future homes of Louisville's culturally aware. The windows in Slyter's office faced Central Park with its magnificent oaks, annual Shakespeare festival, and public tennis courts where determined players hammered scuffed balls over industrial-strength nets for hours on end.

"I've become somewhat of an authority on bad tennis," Slyter would lament.

Slyter had worked at several jobs in electronics, ophthalmology, and photographic processing before launching a career in forensic analysis: studying the signatures or writing on wills, deeds, legal documents, even threatening letters. He'd become an expert in the field, testifying in hundreds of court cases, both for the defense and prosecution. Slyter was elegant, bearded, soft-spoken, but firm and knowledgeable. He radiated competence. He was the perfect expert witness, never one to undersell or oversell his goods.

In April 1992, Lesousky had gone to Slyter's office to clean up some loose ends on a case involving documents written in Arabic. Lesousky enjoyed talking with Slyter; some of his work seemed to border on the occult. Killing time, the men began talking about a case in which Slyter had managed to decipher some writing on a telephone pad where the underlying words had been strongly scratched over.

"I have one of the photographs from that case," Slyter told Lesousky. "Do you want to see it?"

"Sure."

Lesousky looked at the photograph. He was amazed Slyter had been able to salvage legible words buried beneath a thick layer of frantic scratchings. Suddenly a thought popped into Lesousky's mind: Mel Ignatow's pocket calendar.

The calendar, a giveaway from Hasenour's restaurant, had been confiscated in the first search of Ignatow's house. It contained daily notes for all of 1988, almost all of them scratched over.

"Would you mind taking a look at it?" Lesousky asked.

"Anytime," Slyter answered.

Lesousky had been excited about the calendar's potential, as were the Jefferson County police when it was first seized. Ignatow, a compulsively organized man, might have written something relevant beneath the September 23 or September 24 dates before scratching out the entries. County police had looked at the calendar, but the entries were so heavily obliterated it seemed hopeless. The calendar was sent to the FBI laboratory in Washington, D.C., where experts—hampered by a backlog of work and uncertain exactly what they were looking for—were also unable to read beneath the scratchings. It was sent back to Louisville.

Meanwhile, the Ignatow case continued to be affected by

legal and financial problems beyond anything anyone in Louisville could even remember. On June 2, citing a lack of federal money to pay T. Clay and his private investigator, William Cravens, Johnstone said the trial would have to be rescheduled until after October 1, the start of a new budget year. The delay was a blessing to Lesousky, who didn't get the pocket calendar to Slyter until June 29. Slyter's bill would be $3,000, but Lesousky knew it could be worth it.

"This is it," Lesousky told Slyter as he handed him the pocket calendar. "We know Ignatow was at Mary Ann Shore's house the night of September twenty-third. We know he murdered [Brenda] the next night. Why don't you see what you can do with it?"

Slyter used the same equipment the FBI had used: a video spectrum analyzer and a stereo microscope. His advantages were a long familiarity with the case, more time to work on it, and having Sears, Fike, and Lesousky a quick phone call away.

The calendar was small, about three inches by six inches, with about an inch of space for each day of the year. Slyter began with January, eventually spending one hundred hours bent over his equipment. Working with various filters to screen infrared and ultraviolet light, Slyter hoped to carefully penetrate levels of ink only two microns thick, reading one layer beneath the other.

"The thing you would hope for is that the ink used to obliterate the writing is different from the ink underneath it. At some combination of light and filter you can get the obliterating ink to disappear."

Slyter quickly guessed that Ignatow used a Cross ballpoint pen with black ink to make his entries, and to obliterate them.

"I was able to make Ignatow's calendar look like plain white paper with nothing on it," he would say. "But I couldn't find a place where one ink stayed and the other disappeared."

Slyter, careful, meticulous, determined, turned to his microscope. Concentrating on the month of September, he made eight-by-ten photographs of every scratch line in the calendar. Combining the photographs with what he saw under the microscope, he used Wite-Out to eliminate the sweeping horizontal strokes. He would make almost three hundred photographs, each one covering perhaps one inch of the diary. He worked at it hour by hour, his patience finally rewarded; there were multiple entries in September with references to MA (Mary Ann Shore-Inlow) or BS (Brenda Schaefer).

Slyter listed Ignatow's entries, one by one.

> 9/9 call MA
> 9/10 MA poss 11 AM
> 9/13 Call MA 11 AM
> 9/15 9 PM MA
> 9/19 call MA date BS
> 9/20 call MA call BS
> 9/21 call MA BS

The entries were vital because Ignatow had testified before the grand jury he had no contact with Shore-Inlow for months before Brenda Schaefer disappeared. Slyter was elated; his hard work was paying off. Focusing on Friday, September 23, the night before the murder, Slyter got the biggest surprise of all; Ignatow had scratched over that black-ink entry in heavy blue ink, the only time he used a different pen the entire year.

Slyter moved to his video spectrum analyzer and fitted it with a 460 blue filter, which would enable him the layer of black ink below. His mind raced as he saw the entry:

> 9/23 MA catails shovel supplies
> 8 PM call BS

Slyter was elated. This was it, the missing piece; some physical corroboration of Shore-Inlow's story! ''Catails'' had never before been mentioned—would remain a mystery— but the shovel and supplies were clearly written in the pocket calendar. Slyter made large photographs of the entry, large enough for any jury to read. He phoned Sears and Lesousky, who raced to his office.

"It was a rare day," Slyter would say. "You don't often see prosecutors give high fives."

Slyter began concentrating on September 24, the day of the murder. Ignatow had used black-on-black ink. The words were extremely difficult to read, but Slyter thought one was "spank" followed by "eat ltr."

Sears believed that was a reference to Ignatow's plan to go to the chili parlor after the murder and make a big enough fuss to be noticed. The next entry was so faint Slyter was certain it would never be admitted in court; his working motto had always been "If it's not evident, it's not evidence." Yet Slyter felt certain what the September 24 entry said; it fit the crime and it fit Ignatow's psychopathic personality:

beat . . . sex/keep bound in house . . . unrealistic idea.

"Mel was going to keep her bound in the house and go back whenever he felt like it," Slyter would explain. "Then he vetoed that idea."

Ignatow and his attorney, T. Clay, would see the photographs of his calendar entries at an evidence hearing before Johnstone; the blown-up images were suddenly laid on the table in front of them. Ignatow looked stunned; he stared at the pictures. The Schaefer family was at the hearing, found satisfaction as a growing fear played across Ignatow's face; it had been a long time coming.

A smiling Ignatow shrugged off the photographs after the hearing: "I keep a notebook all the time. It's not likely that if I was going to do anything like that I would keep notes about it, do you think?"

Shortly after the hearing, Clay and Ignatow went to Slyter's office to see for themselves how the pictures had been taken. Ignatow had already tried to discount their impact; he told Clay the initials MA were for another co-worker, not Mary Ann Shore-Inlow, and the words "shovel and supplies'' were unrelated to the death of Brenda Schaefer.

By then, Clay and Ignatow had been meeting for months in Clay's twentieth-floor office in the Kentucky Home Life Building in downtown Louisville. His corner office, decorated with pictures of efficient-looking hunting dogs, was cluttered with living-room furniture and boxes of documents. Clay was a legal veteran; he had dealt with liars for twenty years. His first impression on talking with Ignatow was that the Kenton County jury had been right: Ignatow was innocent.

"I believed him," Clay would say. "Mel was a very good client. He was a wellspring of ideas. He was fully familiar with all the facts in the case and the evidence against him. He had sat through the trial; it gave him a tremendous advantage over me."

Clay was installing a new computer system that enabled him to place the entire Ignatow file—thousands of pages of documents and testimony—into its file banks. He hoped to go to trial with a laptop computer before him, all that evidence on instant recall. Once or twice a week Ignatow came to his office to help index the records, work with the computer technicians, relentlessly making notes on his case. Not all of Clay's office staff was comfortable working with Ignatow; his history was well known.

"His arrogance would show at times," Clay would say, "but I've been around people a lot more arrogant."

Clay also planned to attack the credibility of the infamous thirteen-minute tape, which continued to be controversial, puzzling, bizarre. Tom Owen, of Bowling Green Kentucky, who described himself as an expert on tape recordings, had interjected a third interpretation of the tape in a legal hearing; he believed the key word in the phrase "That's not shallow . . . that place we *dug*" or "that place we *got*" was neither word; the phrase should read as "that place we *cut*." The "cut" interpretation was based on a new Ignatow story; it referred to a "short cut" he and Shore-Inlow had taken looking for a suitable place to bury her safe. Johnstone would eventually rule the jury's transcript would be left blank, the missing words left up to the jurors' interpretation.

Clay's defense would be similar to Ricketts's: Attack the credibility of Shore-Inlow, downplay the police and FBI work, hammer at a lack of physical evidence, although Slyter's photographs might make that more difficult. All told, Clay would be paid about $48,000 for his work defending Ignatow.

Slyter found the meeting in his office with Clay and Ignatow interesting. Clay acted concerned. Ignatow was more the goodwill ambassador. He wandered all around Slyter's office, appreciatively touching the equipment; complimentary, ingratiating.

"I can easily see that people would find him charming," Slyter would say. "I knew that he was guilty. He knew that I knew, but he was still very much the salesman.

"I'm basically saying, 'I know you did this, you SOB. I'm going to do my best to put you in prison.' And he's coming on like it's a family reunion or something."

On September 9, U.S. District Judge Edward Johnstone, citing "judicial economy," ruled that the Ignatow trial would begin October 13 in U.S. District Court—not in Chattanooga, but in London, Kentucky, a small town at the edge of the Eastern Kentucky mountains about 160 miles southeast of Louisville.

Ignatow, at least from what Clay could see, seemed confident. Ignatow had managed to find yet another public forum to protest his innocence. Showing incredibly bad judgment, the Louisville Society of Professional Journalists had invited him to speak on September 22 to discuss media coverage of his life.

The man who had twice received a change of venue for pretrial publicity was willing to speak before a gathering of journalists and public-relations people two weeks before his trial. When the Louisville chapter of the National Organization for Women protested, the Ignatow appearance was canceled. He would next be judged by a jury of his peers in London.

CHAPTER
32

Steve Doherty paid little attention to the names of the people who lived in the big brick house at 10500 Florian Road. His main concern was installing the customer's order: forty-six yards of white Berber carpet underlaid with a quarter-inch rebond padding, a mixture of foams glued together for added strength.

Doherty was very conscientious, a hard worker. After graduating from Jeffersonville High School, he had walked on the wrestling team at Indiana University for a year, attended Indiana University Southeast in New Albany, then dropped out to begin laying carpet with his brother, Mike, who owned Sunnyside Floor Covering of New Washington, Ind.

Mike was an installer; he contracted with retail carpet outlets for their work. A lot of his business was through Donna Vogel, who owned Floor Fashions, a carpet store in the Louisville suburb of Jeffersontown. Vogel had sold Ronald and Judith Watkins new kitchen flooring not long after they had moved into the 3,500-square-foot home at 10500 Florian Road in January 1991.

"I remember they said something at the time about the previous owner of the house being in jail," Vogel would say, "but I didn't know who they were talking about; no names were ever mentioned."

The new owners liked the Florian Road house, especially the upstairs bathroom. They'd been told the previous owner spent about $25,000 to add a skylight, whirlpool, mirrors, and expensive bathroom fixtures. The house's landscaping had been neglected but it was obvious the previous owners had expensive interior-design tastes—with an Oriental flavor.

One thing the Watkinses disliked about the house was the chocolate-brown rug that dominated the great room, with its fingers of brown carpeting reaching down the narrow hall past the wet bar into the kitchen. The carpet's pattern was too dated, its mood too dark and somber.

It was June of 1992 when the couple began seriously thinking about new carpeting for the great room, something much lighter in tone. They were in no hurry; they would take all summer if need be. The important thing was to find the right color at the right price. They shopped many stores; the decision was so difficult it was the middle of September— almost four months after they began looking—when they returned to Floor Fashions to talk to Vogel.

"I remembered the brown carpet from the first time I had gone to their house," Vogel would say. "I didn't know how long they had been looking, but from the time they came into the store until their new carpet arrived it wasn't a week, with maybe another two weeks to get it installed."

Installation was scheduled for October 1, a Thursday. The job was contracted to Mike Doherty, with Steve Doherty and two other employees, Joe Blackburn, twenty-four, and Donovan Harold, nineteen, doing the work. About 8:00 A.M. Blackburn and Harold met at Steve Doherty's house, a small, one-story brick home at 1221 Birchwood Drive near grassy Highland Park where the boys had all played while growing up.

The morning was bright, sunny, the temperature in the mid-50s, headed toward a crisp 74 degrees, perfect Louisville weather. National—and local—news was dominated by speculation that Ross Perot, the folksy Texas billionaire, might buy his way back into the presidential campaign. Mel Ignatow had temporarily faded from the local news; he had spent much of that time in T. Clay's office helping prepare his defense for the October 13 trial, only twelve days away.

With Blackburn and Doherty following in separate cars, Doherty drove his tan 1984 Chevrolet van to Elkins-American in Jeffersonville, a trucking firm that hauled carpet from Dalton, Georgia, to Jeffersonville for distribution to local retailers. The three men wrestled the forty-six yards of carpet and padding into the van, then headed south toward Louisville on the Kennedy Bridge, turning east on Interstate 64 toward Jeffersontown.

Doherty picked up the work order at the store, quickly ran through the final instructions with Vogel, then headed toward 10500 Florian Road, arriving about 10:00 A.M. The men carried their toolboxes into the house and quickly began sizing up the job. Doherty glanced around at the creekstone fireplace, the balcony that hung over the great room, the dark brown carpet on its floor.

"Three or four hours," Doherty thought, "and we should be out of here."

Their first chore was to move a couch, a love seat, and a few chairs from the great room into an adjacent room. Judith Watkins was there to assist them; her husband had gone to the store to get some stereo wiring to place under the new padding.

Harold carefully began to take up the carpet from the great room; the Watkinses wanted to save it to use in another area. Doherty—with Blackburn working right behind him—began working in the hallway that led to the kitchen. Using a pry bar, Doherty popped up the flat piece of metal where the carpeting met the kitchen floor, then began working his way down the wall, pulling up carpet as he went.

The hallway had been screened off from the kitchen by two narrow wooden doors that bisected the doorway. The doors, each about eighteen inches wide, were folded back to opposite walls where they rested against brass door stops attached to the baseboard. Working his way to just past one of the door stops, pulling carpet as he went, Doherty was surprised at how tightly fastened the rug had become; it wouldn't budge.

He struggled with it, pulling at the loosened edges. He bent over to take a closer look, jerked hard at the rug until it gave way, his momentum bringing him to his feet.

Standing upright, Doherty looked down in surprise at the narrow, rectangular hole that had been hidden below the carpet.

"A *heat duct*," he thought. "Why in the world would a heat duct be buried beneath carpet?"

There had been no vent cover over the duct. The carpeting had been stretched so tightly over the opening that no hole— or even an indentation—ever showed. The duct opening, about four inches by ten inches, had been cut so close to the wall that it was protected by the open door where it rested against the doorstop; no one could ever have known the duct was there, or even have had reason to step on that part of the hallway.

Doherty looked at the carpet in his hands. It had been fastened with huge staples that looked as if they had been shot from a high-pressure air stapler, something a professional might use. Doherty was embarrassed, unsure what to do next; this must have been somebody's hiding place.

He looked down into the vent, which dropped down only about ten inches before angling sharply away toward the basement furnace. He saw a clear plastic Ziploc bag fastened to one side of the vent with gray duct tape. What looked to be jewelry was in the bag, along with three small black plastic canisters with gray snap-on lids, the kind of canisters used to hold 35mm film.

Doherty got to his knees, reaching into the vent. He gingerly picked up one edge of the bag, but didn't tear it loose. He saw the jewelry more clearly: at least one ring, a necklace, perhaps a tennis bracelet. He looked at the plastic canisters. A terrible thought leaped into his mind: *Drugs*. He had stumbled onto a cache of drugs. Ronald and Judith Watkins didn't look like people who would ever be involved in drugs, but the jewelry and canisters had been very well hidden.

Judith Watkins was in another room. Her husband wasn't home yet. Doherty called over his two working partners and showed them the find. The three men were perplexed. They briefly considered saying nothing—just go on about their work, let actions take their own course. Surely Judith or Ronald Watkins would notice the opening and the plastic bag; they could discreetly do whatever they wanted.

Joe Blackburn settled the issue. He got on his knees, reached into the duct, and pulled out the plastic bag.

"Donovan," Blackburn told Harold, "why don't you go get Mrs. Watkins?"

When she appeared, Blackburn asked: "Do you know what's in the heat duct?"

"No, what is it?"

Blackburn handed her the bag. She peered through the plastic, immediately understanding what she had in her hand, its incredible impact and meaning.

"Do you know who used to live here?" she asked the men.

"No."

"Mel Ignatow."

Deirdre Fike had left her business card at the Watkins home when she asked if the FBI could again search their house; the owners had said no, but promised to call if something showed up. When Ronald Watkins returned home, he immediately tried to call Fike, who was a hearing in the nearby federal building. The call was relayed to her supervisor, Mike Griffin.

"When Watkins started telling me what they had found," Griffin would say, "the hair began standing up on my arms."

Griffin, John Wayne buff, a veteran of dozens of tight spots, felt his heart pound as Watkins talked.

"Who knows about this?" Griffin asked Watkins.

"My wife's here and three young carpet layers."

"Anybody else?"

"No."

"Don't call anybody else until the FBI gets there."

Griffin knew how hard Fike had worked on the case; she had to be the agent to lead the investigation, make the arrest. He almost ran the two hundred yards across the asphalt parking lot that separated his office from the federal building, hustling upstairs to Courtroom 2.

It was almost noon. Fike was with Alan Sears and Jim Lesousky at a pretrial hearing before U.S. District Judge Edward Johnstone when she noticed Griffin frantically motioning to her to come outside. The courtroom, where yet another hearing on suppressing tape-recorded conversations was being held, is cavernous, regal blue and gray, churchlike. It took Fike a few seconds to reach Griffin. He led her into a small witness room:

"I just got a telephone call from the people who live in Ignatow's old house. They found the jewelry and some film canisters in a heating duct."

Fike felt a sudden surge of surprise, elation. She had to sit down, collect her thoughts, get organized. In a few minutes she called Sears outside and told him the news. The two hugged like schoolchildren; finally it seemed as if Mel Ignatow's luck had run out.

Griffin began planning the next step.

"Here's what we need to do," he told Fike. "I've got agents standing by to help you. I want you to go to the house, secure the scene. Make sure we have two or three vehicles go with you to assist."

In another bit of good luck, Cyrus Glover, the man who helped detail crime scenes and had found Susie the mannequin, happened to be in Louisville. He was waiting for an airplane to fly back to Washington, but quickly canceled. He joined Fike, her working partner, Allen "Mac" Bond, and Ed Armento, all members of squad four, the Louisville FBI's violent-crimes squad, in hustling out to 10500 Florian Road.

The Ziploc bag was sitting on the kitchen counter, the same kitchen where Jefferson County police detective Jim Wesley and Jeffersontown detective Robert Perkins had sat four years earlier interviewing an emotional Ignatow; the plastic bag could have been ten feet away from them all along.

Fike was still excited, emotional. She could see the gray film canisters and Brenda's jewelry: the engagement ring, a cocktail ring, a gold bracelet, along with two items the family did not know were missing, a gold necklace and a silver Indian head coin. Brenda's house keys, her billfold, and her purse were never found; they'd apparently been thrown away.

Doherty, Blackburn, and Harold had to reenact the discovery, showing the agents how the carpet was lifted, and the location of the bag. More FBI special agents showed up, providing security, carefully finger-printing all the evidence, taking dozens of photographs of the rug, the hallway, the doors, the open duct, and the plastic bag. Their arrival created a small stir in the neighborhood, where people slowly became aware something was going on at Mel Ignatow's old house. In the middle of their investigation, Donna Vogel called to ask why a simple carpeting job was taking the three men so long.

Even with the jewelry in hand, Fike still had several things to worry and wonder about. The film was at least four years old; how long had it been in the heat duct? Had it been damaged by furnace heat? Could the raw film still be processed?

Fike couldn't even be sure these were the pictures Mary Ann Shore-Inlow had taken the night of the murder, although finding the canisters with Brenda's jewelry made it seem a strong possibility. The discovery also raised several questions in Fike's mind that might never be answered. How long had the brown carpet been in the house? Did Ignatow have help hiding the film under the carpet? Did his mother—or anyone else in the family—ever notice the heat duct had been covered, or even know it had been there?

Ignatow was a man with many shadowy connections, both in Kentucky and the Far East; wasn't there *someone*—a pornographer, a magazine publisher, a trusted colleague—who would have developed the film for a price, especially since

Ignatow's face was not supposed to be in any of them?

Finally, had Ignatow ever plotted to get back into his old house, stage some sort of burglary, grab the film, and leave?

Long before the FBI violent-crimes squad finished its work in the house, special agent Ed Armento called Brian Keller at the Metro Photo Lab, which processed crime film for both the Louisville and Jefferson County police. Armento warned Keller he could be working late.

"He told me they thought they had the Ignatow film," Keller would say, "but nobody would know for sure until we processed it."

About 4:00 P.M., Fike and the other agents arrived at the photo lab, located on the second floor of the Louisville Police Department headquarters. The Kodak color-print film, ASA 200, would be developed by machine—the raw film inserted in one end, the processed color negative rolling out the other end in a long strip. Fike was nervous, excited; the twenty-minute wait seemed like an hour to her. To pass the time she called Sears and Lesousky, who were anxiously waiting for any information at the FBI office.

Finally the long negative strip snaked out of the processor, slid down a ramp, and passed a point of light where Fike could see an image. It was Brenda Schaefer, tied to the coffee table, exactly as Mary Ann Shore-Inlow had described, exactly the way she had reenacted it using Susie the mannequin.

The image jolted Fike; she felt weak, almost ill, a revulsion at what she was seeing mixed with the elation of knowing that what they had all been looking for so long was finally at hand, slowly sliding down a ramp in front of her.

After all three rolls of film were processed, Keller ran the negatives through a video analyzer, which automatically calibrated the printer. He was a little nervous; this was not a normal job. He had processed a lot of crime film, had seen a lot of film of sadism and child abuse, and was amazed at the good quality of the negatives, the perfect exposures, the proper use of flash.

"They were right on the money," he would say. "It was

almost as if the pictures were taken in a studio.''

The 112 photographs were automatically printed on long rolls of copy paper, then sliced up into individual five-by-seven photographs. The whole process, from raw film to finished prints, took less than an hour. The FBI agents took the photographs as soon as they were finished, but Keller had a little time to look at them:

"It was a very detailed, systematic approach; let's document each stage. It was kind of chilling.

"They started out as if Brenda had been arrested; frontal picture, profile, back. They showed the same thing as she removed layers of clothes. You could tell she had been crying. It was humiliating. You could tell she was very humiliated.''

It was close to 6:00 P.M. before Fike got back to the FBI headquarters with the prints. Everyone was still euphoric; not only were the photographs clear and sharp, but they matched most of the posed pictures that had been taken with Susie.

"It was amazing how close they were," Fike would say. "Mary Ann was right.''

Tom Schaefer was called at home and asked if he and Mike could come down to FBI headquarters; there had been a new development. Tom Schaefer, as he often did, had a feeling that something big was about to happen. The men were met at the back door of FBI headquarters by Mike Griffin, then led upstairs, where two packages were handed to them. Mike Schaefer wasn't sure if it was Brenda's jewelry. Tom felt a cold chill run through his body.

"Most definitely," he told the agents. "This is it.''

Griffin was pleased, but cautious.

"Please don't say anything about this to anyone, not even Carolyn," Griffin told them. "We want to keep the lid on this for two or three days.''

Caution prevailed everywhere. Shore-Inlow had done her photography job too well; none of the photographs showed Ignatow's face. Nor did anyone have to be reminded of what had happened the last time the FBI and Jefferson County police had been forced to move in haste; Ignatow had been acquitted.

Sears, Lesousky, and the special agents had all decided not to do anything right away; they wanted to check the film canisters for Ignatow's fingerprints, which could take a few days. It was a little risky, but Ignatow was under surveillance at LaFontenay Apartments; he couldn't get away. This time everything was going to be perfect. Fike called Jim Wesley and told him what they had found, adding they were going to move very deliberately now.

"We wanted to be careful, take our time, be sure we had everything in place before we arrested him," Fike would say. "We didn't want anything to go wrong after we'd come this far. So we all went our separate ways."

It wouldn't be that simple. Late that afternoon WLKY-TV's Steve Burgin, who had been tipped off by a WLKY salesperson—who had been told by a client—that some film and jewelry had been found at Ignatow's house. Burgin didn't have time to go before the 6:00 P.M. news. Immediately afterward he went to the Watkinses' home and knocked on their door.

"They wouldn't tell me anything," Burgin would say.

Burgin went back to the station and began calling people at home, including T. Clay.

"There's a rumor going around," Burgin told him, "that they've installed some carpet in Mel's old house and found several rolls of film and jewelry in a vent. What do you think?"

Clay was stunned, astounded; he knew nothing about it.

"I don't know what to think," he told Burgin.

After Burgin hung up, Clay called Sears and Lesousky at home to see what they knew; they were not home yet. Clay knew something was up.

"I'm thinking trouble," he would say.

Clay tried to call Fike, was told she had just left; she was eating dinner with her husband, also an FBI agent, and his daughter, who was in town for a visit. They were eating at

LaCazuela Mexican Restaurant at 10602 Shelbyville Road, not too far from LaFontenay Apartments.

"Can you patch me in to her?" Clay asked.

"Sure."

Fike wouldn't confirm anything.

"You'll have to talk to the U.S. Attorney about that," she said, then cut her meal short to return to the FBI office.

Burgin had also called Scott Cox, who was at home, asking him the same questions he had asked Clay.

"I don't know anything about it," he told Burgin.

Cox didn't know; he had been out of the loop. After Burgin's call he went to his downtown office to work on another case. He bumped into Sears and Lesousky in the stairwell leading to the parking lot.

"Is there something you guys aren't telling me?" Cox asked them.

Sears and Lesousky were surprised; how did Cox find out?

"Steve Burgin called me," he told them.

The three men went back upstairs to the U.S. Attorney's office. They knew that if Burgin had called Cox, he had probably called Clay, perhaps even Ignatow. Once again the Ignatow case had taken on a life all its own.

"We have to arrest him," Cox urged. "He's either going to try to run, or maybe kill himself."

The men called Joe Whittle, who was out of town, advising him of the developments. They looked through their law books—18 U.S.C., Section 1001—and decided Ignatow could be charged with lying to a federal official in the course of his duty; he'd lied to Cox about the murder in a conversation in Ricketts's office.

The men prepared two legal documents: the specific complaint against Ignatow and an affidavit to be signed by Deirdre Fike detailing the facts of the case. Then Sears had an idea: Have a judge sign an order allowing Ignatow to be stripped and photographed naked, legal under federal statute.

The prosecutors had a backdrop to all their work. T. Clay was calling their office over and over, leaving messages, trying to find out what was going on. Although the three men heard the phone ring and ring, neither Sears, Lesousky, nor Cox would pick it up.

Clay went to bed that night a frustrated man.

"I did call Bill Cravens, the [private] detective who had been working on the case with me," Clay would say. "I figured if I didn't get any sleep that night, he shouldn't either."

Around 9:00 P.M. the prosecutors called U.S. District Court Judge John Heyburn at his home in the exclusive Indian Hills and told him they had some orders they needed signed. Fike met them there, swearing the facts in the affidavit were true. Cox watched the television news at Heyburn's house, wondering if he was going to see the story blow up in front of him.

A little after 11:00 P.M. several teams of FBI agents—perhaps eight to ten people—converged on the LaFontenay Apartments. Their plan was to seal off all entrances to the complex and assign an inner perimeter team for close watch, with special agent in charge Dave Kohl, Griffin, Armento, and Fike among the entry team at 175 LaFontenay Drive, Ignatow's apartment.

Ignatow had kept a very low profile since his acquittal; he feared public rebuke, even worse. FBI surveillance agents had been watching the apartment since late in the afternoon. Griffin believed Ignatow might have had some contact with Charlie Ricketts—apparently after receiving a phone call from Clay. In any event, Ignatow was now home.

Fike was ready, eager to get moving. The team, all wearing dark jackets with huge FBI letters on the back, was in place. The plan was to knock on the door and arrest Mel as he answered. If Mike, his son, came to the door, they would just ask him if his father was there. Everybody was all but certain Ignatow already knew the film and jewelry had been found; no one was certain what his reaction would be.

As Fike and the others prepared to walk up the apartment stairs, Ignatow suddenly appeared from his building, walking toward his car. He was dressed very casually: loafers, khaki-colored walking shorts, a blue T-shirt, and a tan windbreaker.

He had no luggage, didn't appear to be in a hurry. As he got in the car Kohl approached him and told him he was under arrest.

"What do you want me for this time?" Ignatow asked.

Fike hustled across the parking lot, put the handcuffs on Ignatow, and placed him in the FBI car for the trip downtown.

"I was going out to get some ice cream," Ignatow told the agents.

CHAPTER
33

Mel Ignatow was naked, hands held stiffly at his sides, posing for pictures in the photography lab at Louisville FBI headquarters. Larry Thomas, a civilian FBI employee, was taking the 35mm color pictures. With Ignatow in the small, cluttered room were Mike Griffin and Dierdre Fike.

It was very early in the morning of Friday, October 2. If Ignatow's arrest was supposed to be a secret, it was out. The television cameras had been waiting outside the federal building as Ignatow, looking sheepish and mystified by it all, was led though the doors, Fike at his side.

The agents took the elevator to the fifth floor and led Ignatow down a narrow hall where he would be booked, fingerprinted, photographed. The photo session had begun with Ignatow clothed. Then—as Judge John Heyburn's court order had allowed—Ignatow was told to strip and face the camera. The purpose was to try to match the body hair, moles, and other physical characteristics of the man in the photographs taken by Shore-Inlow.

"I'm not going to strip with a woman in the room," Ignatow said.

"Yes, you are," Fike answered. "You have no choice."

"I'm not going to do it."

As lead agent in the case, Fike had a right to be there; she was a professional doing her job. Beyond that she was very much aware of what Brenda Schaefer had gone through: the humiliation of being forced to strip, then be photographed nude. Not only was Fike supposed to be there, she *wanted* to be there.

"Mel, I'm in charge of this case, I have a court order and you will comply."

"I won't do it. I won't be humiliated like this. I want to see my attorney."

Ignatow would be allowed to call T. Clay, but only after he was booked, fingerprinted, and photographed; that was the law. The imposing Griffin eased up to Ignatow's side, whispered in his ear.

"Mr. Ignatow. We have a court order for you to take your clothes off. It won't do any good for you and me to have to roll around here on the floor ripping your clothes off. Your clothes are coming off. I don't want to hear any more."

Ignatow stopped protesting.

"I just want it on the record that I'm protesting."

"It's on the record."

Griffin helped Ignatow get undressed. Standing naked before a white backdrop, he was photographed from the side, rear, and front. Despite his discomfort, Ignatow was still belligerent. Griffin wasn't finished. He had seen the photographs of Brenda, arms behind her head, forced into a prisoner-of-war pose of submission. Without saying it, Griffin wanted Ignatow to know what the FBI had; all the photographs had been printed; they would be used against him.

"Okay, Mel, put your hands behind your head, elbows out."

Ignatow was fully exposed, humiliated. Griffin saw the arrogance drain from his face. Ignatow had always indulged in sexual fantasies, Griffin was thinking; this was probably not one of them.

Griffin and Fike knew that whatever happened now—a trial or a negotiated plea—Ignatow would not escape; his body hair and moles matched the Shore-Inlow photographs, and the expensive gold-and-stainless-steel diver's watch he was wearing in the photographs was the same watch he was wearing when arrested.

Ignatow's arrest—and the news stories about jewelry and film being found in his former home—hit Louisville like an earthquake. The initial reaction was total community outrage. The find verified what most people already suspected: Mel Ignatow had gotten away with murder. That outrage was accompanied by one inevitable, almost cynical question: Why had he kept the jewelry and film?

The more sophisticated questions would come as an aftershock. What if the federal trial had been held in July, as first scheduled, and Ignatow had again been acquitted? What if Ronald and Judith Watkins had waited just two more weeks to buy their new carpeting?

Callers to Louisville talk radio shows demanded some suspension of the Fifth Amendment of the Bill of Rights, the two hundred-year-old "double jeopardy" provision that said, in part: "Nor shall any person be subject for the same offense to be twice put in jeopardy of life or limb."

What those twenty words meant, in effect, was that Ignatow could not again be charged by the state with murder, kidnapping, sodomy, sexual abuse, robbery, or tampering with evidence, although it was becoming patently obvious he was guilty of all those charges. By way of explanation, the *Courier-Journal* ran a small boxed story, along with its lengthy story on Ignatow's arrest, explaining that both the U.S. Constitution and the Kentucky Constitution restrict double jeopardy.

The story quoted a 1978 U.S. Supreme Court decision that said "there is no exception permitting retrial once the defendant has been acquitted, no matter how egregiously erroneous the acquittal." The Supreme Court, in a 1957 case, explained the underlying idea behind the double-jeopardy clause in that the state "with all its resources and power, should not be allowed to make repeated attempts to convict an individual for an offense, thereby subjecting him to embarrassment, expense and ordeal and compelling him to live in a continuing state of anxiety and insecurity.''

Ignatow had played his game as far as it would take him. He had never seemed capable of remorse, only public protestations of innocence combined with a private willingness to use any individual, family member, church, or social organization that offered him a helping hand. His evil cunning and sexual depravity were mixed with a self-righteous piety that placed him beyond the understanding of honest people, made them vulnerable to him.

After four years of lies, self-absorption, and self-pity, Ignatow would now take the only route left to him; he would plead guilty with the same piety with which he had maintained his innocence; his guilty plea would save the federal government money and spare the Schaefer family additional grief. Ignatow would then seek full credit for his voluntary display of kindness and compassion.

T. Clay had just dropped off his wife at work Friday morning when he received a call on his car phone; U.S. District Judge Edward Johnstone wanted to see him right away. When Clay got to the judge's office, he met with Lesousky and Sears. Johnstone had read the morning paper, knew the jewelry and film had been found, suspected that with a little push from him the case could now be settled without an expensive, time-consuming trial.

Ignatow, still dressed in the loafers, shorts, T-shirt, and jacket he had been wearing when arrested, had been led into the federal courthouse that morning in handcuffs and leg irons, a faint smile on his face.

''I don't know anything about it,'' he shouted to reporters as he was quickly led past.

As the morning went on, Sears and Lesousky showed Clay the torture photographs; he would have a right to see them before the trial, anyway. Ignatow never saw the pictures—the prosecutors were determined never to give him the satisfaction of seeing them—but after Clay talked to Ignatow, it became obvious he did not want to go to trial.

''The photograph was the smoking gun,'' Clay would tell the press. ''It was more than one hundred smoking guns.''

Clay was surprised about the pictures and jewelry, but did not take Ignatow's lies personally; he had been a defense attorney too long for that.

"It's like getting ready for an athletic contest. There's so many different things that can thwart you before the trial. You think, 'Okay, I'll prepare the best way I can. If circumstances beyond my control take over, then I'll deal with it and move on to the next case.'

"In fact, if I had been in Mel's position and had done what Mel had done, I probably would have handled it the same way. I would have played it out to the very end, the last possible second.

"No, I didn't have any hard feelings toward Mel at all."

Negotiations were tricky because there were actually three legal items on the table: the original three-count indictment against Ignatow; the newer charge of lying to Scott Cox; the prosecutor's desire to get Ignatow to confess to the premeditated murder of Brenda Schaefer.

After a morning of preliminary talks, Clay, Sears, and Lesousky went to room 258, the U.S. District Court Library, to work out a possible ending to the story. The big library was like something from a movie set: lush, quiet, a thick tan rug on the floor, a long gleaming table down the center, sixteen elegant chairs at its edges. Long rows of lawbooks were stacked along the walls, reaching to the ceiling, their red, black, and beige covers almost gleaming in the rich, diffuse light.

Clay had one thing going for him; no matter how strong the evidence he could still go to trial, force the federal government to spend perhaps $100,000 to put on its case in London, Kentucky.

Along with the cost of a trial, Lesousky and Sears had other factors to consider. On the plus side, if they accepted a guilty plea on the three-count indictment in exchange for a reduced sentence, there was a certainty of conviction—without appeal.

Sears—and U.S. Attorney Joe Whittle—remained worried that Judge Johnstone would somehow hurt their case, or that

Ignatow might convince Johnstone during the sentencing phase that he had never planned to murder Brenda Schaefer, that the whole incident had been a sex-therapy class gone wrong, and her death was an accident.

The prosecutors feared the effect of the graphic photographs, which would be blown up to almost poster size for the jurors. The Schaefer family had suffered enough; made public, the pictures might somehow end up in some magazine. Nor was either side especially happy about a trial in London, a rural area with a population much different from that of Louisville; Kenton County was still on their minds.

Testimony and court documents from earlier hearings indicated Johnstone had never considered dismissing the case. His emphasis had been on the facts at hand; he had to keep reminding the attorneys this was not a murder case. That had already been decided; this was a new case. Johnstone did not issue many advisory opinions along the way to a trial because his style had always been to let evidentiary issues settle themselves out beforehand; he always encouraged attorneys to solve their problems among themselves.

Clay, Sears, and Lesousky could negotiate only within a limited range anyway; they were bound by the 1987 federal sentencing guidelines, which were designed to provide mostly uniform sentences nationwide for similar crimes.

The seven-page guideline booklet looked a little like a college sociology test. The charges against Ignatow—perjury, subornation of perjury, and lying to the grand jury—were given numerical weight, with points added or subtracted for the defendant's criminal history, cooperation with police, and similar factors.

When Ignatow's numbers were plugged into a predetermined sentencing grid, the mandated range of his prison time was from 97 to 121 months—approximately eight to ten years. It made no difference that the three Class-D felonies with which he was charged carried a maximum penalty of five years each; the sentencing guidelines must be followed.

Sears and Lesousky knew that if the case went to trial and Ignatow was found guilty on all counts, his maximum sentence would still be only the 121 months, a little over ten years. They also knew that Ignatow—always a model prisoner—would get 54 days off his sentence for each year served without incident after his first year. Sears and Lesousky argued for the high end, 121 months. Clay wanted the low end, 97 months. Clay's best argument never changed: Deal or go to trial.

Sears and Lesousky had to decide if the cost and pain of the trial would be worth the potential benefit. Even if they won in the new trial, Johnstone might not sentence Ignatow to the full 121 months. The prosecutors, along with Fike, had done a prodigious amount of preparation, were eager to test it. A lot of money had already been spent. They *wanted* to see Ignatow taken apart in public.

The prosecutors argued, worried about the risks, consulted with a federal probation officer, talked by phone to Joe Whittle. Clay went back to Ignatow, then returned with a proposal: If Ignatow was guaranteed the low end of the sentence he would plead guilty to the three federal charges. He would also publicly confess to the premeditated murder of Brenda Schaefer. The new charge of lying to Scott Cox would be dropped.

If Johnstone didn't accept the 97-month sentence, Ignatow had the right to withdraw his guilty plea and go to trial.

Sears, Lesousky, and Clay agreed to the deal; Ignatow would publicly admit to the premeditated murder of Brenda Schaefer at a change-of-plea proceeding before Johnstone at 2:00 P.M.

Events had moved so swiftly that it was about 1:30 before Carolyn Kopp learned that Ignatow was going to change his plea. Mike Schaefer didn't have his car at Fort Knox that day; he had to patch together a sudden trip to downtown Louisville. Tom Schaefer, who was at work in LaGrange about twenty-five miles away, had been advised four or five times by Yulee Shafer that something might happen; he got the final word about 1:30 P.M.

"Mel's pleading guilty, they want me down there now," he told his supervisor.

"Go," he was told.

When Carolyn arrived, she saw Natalie Lisanby, Ignatow's sister, and Ignatow's son, Mike, sitting together on a bench in the cavernous hallway, tears in their eyes. FBI special agent Mac Bond caught Tom Schaefer as he came into the door, pulled him to one side, told him about the deal. Mike Schaefer got to the federal courthouse a little later, joined by Mary Ann Hilbert and her husband, Bernie.

Tom Schaefer, still dressed in his blue correctional uniform, pushed open the huge courtroom door and instantly felt a surge of tension, expectation; the room was full of people. Space had been made for the Schaefer family on the front bench. Most of the others were already full, with spectators, reporters, and photographers flooding out toward the side walls.

The Schaefers saw prosecutors from the Commonwealth Attorney's office, the U.S. Attorney's office, their clerks and secretaries. Many of the federal courthouse employees had pushed into the room to watch the final moment of a four-year drama. Ernie Jasmin looked up at the Schaefers and wiggled eight fingers at them; Mel was getting eight years.

There was a somber air of congratulations in the room. Scott Cox came by to shake Tom Schaefer's hand, wish him well. The buzz was almost like a party, with everyone waiting for the guest of honor. As Ignatow and Clay came into the room from the right rear door, the courtroom went dead silent, all eyes on the men. They took their seats behind a table, not talking to each other, Ignatow, as always, playing with his legal pad and pencils.

Tom Schaefer heard some talking behind him, a muffled burst of laughter.

"I wonder who's going to play Charlie Ricketts in the movie?" somebody had asked.

The change-of-plea proceeding began late, closer to 3:00 P.M. As he had done through the trial, Ignatow occasionally stared at the Schaefers, who stared back, unwilling to give an emotional inch to him.

Sears and Lesousky faced Clay and Ignatow across the

wide room, Johnstone on the bench above them. Sears did most of the talking, Lesousky at his side. It had been a long day for both men, beginning about 8:30 A.M. with the call from Johnstone's office followed by six hours of intense negotiations, including about an hour with Clay and Ignatow together.

For Lesousky the real high had come the night before with the discovery of the film and jewelry, and the processing of the pictures. He had gotten the same feeling the day Brenda's body was found; he was out on the street, performing police work, something rare for a federal prosecutor.

After four months of emotional buildup to the trial, he suddenly had to shift gears, help negotiate a plea change, prepare a lot of very detailed but important paperwork, all of it anticlimactic.

The first part of the proceeding was routine. Johnstone advised Ignatow of his rights, led him through the eight-page plea-bargaining agreement on the three-count indictment that set out in public what had been agreed to in private.

The Schaefers sat together, listening to more of the carefully phrased language of the court, waiting for their time. It came a few minutes later when Ignatow, as agreed, stood before Johnstone, his voice breaking the churchlike silence of the moment.

"On September twenty-fourth, 1988, I did take Brenda Sue Schaefer over to Mary Ann Shore's house on Poplar Level Road and I did physically and sexually abuse her and I did murder her."

Carolyn Kopp cried, her head bowed. The words were bittersweet to her brothers, who were grateful Ignatow was going to jail, forever angry he would someday be getting out.

Sears pushed for more, believing Ignatow could fulfill the conditions of his plea agreement only by giving some details of the murder in open court.

"Would you tell the court on the record what type of sex acts that you engaged in on the evening of September twenty-fourth, 1988?"

"Is that necessary?" Johnstone asked.

"Yes, sir, Your Honor."

Clay moved in to protect Ignatow, saying he thought the answer might go beyond the required guilty plea. Sears rephrased the question.

"Would the defendant admit that the sex acts were done by force and compulsion, not without the consent of Brenda Schaefer?"

Clay jumped in again:

"Does the court desire Mr. Ignatow to answer that?"

Johnstone saw no need for a discussion of the sexual details; that had come out in the Covington trial. His interpretation of the plea agreement didn't include such details; he also felt the need to protect Brenda Schaefer. He told Ignatow to answer the question about forceful sex acts yes or no, then move on. He suggested similar questions be proposed to Ignatow in writing.

Sears tried one more time.

"There's one other question I would like to ask . . . with the court's permission, and that's for Mr. Ignatow to tell us how Miss Schaefer died?"

Johnstone relayed the question to Ignatow.

"How did she die?"

"She died from having inhaled chloroform. She died peacefully."

A shock wave ran through the Schaefers. Ignatow had sexually tortured Brenda for hours, humiliated her, destroyed her pride and dignity. Now he said she died peacefully.

"Bullshit," said Mike Schaefer, spitting out the word. Carolyn Kopp turned away, couldn't look back at Ignatow. At the end of the proceeding, Ignatow asked to make a statement. He turned a little, facing toward the Schaefers and his own family, his voice quivering.

"I assume total responsibility for what I did. What I did was wrong and horrible, and there are reasons, but I'm not going to get into that because there are no excuses.

"I just wanted to say to Brenda's family that I am very sorry this happened. I know all the pain and sorrow and suffering I have caused you. I have felt it myself.''

The last line was classic Ignatow: pulling himself into the circle of grief. The Schaefers did not believe a word Ignatow said; the eight-year sentence wasn't enough, not nearly enough.

Ignatow continued. Just one day before, he had been willing to stand before God and a federal jury to profess his innocence. Now, as he had done so many times before, he would use values that others truly held sacred to further his ends.

"And I want to apologize to my own family for the same reason. I want to apologize to all the law-enforcement agencies and to the judicial system, local, county, state, and federal, for all the grief and burden I've caused them. It was not my intent to do that.

"I just hope and pray that all of you will forgive me as I ask forgiveness from God. And I hope that there's some unknown way that God will bring about some good from this. Because I know the Bible says in all things God works for the good of those who love.''

As Tom and Mike Schaefer left the federal courthouse, they avoided all reporters; they never could have expressed the confusing cross-current of emotions they were feeling had they been asked. That Ignatow would even speak of love, family, and God was blasphemy beyond comprehension. Ignatow was going to prison for eight years, but that wasn't the result they had wanted; it was just the best they were going to get.

It had all ended so quickly. Just the night before, they'd been called to identify Brenda's jewelry, their hopes rising that it soon might be over. They were optimistic, but had been through too much to let their feelings show. At that point in their lives, they wore their stoicism like a heavy coat.

Not one day had passed in the last four years when they hadn't thought about Brenda, Jack, the deaths of their parents. Now, in less than twenty-four hours, Ignatow had been arrested, had publicly confessed his sin, and was going to prison. The Schaefers had been pushing against an emotional wall for so long it was hard to stop. Nor would the confession bring back Brenda, restore their family; Ignatow had taken away those things forever.

Tom Schaefer was grateful, angry, resigned, frustrated, dissatisfied. He felt good, but the feeling was hollow at its core. So many people had come forward to help the family, had devoted months and years of their personal and professional lives to the Schaefers. There was no proper way to thank them. They deserved better. Brenda deserved better.

Mike Schaefer shared those feelings; all the Schaefer lives had been touched by good people who had come to them in hard times. He wanted to pay them back, reach out to them, but his hands were empty; a simple thanks didn't seem like enough.

In time, Mike Schaefer would come to believe that Ignatow's confession, as self-serving as it had been, was the best possible solution. It avoided the agony of another trial. It forced Ignatow to admit in front of God, the membership of Southeast Christian Church, the jurors in Kenton County, his character witnesses, and the entire community, that he had tortured and murdered another human being. His confession left no doubt in anyone's mind.

The Schaefer family's healing—and it would take a long time—would have to grow from there.

EPILOGUE

The damage Mel Ignatow had done to so many lives and families, including his own, was incalculable, but the story did not end with his confession. It continued to twist and turn for years afterward. Nothing about the case ever seemed settled, final, or satisfactory. Nor was there any evidence Ignatow had changed, or would change.

Jefferson County police sergeant Jim Wesley, who had chased Ignatow for four years, did not hear his confession. Wesley had no idea events would move as fast as they did; he had taken his wife, Anne, and their daughter, Meredith, to a daylong outing at the Louisville Zoo. Wesley's superiors, the FBI, the Commonwealth Attorney's office, and the U.S. Attorney's office all had frantically tried to reach him. Wesley, a uniformed shift commander, no longer carried a pager when off duty. He heard Ignatow's confession on WHAS radio as he drove out of the zoo parking lot.

"I was in shock," he would say.

Wesley's joy was tempered by one recurring thought: Two long, methodical searches of Ignatow's house had failed to produce the photographs. Wesley would forever be bothered by that:

"It just never occurred to anybody to look for a heat duct

under a rug. I guarantee you we'll look the next time.''

Charlie Ricketts said he learned about Ignatow's guilt when his son, Mike Ignatow, obviously crying, called Ricketts while he was in his office.

"Charlie, this is Mike. Dad did it."

"Did what?"

Mike Ignatow could only repeat himself.

"They found the film and jewelry. Dad did it."

Ricketts would maintain he had always thought Ignatow was innocent, that his first thoughts after Mike Ignatow called him were of the two families, the Ignatows and the Schaefers.

"I'm human as well as a trained advocate. As corny as it sounds, my mind went heavenly. I prayed a lot. I asked the Lord, 'What purpose was all this?' "

Part of that purpose, he believed, was a defense attorney doing his job.

"I didn't feel guilt. I did what I was sworn to do. To the extent that is required by the commonwealth, I did my job. There is not anything in that record that suggests chicanery, foolishness, or unethical behavior."

The Saturday after Ignatow confessed, T. Clay met with Ignatow in a visiting room in the basement of the Hall of Justice. Clay believed Ignatow might need someone to talk to, but Clay also had personal reasons. There were dozens of questions that needed answers: When did Ignatow decide he would murder Brenda? How did Mary Ann get involved? Was there a final disagreement that caused him to murder Brenda? Clay was also curious about the sequence of events: What had really happened?

The men talked for two hours. They talked about many areas of Ignatow's life: his friends, his family, events surrounding the murder of Brenda Schaefer, the things Ignatow had discussed with members of Southeast Christian Church. Clay taped the conversation, but always said "no comment" when asked about its contents. A few weeks later, as a condition of his plea-bargaining agreement, Clay said, Ignatow made a second tape to help clear up unanswered questions.

Present at that taping were Clay, Sears, Lesousky, and U.S. probation officer David Spoelker. That tape wasn't made public.

On November 13, 1992, Ignatow sent a letter to Clay discharging him as his attorney. Written in very detailed, very legal terms, Ignatow's letter made it clear that Clay had no right to use any information Ignatow had given him for any future publication. Ignatow asked that his entire case file be sent to the law office of Ricketts and Travis, which was acting as trustee and custodian. Legally, Ignatow could not fire Clay; Judge Johnstone would have to approve his withdrawal, which he did. Both Clay and Ricketts would eventually express interest in writing a book about the case, but neither would.

In Kenton County, David Whaley, foreman of the jury that had acquitted Ignatow, heard Ignatow's confession on television. Whaley was surprised, had some regrets the jury hadn't taken a little longer to consider the evidence, but still believed the jury had done the right thing.

"I felt the job that I did while I was sitting there was the best job that I could do," he would say.

Jerry Sebastian wouldn't second-guess himself. He remained firm in his convictions. Had he known about the pictures and jewelry, he would have voted to find Ignatow guilty. Given the same evidence he saw and heard, he would again set him free. Andrew Wilder had a different slant. He told the *Courier-Journal* that since new evidence had been found, and Ignatow had confessed to the crime, then justice had been done after all.

Lois Reber, one of the last two holdouts, had lived with a guilty feeling since the day of the verdict; she had given in to peer group pressure, would never forgive herself.

William Miller, the other holdout, felt a little vindication mixed with his guilt over giving in to the other jurors.

"I still think about it," he would say two years later. "I knew that I should have stuck with what I wanted to do. It made me feel good that the rest of the jurors said he wasn't guilty, then they found out he was guilty."

In spite of the double-jeopardy prohibition, Common-wealth's Attorney Ernie Jasmin, sounding more like a poli-tician than a prosecutor, pledged to bring additional state charges against Ignatow "as soon as humanly possible." Jas-min was relieved of that burden on November 10, 1992, when he was appointed a circuit judge by Kentucky governor Brereton Jones, becoming the only black circuit court judge in Kentucky.

Jasmin's appointment allowed him to avoid a reelection campaign that might have been made difficult by the verdict in the Ignatow trial. Jasmin's likely opponent was Louisville trial attorney Nick King, who subsequently was appointed to replace Jasmin.

Public pressure for King to find more charges against Ig-natow was enormous. A *Courier-Journal* editorial headlined MISCARRIAGE OF JUSTICE again ripped the Kenton County jury's decision, called Ricketts's claim that the system had worked "ridiculous."

King took the task seriously. Ignatow already was a con-victed tax evader; if found guilty of another state crime, he could get an additional ten years in prison for being a per-sistent felony offender. On November 20, 1992, standing be-fore a mountain of twenty-one boxes filled with court records, pleadings, and transcripts, King held a news con-ference at which he pledged to review every word on the thousands of pages. A thirteen-member team of investigators, including five of his attorneys, the FBI, the U.S. attorney, the Kentucky attorney general, and Jefferson County police would meet regularly to find more charges. He also said new charges against Mary Ann Shore-Inlow were being consid-ered.

On December 17, with a dozen task-force members stand-ing behind him in a somber Hall of Justice courtroom, King gave his answer:

"The task force unanimously concluded that any addi-tional charges against Mr. Ignatow would be prohibited by the United States Constitution, the Kentucky Constitution, and other appropriate Kentucky law."

King had prepared a three-by-five-foot piece of white cardboard with eight possible charges listed, among them criminal conspiracy to commit murder, rape, sodomy, intimidating a witness, and receiving stolen property. Further charges were impossible because of double-jeopardy standards, and the issue of collateral estoppel, which provides that if a fact has been questioned and determined in a court proceeding, that fact or determination cannot be challenged in a subsequent court proceeding. A federal civil-rights charge could not be filed because that statute dealt only with public employees. King added there could be no additional charges against Shore-Inlow; she had kept her part of the bargain; there was nothing to charge her with.

Circuit Court Judge Martin Johnstone heard about Ignatow's confession while watching television.

"I got very sick to my stomach," the judge would say. "I didn't throw up, but I came as close as I ever did. It confirmed everything I had believed from the beginning. I was reliving the experience. It confirmed that Mary Ann Shore was right on target."

In May 1993, Johnstone, forty-four, left the trial bench to take a seat on the Kentucky Court of Appeals. He had been a popular, respected, highly rated circuit court judge; he had been feeling burned out, but it was the Ignatow trial that pushed him into the decision.

"It was such a draining, heart-wrenching experience I made up my mind to get out of trial work. You can only take so many bites out of the apple and I was down to the core.

"Everybody always talks about someone getting away with murder, but here was a real, live case. The system was a colossal failure. The man got away with murder and there was nothing anybody could do about it."

Scott Cox and Jim Lesousky remained with the U.S. Attorney's office. Both moved on to other cases, but Lesousky would always wonder what would have happened if the case had gone to trial. Alan Sears moved to Arizona, where he worked with a nonprofit charity group.

FBI special agent Mike Griffin retired in 1993 to open the Big Sky private detective agency and write a novel based on his FBI experiences. Maury Berthon was transferred to the Miami Bureau. Deirdre Fike stayed in Louisville. Like Lesousky, she always had some regret the case didn't go to trial.

Roy Hazelwood retired from the FBI Behavioral Sciences Department in January 1994 to begin a career as a national consultant, expert witness, and teacher in areas of police liability, premise liability, criminal sexual behavior, and sexual sadism.

Dr. William Spalding worked in a low-income family clinic operated by the Louisville-Jefferson County Board of Health until he retired in July 1993 after becoming disabled with asthma. He tried hard not to think about Brenda Schaefer and Mel Ignatow, but said he never felt safe anymore on Louisville streets.

Mary Ann Shore-Inlow was scheduled for her first parole hearing in January 1993, about a year after she was sentenced to five years in prison on her tampering-with-evidence charge. Just before that hearing she announced that she would waive her right to the hearing and serve the rest of her sentence to spare herself and the Schaefer family the ordeal of rehashing the crime.

The Schaefer family didn't believe her; it again gathered in Frankfort, Kentucky, to testify against any parole, but Shore-Inlow did not appear. Two years after her sentencing, she was working in the laundry at the Kentucky Correctional Institute for Women and living in the Lonnie Watson Annex, a big brick building outside the main prison fence near the parking lot. If she accumulated the maximum sentence reduction for good behavior, she would serve about three years of her five-year sentence, being freed in late spring or early summer of 1995.

On November 13, 1992, Mel Ignatow was sentenced to eight years and one month in prison by U.S. District Judge Edward Johnstone. Under the terms of the plea agreement, he was to serve sixty months on the charges of perjury and subornation of perjury, with another thirty-seven months for making false statements to the FBI. There was no chance of parole, but fifty-four days would be knocked off his sentence for every year of good time served. He was also fined $150.

With Mel Ignatow's open-court confession, it was easy for the public to believe he was somehow being punished—albeit with a very light sentence—for the brutal murder of Brenda Schaefer. This wasn't the case. Although he had admitted to a sordid sexual torture and murder as part of his plea bargain, no in-prison psychiatric counseling was ordered for him in the federal system; it would have to be done on a volunteer basis. Johnstone did sentence Ignatow to a three-year, community-based health-counseling program to begin after his release from prison, and forbade any contact with the Schaefer family.

Ignatow had written the Schaefer family a sprawling, two-page letter about a week after his confession. He apologized for the suffering he had caused the family, saying Brenda's murder had come as the result of a life lived away from God; the murder had occurred while he was being influenced by the devil. Ignatow asked forgiveness from the Schaefers, as he was already certain that God had forgiven him.

Ignatow's sentencing hearing lasted only five minutes, Ignatow saying "No, sir" when Johnstone asked him if he wanted to make a statement. Tom Schaefer had requested to make a statement, but his wish was denied; Johnstone wanted to keep the hearing brief.

Ignatow was quickly led out of the courtroom by federal marshals. As he was led from the courthouse in handcuffs, Bud Kraft, a freelance photographer for the *Courier-Journal*, took a picture of Ignatow with a smug, almost beatific smile on his face, a picture that would last in the minds of many Louisvillians a long time.

Ignatow was first sent to Federal Correctional Institute McKean, a new prison near Bradford, Pennsylvania, in the northwest part of the state. He was held in its medium-security facility with about 1,150 inmates, most of them guilty of white-collar or drug-related crimes.

On April 15, 1993, Ignatow filed a motion in U.S. District Court in Louisville arguing that he should get a reduction in his eight-year-and-one-month prison term because he had pleaded guilty the day after his arrest, sparing the government "the trouble and expense of preparing for a trial."

Included with the motion was an affidavit showing Ignatow was earning forty-six cents an hour from UNICOR-Federal Prison Industries for prison work in a laundry, and a certificate of completion from Prison Fellowship signed by, among others, Charles Colson.

The certificate included a passage from Philippians 3:12–14: "... there is one thing I always do; I forget the things that are past. I try as hard as I can to reach the goal that is set before me...."

Ignatow filed his motion from McKean without a lawyer. Assistant U.S. Attorney Alan Sears blasted the motion, telling the *Courier-Journal,* "The outrageousness of the motion is only exceeded by its lack of merit.

"He is a man who escaped the electric chair. He now faces at most ninety-seven months in prison and he is complaining."

On April 23, 1993, U.S. District Judge Edward Johnstone denied the motion.

A week later Sears learned he was wrong about Ignatow's sentence; the *Courier-Journal* printed a front-page story saying Ignatow would be released from prison two years earlier than expected because he would be given credit in the federal correctional system for the two years he served in jail in Jefferson County waiting for his state trial.

The news shocked—and embarrassed—everyone in the U.S. Attorney's office who had been involved in negotiating Ignatow's sentence, Sears, Lesousky, U.S. Attorney Joe Whittle. None of them knew about this aspect of federal sentencing guidelines. Even T. Clay, who had helped negotiate Ignatow's sentence, was unaware he would be given credit.

Michael Willis, inmate-system manager at McKean, said federal law requires the corrections bureau to give an inmate credit for time spent in custody after the offense—even if he was in custody on a different charge. In Ignatow's case the federal offenses occurred before Brenda Schaefer's body was found and he was arrested; he had to be given credit for the two years served.

With two years taken off his sentence—and if he continued to earn a fifty-four-day reduction for his year served—Ignatow would be free on November 3, 1997. His total time served would be about five years.

In August 1993, Ignatow was transferred to Allenwood Federal Correctional Institute south of Williamsport, Pennsylvania, another medium-security facility, where he could qualify for temporary furloughs from prison.

For Ignatow, even five years in prison was too long. In February 1994, he filed a motion in U.S. District Court in Louisville maintaining he should have been sentenced to only ten to sixteen months in prison because federal authorities had incorrectly computed his sentence, and that T. Clay erred by failing to notice, thus providing ineffective counsel. Johnstone also denied that motion.

In December 1994 Ignatow was transferred to the Federal Correctional Institution in Petersburg, Virginia, apparently to be closer to his family on the East Coast. The low-security facility had about 1,150 inmates, most first and second offenders.

Seven years after Brenda's murder, the Schaefer family was still trying to deal with all that had happened—and was still happening. Brenda's sister, Carolyn Kopp, had recurring anxiety attacks and had gone into a deep depression after her mother's death; she did not want to leave her bedroom, care for her family, even dress or care for herself. She was hospitalized for two weeks at Our Lady of Peace in Louisville, then began taking Prozac, which helped bring her life into balance.

After the Kenton County trial, she had felt emotionally drained for a long time. By the summer of 1994, Kopp was feeling stronger. She had a dream about Brenda that helped:

"I dreamed I saw Brenda in a white terry-cloth robe. She

smiled and said, 'I'm happy. Don't worry about me.' I know it was meant to help overcome my sadness and grief. I'm getting better, but I've got to have something to do every day.''

Tom Schaefer lived alone in the family house on Warner Avenue for three years after the death of his parents. Many of the things that had belonged to his parents, and to Jack and Brenda, were there with him; their clothes, pictures, items of handiwork, letters, and records.

He continued working as a corrections officer at the Kentucky Correctional Psychiatric Center near LaGrange, and was still dating Linda Love. In 1993 he bought six acres of land and a mobile home near the Trimble-Oldham county lines east of Jefferson County. In the spring of 1994 he began cleaning out the family home, preparing it for sale. The home was in a good neighborhood; he expected it to sell quickly.

"What we went through will never go away," he said. "I have a feeling that when Mel gets out it may even be harder. He likes the publicity, he likes to flaunt it. It's going to be hard to deal with."

Mike Schaefer remained a technical-publications editor at Fort Knox. He would explain how he was dealing with the family's long struggle in a brief letter.

THE CHRISTMAS AFTER IGNATOW'S CONFESSION WE PLACED A LARGE, PINE WREATH ON THE SCHAEFER GRAVE STONE IN CAVE HILL. THE WREATH WAS ABOUT 24 INCHES ACROSS AND HAD PINE CONES AND A DARK VELVET BOW. TOM AND I MAKE SURE THIS IS DONE EACH CHRISTMAS SEASON.

WE VISIT CAVE HILL EVERY FEW WEEKS AND TAKE FLOWERS ON SPECIAL OCCASIONS. WE USUALLY BUY FLOWERS AT NEARBY SCHULZ'S FLORIST ON CHEROKEE ROAD. ON MORE THAN ONE OCCASION THEY HAVE REFUSED PAYMENT WHEN THEY KNEW WE WERE TAKING THE ARRANGEMENT TO MOM'S GRAVE.

TOM AND I EVEN RUN INTO EACH OTHER AT THE GRAVE SITE. WHILE WE ARE THERE WE SOMETIMES

VISIT JIM RUSH'S GRAVE. MY VISITS TO THE CEMETERY ARE OFTEN FAMILY AFFAIRS. I TAKE MY YOUNG SONS, JESSE, 8, AND JOHN NELS, 11, SO THEY WON'T FORGET THEIR GRANDPARENTS AND AUNT BRENDA AND TO REMIND THEM THEY HAD AN UNCLE JACK WHO LIVED AND DIED YEARS BEFORE THEY WERE BORN. WE OFTEN GO WITH MY FRIEND, EVELYN, WHO UNFORTUNATELY NEVER HAD A CHANCE TO MEET ANY OF THEM. WE ALWAYS END UP EXPLORING OTHER SECTIONS OF THE CEMETERY, EXAMINING ANCIENT GRAVE STONES AND ADMIRING THE DUCKS AND GEESE.

VISITS TO CAVE HILL ARE NOT SAD OCCASIONS. THEY ARE A TIME TO REMEMBER AND REFLECT ON WHAT HAS BEEN AND WHAT MIGHT HAVE BEEN. NO ONE BURIED IN THE SCHAEFER PLOT WOULD WANT US TO MOURN OUR LIVES AWAY.

I N D E X

Compelling True Crime Thrillers
From Avon Books

DEATH BENEFIT
by David Heilbroner
72262-3/ $5.50 US/ $6.50 Can

FREED TO KILL
by Gera-Lind Kolarik with Wayne Klatt
71546-5/ $5.50 US/ $6.50 Can

GOOMBATA:
THE IMPROBABLE RISE AND FALL OF
JOHN GOTTI AND HIS GANG
by John Cummings and Ernest Volkman
71487-6/ $6.99 US/ $8.99 Can

CHARMER: THE TRUE STORY OF A
LADIES' MAN AND HIS VICTIMS
by Jack Olsen
71601-1/ $6.50 US/ $8.50 Can

DOUBLE JEOPARDY
by Bob Hill
72192-9/ $5.99 US/ $7.99 Can

BY TWO AND TWO
by Jim Schutze
72177-5/ $5.99 US/ $7.99 Can